One Hundred Voices

Volume Three

Centum Press
Dover, NH

One Hundred Voices Volume Three
Copyright © 2017 Centum Press

All rights reserved. Printed in the United States of America. No part of this book may be used or reproduced in any manner whatsoever without written permission except in the case of brief quotations embodied in critical articles or reviews.
The stories in this Anthology are works of fiction. Names, characters, businesses, organizations, places, events, and incidents either are the product of the author's imagination or are used fictitiously. Any resemblance to actual persons, living or dead, events, or locales is entirely coincidental.

For information contact:
Centum Press
http://www.centumpublishing.com
email: info@centumpublishing.com

ISBN:

978-1945737-02-2 (Paperback)

978-1945737-07-7 (Hardcover)

Cover Design by J Ashley Designs

First Edition: August 2017

10 9 8 7 6 5 4 3 2 1

EDITOR'S NOTE

Out of respect to those represented in our book who reside in Canada, the United Kingdom, Australia, Egypt, India, and other English-speaking countries that do not use American English, we have not sought to impose American punctuation styles throughout the book.

TABLE OF CONTENTS

9	Riham Adly	The Ladder
12	**Edward Ahern**	Touching Memory
15	Dina Arrelle	Late Again
19	Josephine Asturias	Scenes from a Fire
22	Hall & Beaulieu	Last Line
25	Jesse Booth	Off the Hook
31	Victoria Bovalino	341 Days
35	Nimue Brown	Creature Comforts
38	Warren Bull	The Lesson
40	Sarah Tracy Burrows	Asking for a Puppy
46	Jeremy Bush	Sleepover
50	Susan Carey	A Bit of Sparkle
52	Bob Carlton	Thorns and Thistles Shall it Bring Forth
55	Steve Carr	The Old Chapel Road Story
58	Patricia Carragon	Mural Man
62	Jean M. Cogdell	Precious Memories
66	Brett Cullen	**Waning Ripples**
68	Dave D'Allessio	Ocean's Eleven
72	Pradyumna N. Chaudhuri	The Three Chambers
77	C.J. Cole	A Pig in Court
81	Jeanne Davies	The Day the Pony Went
87	Pat Jeanne Davis	A Surprise Find
91	Alana Guy Dill	Bird's Eye View
98	Rachel Doherty	E Train: Jamaica to WTC
101	Glen Donaldson	Dog on a Hot Tin Roof
103	Loretta A. Folz	Bonsai
107	Joanna Friedman	Orange Blossoms and Telescopes
111	Sharyl Fuller	The Suitcase
114	Joni Gadner	Farmer's Market Day
116	T.C. Gardstein	The Kitten in the Rye Bread
120	Shelia M. Good	Maggie's New Beginning
124	E. Margareta Griffith	**Love by a Sky-Blue Thread**
127	Eric Hirscher	Last Call
132	Timothy C. Hobbs	Love Eternal
136	**Charlotte Holloway**	A Mockery of Tears
138	Susan Imboden	Crazy Comes First
143	Kilmo	Tic
149	E.E. King	The Weight of Fiction
152	Cass Sims Knight	Pop It
157	Darin Z. Krogh	The Coot Pond

161	Stephen Landry	Going Up
164	Q. Lei	The Station
166	Kari Livingston	The Collector
171	Calley Luman	Invisibility
173	Bridgett Magee	A Dog's Tale
177	Jackie Davis Martin	The Supplemental Turtle
180	Paul McDonald	Swiftly the Swift
182	Anne McGrath	Push the Lobster
186	Joanne Jakle McKinnis	The Eyes Have It
190	C.J. McPherson Heaney	The Christmas Ornament
194	Alan Meyrowitz	I Am Here for You
196	Eddie D. Moore	The Hatchling
199	Alex Morgan	April
204	Zachary Mulcahy	Foreign Familiarity
208	Ted Myers	For All Eternity
211	Clarke O'Gara	My Uncle's Magic Hands
216	Carl Palmer	Her Fella
218	**J.M. Paul**	Anxiety
220	**David Perlmutter**	Hilaria in Winnipeg
222	**Melissa Quigley**	Holidays
229	**Sally Ramsey**	Grandmother's Typewriter
232	Anna Reichert	The Go-Away Bird
235	Ellena Restrick	**My Brother's Keeper**
238	Jon Robinson	Run
243	Naomi Brett Rourke	Rockstars and Broken Dreams
247	Valerie J. Runyan	Last Page Front
252	Jo-Ann Russell	Curious
256	Matt Scott	Good Samaritan
259	Pamela A. Scott	Reign of the Forest
264	Dennis Sinar	My Soulmate
269	Fiona Skepper	The Divine Wow Wow
274	**Allison Spector**	Better Than Dread
278	Patricia Lesley Stammers	Cows of Nether Alderley
284	M.E. Syler	Turning Point
289	Pat Simmons	Gryph
295	Carl Smith	Flashes
296	Lauren Suchenski	The Earth Cracked in Two
298	John Taloni	A Galaxy Fur, Fur Away
302	Caroline Taylor	What is This Thing Called Like?
307	Trudi Young Taylor	Memories of Not Greece

311	Rozko Iliev Tzolov	The Chess Game
315	Robert Ullrich	Radar Love
319	Judy Wang	Hot Tracks
323	Kathryn Wells	The Bitter Crimson
325	Edel Williams	How to Cook Eggs
329	Iona Winter	Bystander

THE LADDER

RIHAM ADLY

"You're my sweetheart". He tells me so all the time.

Daniel calls me "Little Miss Sunshine" because of the way I smile. Our relationship was like going up and down a ladder, but he's never given up on me, he's never let go. He would always say that I brought in the sunshine wherever I went and that I have the soul of a child. I love him, words just can't do justice. I love watching him walk into my room every day. He came in today wearing this funny tight hat that clung to his head; his stubble was maybe a day or two old. Those new frameless glasses suit him really well, and the color of his scrubs complimented the cerulean blue of his eyes. Today he smuggled in a citrine pyramid. He knows how much I love crystals and that citrine's my favorite. Last week he brought me dandelions. He knows I'm not a roses girl. I love it when he holds my hands the way he's doing right now, whispering poetry to my sleeping frame. I know he knows I can hear him. I'm not always around, but I do come when I sense him.

When I'm not around, I usually sit in my garden with the soft- scented dandelions everywhere. Tall trees sway to my singing, the smell of grass earthy and strong. I like making wreaths of my dandelions, just like when I was little. Daniel used to love it when my hair was loose, framing my face. He loved to kiss my half-closed eyelids. He would tell me I looked like honey and hazelnuts and that I always smelled like the early notes of spring.

Sometimes when I miss him, when the urge to be around him is strong enough, I come back. I don't go back to my room, instead, I follow him. Today, I feel near enough. I watch him scrub for his coming surgery, my surgery. I observe this intense look in his eyes as he says "scalpel". His eyes turn to a faint shade of blue, sometimes gray when he's concentrating on a task. The nurse wipes the sheen of sweat on his forehead before it trickles down his face. I love to watch his hands, there's lots of love in those hands. He's a giver. Daniel's a selfless giver, a life saver, but not today he won't.

I hate it when he comes into my room and cries, he's done it before. Usually, he holds up the tears in the corner of his eyes for the longest time before he lets them escape, but today he screams and sobs with such anguish, almost like a wounded animal, like a madman. I'm usually content with this state of existence, but in times like these, times when Daniel loses it, and when his tears wet my face and the pillow underneath I wish to be set free. The sound of his sobs punctures my very soul. I hate this body sleeping in a hospital bed, a useless cage as it is, tethering me to this world. I hate the tubes hooked to every part of this broken-down me. I hate the sound of the beeping monitors. Why can't they stop, and just shut up? I hate the machine that breathes for me. I hate lying here indefinitely. Daniel sleeps right now, he's sedated I think. They had to hold him still to shoot the sedative in his arm.

"Let me go, Daniel," I whisper in his ears.

I want to be around him forever, and I want to make it up to him for not saving me. It must be killing him, but some people are not meant to be saved. I want him to pull the plug and set me free. I want to climb that ladder all the way up there, to the other side, to my garden and never come back.

"I'll miss you, Daniel, I know it's hard, but you can do it. One day you'll be able to join me and we'll be the couple we were always meant to be." I whisper softly.

I see him now, agony and hesitation flitting across his face.

"Yes Daniel, do it. Do it for me, for us."

Deep lines etch the skin between his brows. His jaws clench and unclench, his eyes are wet with tears that don't stop.

Will he switch off the machines? What's the point of keeping my useless body going?

I see him standing tall over me, his hands holding mine.

"Let me go, Daniel. Let me go. Let the Angels come and get me, let me climb that ladder to the other side."

TOUCHING MEMORY
EDWARD AHERN

"We'll use the skin from his back for the book's cover."

Janice waved away his patter and interrupted. "I think I've got it. You're going to grind up Sam's body parts and make a memorial book."

Bosworth was a seasoned undertaker, but his expression flickered into annoyance before settling back into unction. "Yes. As I was saying, the hair and bones provide the fiber substitutes for the pages and the cover boards, the body fluids and soft organs provide paper binders and glue, and the best skin provides the cover vellum. Does Sam have any tattoos you'd like us to incorporate into the cover design?"

Janice leaned forward in the leather chair, wondering if Bosworth had used excess skin to upholster the funeral parlor furniture. "No, no tattoos, just aberrations. How does the cost compare to old-fashioned cremation?"

"Surprisingly, not that much more. We use a digital printer and automated binding. The additional cost is in the preparatory work—"

"Hacking up his body."

"Um, we refer to it as funeral surgery. Consider that instead of a nondescript urn with ashes you have a luxuriant coffee table book commemorating Sam's life and your love together. And there's the positive environmental impact. Instead of a polluting incineration we recycle Sam for future generations. It's become quite popular."

Janice flipped through the book Bosworth had handed her. "The pages are kind of gray."

"We refer to that as antique vellum. Only the finest paper and our own timeless organic material achieve that shade. Notice how sharp the color reproductions are. You could have portrait quality pictures of Sam in your book."

She snapped the book shut. "Sam's ugly. Out of focus would be better."

"Ah. The paper takes ink extremely well, the result of its complex proteins. You could write a beautiful tribute or dedication by hand.""

Janice nodded. "That is a thought. For sure I'd want to write something."

Bosworth interlocked his fingers. "If you're concerned about writing up a biography, we have several templates available, targeted at various ethnicities and social stratum. You just fill in a questionnaire and add some anecdotes. The computer does the rest."

Janice stared at him. "Tell me, Bosworth, do I have client privilege?"

He stared in turn. "So long as it's nothing illegal, I can assure whatever we discuss does not go beyond this room."

"Good. Sam's a jerk. I've kept a diary on the son of a bitch, and that's what would go in your book. Some of it has to do with deviant behavior. Do you have a problem with that?"

"Oh. I see. In speaking ill of the dead, there's little chance of a suit for defamation unless family members bring it. Do you have children by Sam?"

"No, thank God."

Bosworth had begun to sweat. "We would probably ask you to sign a disclaimer, vowing you would not sue us for any repercussions."

"No problem. So, how much extra for an embossed cover title?"

"That would depend on the number of letters."

"It would read '*Good Riddance*'. There's also some rather explicit pictures I'd like to incorporate in the book."

"That would be approximately a hundred and fifty dollars for the embossing, perhaps another two hundred for the pictures. Mrs. Stiltworth, I wonder if you might not want to also evaluate other funeral houses, just to get comparative quotes—"

Janice waved her hand again. "No, no, Bosworth. You need to go on a monster diet, but other than that I like you. Just prepare the quote for me."

Bosworth pulled an estimate sheet from a tablet and took out a pen. "We should get the larger items decided first, the number of wake times, religious services, choir and organist, and so forth."

She laughed. "He's lucky he's getting time on your slab. Just the butchery and the book, please."

"Oh." Bosworth did some calculations. "With the tax, fourteen thousand five. I've included the cost of up to ten pictures."

"And how long is your quotation valid?"

"Thirty days. But I don't understand. Didn't your husband pass on yesterday?"

"Hell no. But thirty days ought to be enough time for me to make arrangements."

LATE AGAIN
DINA ARRELLE

Margaret Smith's mother came into the bedroom and pulled back the curtains. "Margie, get up," she called.

Margaret covered her head with the pillow.

"Margie, I said get out of that bed!"

From under the pillow Margaret mumbled, "Don't wanna get up."

Sighing, Mrs. Smith tucked some loose hair back under a roller and yelled, "Margaret Catherine Smith, you better get out of bed right now! You know today is the first day of school!"

Margaret knew when her mother used her full name, it was time to respond. She threw the pillow from her face and sat up. "Mother, I don't feel good. I thi--"

"Well," Mrs. Smith corrected. "I don't feel well."

"Then that makes two of us." Margaret said in a hopeful tone. Seeing the look of annoyance on her mother's face, she started again. "Mother, I don't feel well, I'm too ill to go to school."

Mrs. Smith started to laugh.

Margaret, still sitting in bed, was shocked by this outburst.

Finally, Mrs. Smith stopped laughing, wiped the tears from her cheeks and said, "Oh come on now. You really have to get more original, you use that excuse every year."

"Well it's true," Margaret whined. "I'm sick!" She flopped back onto the pillow and dramatically threw her arm across her face.

"Sick of school?" her mother asked.

"Yeah, sick of school."

"Well Margie, you know you have to go. We all have to do things we don't enjoy. Life's just that way."

Margaret sat up again and snapped, "Oh really, Mother!"

"Come on," Mrs. Smith coaxed. "Get dressed and I'll make a good breakfast and pack you a special lunch."

"Well..."

"That's my girl, I knew you'd come around."

Margaret got out of bed and shuffled to the bathroom. She took an extra long shower and slowly brushed her teeth.

Several minutes later her mother called from downstairs, "Margaret stop wasting time. Your breakfast is getting cold."

Margaret sighed, "Ah Mom, stop treating me like a baby,"

"Then stop acting like one and get down here,"

Sulking, Margaret stamped down the stairs. Her mother had made her favorite breakfast. The aroma of French toast and bacon enticed her into the kitchen.

"Doesn't that look wonderful?" Mrs. Smith gushed. "Let's eat all of it so we'll have energy for a full day."

Margaret was tempted to ask her mother if she were joining her, but decided that the humor wouldn't be welcomed. Instead she started eating. The meal did make the day a little brighter, but still she said, "I really do hate going to school. I've been going to school almost all my life and I don't want to go anymore."

"Now Margie," Mrs. Smith sighed. "You don't mean that. We have this argument every September. Once you're there everything will be fine."

"No it won't. I hate it there."

Mrs. Smith rolled her eyes.

Margaret got angrier at her mother's familiar gesture. She shrieked, "I hate my principal, and all the teachers! I even hate all the kids and I'll tell you something. They all hate me right back!"

"Don't yell at me," Mrs. Smith snapped. "I've had enough of this nonsense. Now, you are going to finish and leave. Remember you had better not be late."

Margaret got up, her faced flushed with anger and ran up the stairs. Five minutes later she stormed from the house. Once she was outside in the warm sunshine she slowed her pace. She kept wishing for one more week of summer, but all too soon the brick school loomed in front of her. Too late for wishes, summer was officially over.

There were no children in the yard so she knew she was late, not to mention in trouble. She tried to sneak inside but just as she entered one of the teachers leaving the office noticed her. "Hey look," he laughed. "Margaret's back and she's late again.
Margaret, I thought you said that you weren't coming back here ever again."

Margaret ignored him and continued walking. When she got to her classroom, the principal was there speaking to the class. Seeing her enter, he said, "Well, well, Miss Smith, I see you're tardy again this year. We will certainly talk about this after school."

Margaret stared at her new shoes, her face hot with

embarrassment and softly said, "I'm sorry, Sir. It won't happen again."

Then she turned to the class, looked at the children and said, "Good morning, I'm Miss Smith, your third-grade teacher."

SCENES FROM A FIRE
JOSEPHINE ASTURIAS

He saw us first. Then we saw him. We both wanted him, but we knew the other wanted him more. We pretended not to be interested, but he knew. He knew as soon as he met us in that bar on 7th Ave that he would have us. One he would own, the other he would love.

My friend laughed, kept the conversation going, touching his hand lightly as she spoke. She can have him, I decided. She wants him more than me, I thought. I excused myself saying I was tired and my bed was calling. My friend hugged me. Pulling me in close she whispered, "Thank you," and smiled. Her eyes danced in the dim light of the bar and I left, knowing I had done the right thing. My friend was happy.

I stepped outside, closed my leather jacket against the night chill and got out a cigarette. I debated going back in. A lighter appeared in front me. A man. He said he was friends with the guy that was talking to my friend. The guy my friend was currently lusting over, wanted me to have his number. I shook my head. The way these men will play I thought. But…. I took the number and walked the three blocks home. All I saw was his face, those dark brown eyes, topped with perfectly shaped eyebrows, unfairly bestowed to a man. I felt warm inside. All inside. I went to bed telling myself I would burn the number. Throw it in the ashtray and light it up.

Morning came, but sleep had never come for me. I thought of nothing but him. The warm feeling had built to a hot throb, an unbearable ache. He possessed me, yet he was a stranger. I called him. He came over, and we collided. Tongues, fingers, arms, legs, grinding, causing a flame to flicker, then spark and rage. Everything went blue, and, our bodies exhausted and soaked with sweat, we panted for breath.

Over the weeks, my friend saw him and he saw me. He dated her, courted her. Took her to Broadway plays and fancy restaurants. But after, always after, he would come to Brooklyn. To my little apartment, and we would blaze our bodies through the night. He said he never touched my friend except to kiss her. She was a nice girl. I knew. She had always been a nice girl.

My friend had no idea. How could she? She would tell me everything. She was in love. She wanted to marry him and have his baby. She just knew he was going to ask her and he did. He stopped coming to me. He never spoke a word. He just stopped coming, and the ache from the night when I first met him came back. I would try other men to help with the ache, put out the flame like the small of two fingers to a match, but none could sooth me.

Weak. I called him. "Get it together," he said. "We are getting married. She is your friend. It was fun, but it's over. Everyone serves a purpose. Goodbye." He had disconnected the call as if I never meant anything to him. I stood in the same spot holding the phone, looking out the window. The sun started to set and the sky turned that brilliant blood orange fiery color. It was beautiful. I don't think I ever noticed how beautiful. I still stood frozen and watched the sky continue to change colors as night came. I needed him to fix me, and he wouldn't.

I was still in the same spot when there was a knock at my door. I couldn't move. I heard keys jingling and saw the lock turning open. My friend had come. She took my phone from my hand and set me down on the couch. She wrapped a blanket around me because I was shivering despite the heat. It was summer. My apartment had no air conditioning, but my body was so hot I felt cold. She made me tea. Then she sat beside me on the couch and told me. That night at the bar when I had left. She told the man, my man, the one that was going to be her husband. She told him she was looking to give a man a special life, but she needed to get to know him in a special way. She knew a man had needs and her friend, me, was wonderful at satisfying needs. So, he had his friend give me the number. They both knew I would call. My friend knew me so well, and he could already feel my body humming, vibrating, and waiting. For him.

She was sorry. I was part of her experiment but it had worked. She hugged me. Whispering in my ear, "Please be happy for me Gina. He loves me. What he had with you is nothing to me. I knew you wanted him the way you always want men. I let you borrow a piece of him, but I have to take it all back. He is to be my husband and I'm to be his wife," she said.

As she hugged me I hugged her back until she cried out in anguish, and my hands felt warm and sticky. Liquid rushing over them, warm and soothing. The strong smell of metal tickled my nose. The ache had stopped. My body hissed like the sound of steam leaving an iron. I was spent. I had made it stop. I held onto to my friend as her body sagged against mine, and placed the red stained letter opener back on the table behind couch. I was whole again.

LAST LINE
HALL & BEAULIEU

"I am well aware that you don't have a choice in the matter," Luna shouted, tears streaming down her face. "That doesn't change the fact that we will never see each other again."

"You don't know that's actually true," Reyn responded.

"Okay, fine we might see each other again, but if we do I will be, like ninety-five years old and you'll still be a twenty-four-year-old kid."

Reyn was recently assigned to a peacekeeper assignment on an outpost several lightyears away. Of course, neither of them expected this to happen. It was so rare any officer would be forced off-world, especially into another galaxy. Lightspeed travel was still fairly new, only a few centuries old. Each hour that passed aboard a ship travelling at lightspeed equaled years for those planet-side—decades even.

"It's easy for you to act so calm, you aren't giving up fifty years of your life. This trip will only cost you a few weeks." Although Luna was still crying, anger began to rise up as the dominant emotion. She threw things, unable to find a better way to cope with her feelings.

"Oh, give me a break!" Reyn was shouting now too, trying to make his voice heard over his wife. "You think I want to leave? How is it any harder on you than me? I am still losing you and there's nothing I can do about it. As you said, I don't have a choice. It's not my fault the peacekeepers couldn't keep peace on Gressin. It's not my fault the people are rebelling. What should I do? We both signed papers. We both agreed to serve the Star System when I became an Elite Guard."

"What is the point? By the time you get there, it'll be a new generation and they'll have established a new government. No one will even remember the uprising. Just let them live their lives!"

Reyn believed she was right. But the council believed Gressin must be made into an example. If they weren't punished, who would stop any colony from rising up to established their own leaders and law?

"No one told me they'd tear you away from me." She calmed down a bit and had crumpled over on the bed sobbing.

Reyn placed his hand on her shoulder, speaking softly. "I didn't expect this either. But it is this, or I get tried as a deserter. Either way, we lose each other."

"Why can't we just run away together. We talked about running before we got married. You know my dad hated you. That was the easier option."

"Yes, it was the easier option. But one with the least integrity. I swore honor and integrity when I stood before the council. I plan to—"

"And you swore vows to me as well, Reyn!" Luna was shouting again, but Reyn put his arm around her, consoling. "I just don't understand why I can't come with you."

"I don't either, but rules are rules, my love."

Engines revved in the street in front of the small apartment. A knock rapped on the door. Luna shouted uncontrollably. "No! No, you can't go!" She clutched his legs as he started toward the door. It opened before he reached it.

"Time to move out," ordered a large man wearing full combat gear.

Luna stood, then lunged for the man standing at the door. Two more soldiers stepped in, restraining her.

"Luna, please," said Reyn, "I don't want to remember you like this."

"You won't remember me at all!"

Reyn turned to the men in the doorway and spoke a few hushed words. The large one nodded slightly, motioned to the others and all went outside.

"Luna, I will think about you every moment of every day for the rest of my existence. I love you with all that I am and all that I will be."

"I will wait for you," she said.

"No, you won't. You are far too beautiful, too perfect to wait around for me. Live your life. Get remarried, have children, live and love life. I know you'll never forget me, but you'll be able to move on. You have my love, my heart."

He passionately kissed his wife, then walked toward the door.

"I love you," he whispered.

"Reyn," Luna said, "I'm pregnant."

OFF THE HOOK

JESSE BOOTH

Hey you! Yeah, you. Human being sitting on the other side of the ice on an orange bucket, dropping an "invisible" line down through a hole you drilled. I ain't biting that thing at the end of it. Fool me once? Hook in the jaw. Fool me twice? Sizzling on that portable grill you brought along with your buddies. It ain't gonna happen, angler. You know why? I've got buddies, too. And today, we're going to fight back.

You're probably thinking, *Here stupid fishy, fishy, fishy.*

Well, guess what? You're sitting there, wrapped in layers, freezing in your boots. You're shivering and sniffling, cursing the weather for being so cold.

So tell me, who is the stupid one?

I can't say I'm particularly jealous of your warm blood right now. The water fills great, rushing in and out of my gills. You honestly believe you evolved from something like me?

Ha!

We're smart. Smarter than you realize. Just like you, we have schools. You even know about them. But you don't know what we do *in* them. We've led you to believe our schools are nothing but asinine groups. And you have taken the bait.

Chomp, chomp.

My school begins the first phase of our plan of attack. Anything smell fishy to you?

"Bateman, I think I gotta bite," you declare triumphantly.

Bait-man? You mean that's your buddy's actual name? You've got to be joking me.

"Me too," Bait-man says with just as much excitement.

If only you could hear our laughs erupt from the bubbles that are popping in your perfectly-drilled hole.

"My hook's set," you yell over your shoulder.

"So's mine!"

The ice that separates us is my window of entertainment. I feel as giddy as a school guppy!

"Nice'n easy, Bateman," you say to your buddy with such surety, as if you've done this hundreds of times. Which you probably have, jerk-face.

"Oh, it's startin' to fight me," Bait-man announces. "It's gettin' stronger!"

"So's mine," you say. "Must be some mighty big fish in this here lake!"

The anticipation that causes your mouth to circle makes you look more like a fish than I do.

"This fish is probly bigger than your mom, Gilson," Bait-man says to you.

Gill-son? Seriously? That's honestly your name?

"And prettier!" one of your other buddies adds.

"Hey, you two, you know I get crabby when you start talkin' about my mom like that."

My wide eyes pull away from you idiots and look at your tangled, knotted lines. My school did really well spinning them together. I can't help but stretch my mouth a little more into a smile. We got you both real good with this one.

"Sorry, mate, we was only playin'," Bait-man apologizes.

You shrug, then say, "Boy, this fish is bendin' my pole somethin' fierce. I hope I'm usin' a strong enough line…"

Thunk, thunk.

I follow the sinking lures down, down, down, until they clink softly into the pebbles of the bottom of the lake. They reflect sunlight bent by the water, and I claim them as my personal trophies. We've won the first stage of this battle.

"Hey, my line broke," you cry out as you reel in. "That fish really must've been huge."

"Same with mine, Gilson," Bait-man says dejectedly.

"Well, reel in fast," you reply. "Let's get new hooks and fresh bait on these things and get back down there. These fish must be huge!"

We're not, actually. I'm about the size of your hand. But thanks for the compliment: I wasn't even fishing for it.

You humans have such big brains, I'm so jealous. I guess that makes me a jellyfish.

I'm really a trout. A rainbow trout, to be precise.

You dip your freshly-baited hooks back into the water, and I'm almost tempted to have my school tangle them up again before they get all that deep. But that would just be boring, pulling the same prank twice in a row. Time for phase two.

I've seen your guppies, your little ones running around in the summertime, spraying each other with water guns. So much fun, right?

We're going to scale that idea up a notch.

"Hey… there's a fish starin' up at me from my hole," you say. The confusion splashed on your face is priceless.

"There's a couple in mine, too," Bait-man says. "Weird. What do you think they're doin'?"

I'm so glad he asked.

The ice-cold spraying commences, but don't worry, you guys aren't the only ones getting wet. We're hitting every fisherman out on the ice with this phase.

You fall off of your orange bucket and smash into your tackle box, scattering the contents across the ice.

Whoops.

"They're crazy," you cry out. "The fish are crazy!"

"They're not stoppin', man," Bait-man says. "I'm soaked! Make 'em stop!"

The shouts of alarm across the entire lake are enough to warm my cold-blooded heart.

"It's almost like the fish know we's tryin' to catch 'em, and they're fightin' back" Bait-man mumbles as he wrings out his gloves.

Your buddy figured it out! It only took until the completion of phase two. And here I was, thinking we were off the hook.

"The fish wanna fight?" you say rummaging through the mess on the ice that should be in your tackle box. "I'll give 'em a fight!"

You withdraw a can from the disarray and wield it high above your head. Through the ice I can just make out the label. Too bad I can't read your silly letters. But I don't need to -- I know exactly what those yellow morsels are.

• • •

"You can't use that, Gilson," Bait-man says. "It's illegal."

Eel-eagle? What a terrifying name for the ultimate bait. I can almost taste the sweetness of the golden treasure contained in the can.

"They ain't playin' by the rules, Bateman," you say through gritted teeth. "Neither are we."

"But Gilson, if we get caught chummin', we'll be in real trouble."

"Your brains must be smaller than the fishies'," you reply. "We ain't chummin', we was just usin' the corn kernels as bait on our hooks and the can fell in by accident."

Did you just insult our intelligence? Need I remind you that we're both wet right now, and you're not supposed to be?

Through the ice, I see your silhouette walking towards the hole. And I know once you dump the can of eel-eagles in this hole, it's all over for me and my buddies. Those things are overpoweringly yummy. Every fish in this lake will be over here, and you'd be able to catch any number of us that you'd like. I can't let you do that.

Time for phase three.

We're going against nature on this one, but if a few tricks won't scare you away, desperate times call for desperate measures.

I dive out of the water, holding my breath as I soar through the air, colliding with your face, making sure my tail smacks you reel hard in the nose before I plop onto the snow-covered ice.

"What is goin' on!" you scream as you hold your nose.

It's really difficult to see anything as I swish back and forth on the snow, making my way back to the hole, but I can tell you've dropped the can of heavenly gold pieces. Judging by the sounds echoing off the ice, my school is doing their job too.

"These fish are insane," Bait-man cries. "I've been slapped a dozen times."

"They're just fish," you yell back. "They're exposed on the snow. Don't let them wiggle their way back to their holes!"

I panic. I had hoped we could escape easily after surprising you and your buddies. I may have miscalculated

"I don't care what you say, Gilson," Bait-man says. "I'm outa here!" I hear heavy footfalls running away, and the ice groaning at the pressure.

"Bateman, you left all of your gear!" you call out to him. I wish I could see his reaction, because I hear no reply.

I'm so close to the hole, just another inch or so…

And then you snatch me up into a firm grasp and hold me up, forcing my face close to your own. If you think I look scary… take the time to look at your reflection sometime.

"It's over, fish," you cackle. "You're my next meal."

Before you can do anything else, I use my last defense. Opening my mouth, I spray that last bit of water I've kept inside right into your eyes. To my delight, I feel the weightlessness of falling, followed by a padded plop back into the snow, right next to my hole back into the lake. Next to me is the can of eel-eagles. I nudge the opened can in, then follow it back into the water.

"Wait for me, Bateman!" you scream as you flee.

Time to celebrate.

Something tells me you'll remember this day, Gill-son. Never forget: if the fish ain't bitin', they'll be fightin'.

341 DAYS

VICTORIA BOVALINO

She woke up with the alarm at half past five. The duvet on the bed was carelessly thrown from the space next to her. The emptiness there was cold. In the darkness of the rising dawn, she could hear the patter of the shower running in their bathroom.

The wife rubbed her eyes with her hands. The day she had been dreading had finally arrived. Her husband's packed suitcases stood by the door like gravestones, sealing her fate. She missed him already. She sat up in bed and tucked her knees against her chest. Icy despair curled in the pit of her stomach, and the wife pulled the duvet up and around her shoulders.

In the next room, the water shut off. There was the sound of slippery stepping, of teeth being brushed, of a man clearing his throat. He stepped out of the bathroom in a cloud of warm mist that smelled like his shampoo. A white towel was securely wrapped around his waist.

"I'm sorry if I woke you," the husband said.

"I had to be up anyways," his wife answered.

He nodded. He walked to the bed and sat beside her. She felt his damp warmth against her shoulder, and settled into it. He kissed her temple. He hadn't shaved yet, and the prickles of a new beard tickled her skin.

"I don't want you to go," she said. Morning light was spilling over the windowsill and into their North London flat. It was a thin, watery light, the kind that follows days of endless rain and shows the first sign of a clear day.

He ran a hand down the length of her hair. Her hair flowed down her back and curled at the ends, just at her waist. "I don't want to go, either." The husband ducked his head and kissed her shoulder. "You know I have to."

She did. The American branch of his company had a position open for only a year, to help with a deal that would seal the success of the company for years to come. The position had been offered to him. If the deal went through, the husband would get a huge promotion at work, and the couple would never again have to worry about security.

She turned towards him. "I cannot handle not having you with me for a full year."

He wrapped his arms around her. "We will have Christmas, and you can visit me on holidays."

She made a sound in her throat. They both knew that her strict hours at the law firm wouldn't allow for much vacation time.

"I know what will make you feel better," he said, nuzzling her hair. "Let's get dressed and go to that coffee shop that you like."

"Alright," she said. She glanced at him. His eyes were already a thousand miles away.

***

They took the Tube to the heart of the city. The wife paused at the exit to the station. She always had to take a breath when she walked into the busyness of the London street, even though she had been living in the city through the two years of their marriage. The mix of ancient brick and new steel were daunting to her. She stared at one of the buildings that rose in the distance, flanked by a church and a pub. Sensing her hesitation, he shifted his suitcase and took her hand.

There was very little traffic. He pulled her across the road, towards the little coffee shop. There was no line inside.

They both ordered black coffees and croissants, and settled into a small table.

Their coffees were delivered. She watched his face as he picked his coffee up and took a careful sip. He grimaced slightly, as he always did when drinking black coffee. He hated the taste of coffee, but always ordered it. She never understood why. "I've heard that they drink coffee every day in New York City. Sometimes even multiple times a day."

He nodded. He was running the tip of his pointer finger along the rim of his coffee cup. "I can get used to it."

She shifted her gaze to the window. Most of the people passing at this time were businessmen and women, dressed in dark suits with ties, with their Nokias and Sonys pressed to their ears. These people came in all colours, shapes, and sizes, yet were united in perfect harmony as they barked into their small cellphones and checked their watches on the street corners while waiting to cross. Stocks were the great equalizer.

"How do you think it will feel, being so high in the air?" she asked. She scanned the skyline. None of the buildings here compared to the North Tower, where he was going.

He shrugged. "It's high, but sturdy. I shouldn't feel anything different, I suppose."

Across from her, her husband was also checking his watch. "We should go soon. I don't want to miss my flight, love."

She left her croissant half-eaten on the table with his full cup of coffee.

***

They waited at his gate at Heathrow. She spent the time split between memorizing the lines of his face and watching the planes touch down, dreading the moment that his be called to board.

He was reading the newspaper. His hands were shaking. She picked up his left hand and traced his wedding ring. Was it sensible for a couple to be separated for so long, so early in their marriage?

The speakers crackled, and the attendant called his flight.

Panic settled in her heart. The pages of his newspaper rustled as he folded it and set it in the seat next to him. They stood up together.

He brushed her hair off of his shoulder. "At this time on October 5th, 2001, just one year from today, I will be right here again, waiting for you."

She squeezed his hand as tightly as possible. The wife searched his face, wondering if he was trying to memorize her face as hard as she was trying to memorize his. From her pocket, she drew a packet – a small clipping of a studio photograph she had had done for him to put on his desk.

"I don't want you to forget," she said between tears.

He carefully placed it into the breast pocket of his shirt. "I could never forget."

The call for boarding came. He kissed her forehead, her cheeks, the tip of her nose. "I'll call you when I land," he said before he kissed her lips.

"I'll be waiting," she said.

She stood at the gate for a long time, even after the plane pulled away from the airport, and took off into the gloomy sky.

CREATURE COMFORTS
NIMUE BROWN

I knew 'pigeon chest' meant me long before I knew what it signified. Arms like an orang-utan. Teeth like a rat. Big feet. Minnie Mouse feet, but walks like a duck. An ugly duckling. Ballet classes did not bring about a miraculous fix for my shortcomings. My body declined to look good enough in anything bought to try and hide it, which made clothes shopping a form of torture. Too fat some places yet too thin others.

"Could you just try and be a bit less..." or "be a bit more..." were the demands that echoed through my childhood. We were all very clear that, had I been a horse, they would have shot me. From the age of about four, I fantasised about being a horse. Even an ugly, useless horse would be a coherent creature. I grew up thinking of myself as a misshapen amalgam, a freakish cobbling together of life-forms. Something that should never have been. I don't know why but it never occurred to me to fantasise about just being a regular child, much less recognise myself as being one.

Aged nine, I found a one-eyed kitten in a dustbin, and, feeling sorry for the poor little thing, took her home with me.

"Of course, you can't keep it. Don't be so ridiculous, Dorothy," my mother said, hardly bothering to glance at my pitiful, mewling find.

Then she stopped what she'd been doing, and did an over-the top double-take, followed by squawking laughter. "It's even uglier than you!" she eventually managed. "Well, there's a turn-up for the books. If we keep it, you won't be the worst thing to look at any more. Won't that be nice for you?"

The idea evidently pleased her, and my kitten was allowed to stay.

Minnie the Moocher rapidly changed my young life. She ate ravenously, and I saw that being hungry was just what small things do. She grew into a large, friendly fuzz, always inquisitive, never apologetic about her missing eye. I discovered that I could love her for being an asymmetrical, one-eyed mess of a cat. Not in spite of how she was, but because of it. I loved her with every ounce of intensity my pre-teen heart could muster. Which is to say, a lot.

They could tell, somehow. The damaged and deformed, the lost, broken, ravaged, wounded and otherwise messed up. Over the years a one-legged, half tame crow, and a lame fox with a scarred nose became part of my family. There was a succession of rodents – some may have been Minnie's fault. Some were mortally wounded, but a few survived to stare at my kitty from the safety of cages and aquariums. One year, I bought a deformed hamster who couldn't walk, but could swing himself about Tarzan-style from the bars of his cage. Other creatures came and went, either recovering enough to move on, or dying and joining the little graveyard in the garden.

My mother complained endlessly about the cost of 'the zoo', and how I'd taken over the garden, the shed and my own bedroom with it. This made a change from her previous habit of only complaining about me, so I didn't really mind. It felt a bit like progress. I took a part time job to fund their meals, working after school. I can't say it did my grades any good, but I'd never been a star pupil so no one much cared. Me included.

The badger finished my mother. Or rather, the smell of it did. The poor thing had TB, and had crawled under her bed to die there. When she eventually found it, the poor dear wasn't in a very good state. She said they had to go. All of them. All of my beloved family of damaged, mangled, rescued creatures.

"Drown them, starve them, hit them with bricks, I really don't care. Just get rid of the lot of them. Or if you don't, I will. You've got until tomorrow."

I never hated her before that moment. Through all the years of her unkindness and mockery, I'd just gone along with it. Accepted is as fair and normal to complain about my rat's nest hair and my gorilla legs. This had gone beyond complaining though, and the threat to my family seemed very real indeed. I admit, I panicked. Hare-brained, for a while there. If hares used kitchen implements.

Most people misunderstand animals – even the pretty ones. For example, there's a common misconception that foxes are hunters – they get a bad press when it comes to lambs and chickens. Really, foxes are opportunists and will scavenge a free meal any time they can. Hunting is mostly limited to mice. Foxes, it must be said, will eat meat that is a long way short of fresh. Crows like a bit of carrion, too.

Badgers are good at digging, and my departed friend with TB wasn't the only badger in my life at this time. Animals are far more insightful, far more willing to do a friend a favour than most human-animals tend to think. Over the course of a night, a little bit later in the month, the badgers dug up the lawn for me. Not that there was much to bury in the end. Bird boned – my mother – it turned out.

THE LESSON
WARREN BULL

"Master, a Demon has told me I will die on December third."

"Congratulations, Student. Demons do not bother persons of no importance."

"Master, I do not want to die then."

"Then step forward. I will kill you now."

"Master, I do not want to die at all."

"Don't be foolish. Everyone born will die at some time."

"Wise teacher, I want to live past December third of this year."

"I will consult a book of knowledge. Then we can continue your lesson."

"You told me wisdom is greater than knowledge."

"Good remembering, Student. It is wise to know when to consult a book of knowledge."

***

"Master, have you consulted a book of knowledge?"

"Yes. If you wish to live past December third of this year, you will begin your lessons with Master Lau in Christchurch, New Zealand on December fourth. "

"Master, won't I be dead by then?"

"Would I send Master Lau a dead student?"

"No, Master."

"Here is information about the flight you must take and the visa you must apply for. Take them. Prepare for your journey."

"It is an honor to be your student."

"Of course, it is."

***

"Teacher, may I speak to you?"

"Of course, enlightened one."

"Your student told me you are sending him to study with another teacher in order to save his life."

"That is his understanding."

"May I ask how your action will save his life?"

"He thinks it will, but of course it may not."

"Please explain."

"A demon told him he will die on December third. By flying across time zones, he will leave on December second and arrive on December fourth without ever being in December third."

"But this may not save his life?"

"He will have no December third this year. However, the Demon did not say in which year he would die."

ASKING FOR A PUPPY
SARAH TRACY BURROWS

It was summertime. Early week. I sat at the kitchen counter at 'camp,' aka our summer cottage in the Adirondacks. A warm breeze blew through the windows. The lake sparkled and lapped at the rocky shore. Not only was I young, the camp was, too, built just a few years before. Come to think of it, my parents weren't old, either – younger than I am now.

My Mom, a dark-haired beauty, fussed in the kitchen, wiping the counter with her dishcloth, as I took up my ballpoint pen and wrote on the yellow lined legal pad:

Dear Dad,

I really want a puppy, a Golden Retriever. I'll feed and take it for a walk. You and Mom won't have to do anything...

Love,

Sarah

I slipped the letter in an envelope, addressed to my father's firm, two hours away. I looked at my mother. She smiled, nodding approval. It was best Dad receive it at work. Better than when he arrived home, tired, to an empty house, which felt all 'hot and steamy.'

Enjoy the lake! The city is brutal!

Yes, I wanted him to be in a good mood when he opened my letter.

After all, I'd asked for a puppy for several years. My grandfather had Libby. He stroked her head, told her she was a good girl. I'd never thought of asking, until the camp was being built. The builder and his son had two Golden Retrievers, Sandy and Corn. That summer the sound of Crag Point gravel announced father and son's arrival. Their red pickup would pull into the driveway with Sandy and Corn in back, open to the air, tails wagging, mouths panting, each anxious to jump out. I loved it when they did. It meant they were here for the day and I got to watch them, play with them, and fall in love.

After swimming, Corn would roll on the pine needled shoreline and shake, curling his golden fur. Sandy was sweet and snuggled. Each had white faces.

But with summer's end, the camp finished, off they went.

I missed Sandy and Corn!

In fact, I ached for those dogs. The photos of me, them, and the construction hanging on the knotty pine walls weren't going to cut it!

So, the letter asking for a puppy was mailed to my father.

That Friday night, just before dinner, I waited for Dad at the bend at Punkey Bay, quarter mile from camp. I sat high up on the boulder around which the road curved, the towering pines swayed, looking below to the secluded bay dotted with beaver huts. The water was quiet until a loud slap and splash sounded. A beaver had smacked its tail. As I watched it swim toward the hut, with only its head above water, gliding along leaving a small wake, I picked wild blueberries and ate them, like popcorn at the movies.

The next sound was Dad's BMW rounding the road from the other side of the bay.

What's he going to say about the puppy?

I shimmied down as fast as I could. He drove up the hill. Seeing me, he stopped. I jumped in. Dad was still in his suit. He put the car into gear. We turned the bend toward camp.

I felt anxious but didn't ask.

Without looking over Dad said, "I got your letter, Sarah. You can have a puppy."

My heart soared!

The puppies, bred by a veterinarian, arrived. We picked a female. Named her Taffy. I was in first grade. I loved that school year, my teacher, Mrs. Rogers, too. She got a puppy as well. We brought them in for Show and Tell.

Just like I had Sandy and Corn, I adored Taffy. She listened to me when I needed her, became my best friend.

Some of the trouble she got in, like all dogs do, included jumping the backyard fence to run down Farmer Street. One time, a car hit her, breaking her leg. I was relieved she lived and thought her cast was cool. I played veterinarian, using my Dad's toolbox.

I had it all planned out.

Cornell Veterinary School!

I liked dressing her up in my ski hat, goggles and gloves, taking her photo. I'd bring her to play with neighbor dogs, on boat rides at the lake.

I upheld my promise. I took good care of her. But I was mistaken my parents wouldn't have to do anything. I recall one instance Mom crying while my brothers fought, I asked for dinner, and Taffy chewed the kitchen chair rungs. Another when Dad wrote a $200 check to replace our neighbor's Afghan sweater that Taffy stole, shred, then buried. The time, too, Dad risked his life to pull Taffy from the ice when she fell through.

Taffy turned seven when I was in 8th grade, and sick. She wouldn't eat. Her eyes clouded over. Dad's toolbox wouldn't fix her. Three days later Dad and I were at the vet's. Cancer. I held and pet her, told her what a good girl she was while Dad cried beside me and the vet inserted the needle.

The house had already been quieter. My brothers were at college and work. The chairs replaced. I wanted things the way they'd been.

I want Taffy back.

Dad was so broken up he couldn't speak about another dog.

A letter won't work this time.

A few years later, though, when I was a junior in high school, my parents, with my impending college departure looming, decided to get another Golden Retriever.

We picked a female. Dad named her Ginger. He swore there was never a better dog. I compared her to Taffy but she soon captured my heart. Two years later, it wasn't easy leaving for college.

When I graduated, Ginger was six. We spent that summer at the lake together. Running through the woods. Relaxing on the dock. When I moved to Boston to start a job, I was excited but sad to say goodbye.

She lived six more years.

When you lose a dog too early, like we did Taffy, you fear losing the next too soon. Twelve seemed respectable, not easy.

Mom and Dad called to let me know she'd died. I was married. We had our first son.

When our youngest was in kindergarten, all three boys asked for a puppy. They wanted a Golden Retriever. We told them we'd find a breeder that fall. But early spring, while their father and I were at the mall, we passed a pet store we'd never noticed or looked for. A Golden Retriever puppy was in the front window.

Everything I'd learned told me not to buy from there, but go to a shelter or breeder. Yet the four-month-old was beautiful. He had long legs, big paws and reddish fur reminding me of Taffy and Ginger's. He leaned into me, was mellow and sweet.

The boys never wrote a letter but they signed a 'contract.'

Yes, we'll take care of him.

They decided on the name Biscuit.

Over the years, a friend told me, "you won the lottery with him."

Biscuit never chewed the rungs of the chairs though he made his own trouble sometimes. And that was good and fun. I may have cried, just like my Mom.

The day before our oldest was to head to college freshman year, Biscuit, just like Taffy, fell ill. He was nine. We raced him to the vet. A cat scan determined cancer. Hemangio Sarcoma.

There's nothing we can do.

Too weak to stand, I pet Biscuit and told him what a good dog he'd been, 'the best.' He never took his eyes from me, or me from his, as we said goodbye while the vet put the needle in.

My spirit broke. He was snatched from us. The house quiet, changed.

For two months, our youngest cried every night. His older brother was already a high school junior.

Why wait?

On a whim, I sent a letter to a breeder whose website 'Pathfinder Goldens' caught my eye. I began:

I need to share a story...

I told her how much we'd loved our dog that he was taken with no warning by cancer. I mentioned I'm a writer (not a veterinarian) including our military history.

She wrote back. One of her Goldens' was in a study to find out why dogs are dying from cancer. 'Pathfinder' represented the breeder's father who'd jumped out of planes during WWII, leading the way for the men behind him. Her female, Story, had just been bred. Six months before, Story had won Westminster's Best in Breed but better than that, would hopefully become a mother and comfort dog.

For me, the Universe collided. A sense of relief and hope washed over me. I felt I was meant to find Story. And that Libby, Sandy, Corn, Taffy, Ginger, and Biscuit were right beside me.

Turns out, Story was expecting. We now have Scout, a blessing.

SLEEPOVER

JEREMY BUSH

Alma, her agitation overwhelming her, unconsciously grabs her own hair and starts pulling on the ends of it. She shoves her oversized glasses, which have started slipping, back up her nose. "You are a no good, lousy blackguard!"

"I don't even know what that means."

"It means, to put it in simple enough language so even you can understand, that you are nothing but worthless, putrid scum!"

"Putrid?"

"Ahhhh!" Alma throws her hands up in the air in frustration. "I'm so sick of you! I've had *enough*!" She storms out of Alfred's room, slamming the door behind her. Alfred turns to his friend Gregory and winks while they both listen to her angry footsteps pound down the hallway. Then they hear her bedroom door slam shut, and they both burst out laughing.

"Al, you…you really oughtta be nicer to her," Gregory manages to get out through his laughter, "…she *is* your little sister."

Alfred wipes the tears away, "Yeah, but—but she deserves it. You heard her, didn't you? She called me a 'blackguard.' Any twelve-year-old who talks like that—heck, anyone who even *thinks* like that deserves whatever I dish out to them. Come on, she even called me 'putrid scum.' Not just scum; I'm worse than just plain old scum—I'm *putrid* scum." Alfred starts laughing again so hard that he has to wipe the tears from his eyes for a second time.

"Well, you deserved that. I mean anyone who on a regular basis sneaks into their little sister's room to rummage through her stuff and then steal her dolls and make them 'disappear'—and gets caught red-handed at it—deserves to be called putrid scum. And," Gregory stops, his laughter momentarily overtaking him again, "And I don't know exactly what a 'blackguard' is, but I'm guessing you would definitely qualify as one."

"It's all for her own good."

Gregory rolls his eyes, "Oh...*really*? And how's that?"

"You know, toughening her up. Makin' her ready to face the harsh world we live in...or something like that anyway."

Gregory grabs his pillow he brought to spend the night at Alfred's house, and smacks him over the head. "I'm glad you're not my brother. 'The harsh world we live in.' Give me a break. You're only a year and a half older. Like you would know any better." He gives Alfred another whack over the head with his pillow.

"You're only saying that because you like her." Alfred grabs his own pillow and swings baseball bat-style at Gregory. "You like my sister—you like my sister," he says sing-song, taunting his friend while hitting him with his pillow.

Gregory blushes, and he begins swinging his pillow like mad, "I do not!"

"You like my sister—you like my sist—" A well placed pillow to the gut cuts his teasing short.

There's a knock on the door, and Alfred's mother sticks her head in, smiling when she sees the boys. "Alright, you two. Don't get all wound up just before bed."

"Yes, Mrs. Stewart."

Alfred's mother smiles again and shuts the door.

"*Yes, Mrs. Stewart,*" Alfred imitates. Then he starts in with a new chorus, "You like my mother—you like my mother."

Gregory laughs and throws his pillow at Alfred's head. "Oh, shut up...just because I'm actually polite to her, unlike you."

"Hey, is that a new sleeping bag?" Alfred looks genuinely impressed. "I didn't notice it before. It looks pretty cool."

"Oh yeah. My uncle just gave it to me for my birthday. I haven't even had a chance to try it yet...except in my bed at home for a few nights." Gregory's face turns slightly red, afraid that this admission might not be seen by Alfred as being "cool."

But Alfred's face doesn't show any scorn, only approval. "My sleeping bag is old. And pretty worn out, too. But yours is nice."

"My uncle always sends us, my sister and me, birthday presents every year. He lives out in California; he's in the Air Force and lives on a base out there. The only problem is he can't remember when our birthdays are, so he usually just ends up sending them whenever he thinks of it...actually it's pretty fun. We never know when we might end up getting a package in the mail from him. It can be any time of the year when it might show up." Gregory feels a little self-conscious, telling his friend about things that are so very personal to him. He almost cuts himself short, worried he might get teased, but then bravely plows on with what he wants to say. "It—it doesn't even matter what he gets us, really. I mean, it could be something I don't really even like. It's just that it's coming from him, and that he actually thought of us and took time to get us something...it's—it's just special. Whatever he gets for us is always special..." Gregory falls silent, his face a dark crimson from all he had just confessed to his friend.

Alfred had lain down on his bed, with his hands resting behind his head, and he was staring up at the ceiling. "Yeah, I know what you mean. It's like that with my grandma. My grandma is real old. And she always sends me stuff for my birthday and Christmas. She buys presents—well, she just doesn't know because she's real old—she buys stuff that would be for little kids…Sesame Street and Barney. But it's just so nice of her to think of me and go out and get me anything. I keep all the stuff just because it's from her. I mean, it's…it's just so sweet of her…"

Down the hall Alma lets out a screech. "Mommm! Alfred beheaded my favorite doll! I'm going to kill that troglodyte!"

Gregory whispers, "Alfred, you didn't…" as he watches Alfred pull the doll's head out of its hiding place, a huge smile on his face.

A BIT OF SPARKLE
SUSAN CAREY

'Sitara, get in the cupboard!' Tariq ordered. Sitara squeezed into her usual hiding place, the broom cupboard beneath the sweatshop stairs. Looking through the keyhole she saw the inspector with his clipboard.

'How old's that one?' He pointed at Nanda.

'Old enough,' Tariq squashed a wad of notes into the inspector's top pocket. As the inspector counted the rupees he shrugged his shoulders, gave a cursory glance at the other workers and left.

Sitara's tummy rumbled. Something light and furry ran over her sandaled foot. She stifled her scream. Tariq knocked the all-clear and she came out.

She sat down and picked up the emerald green fabric. The colour reminded her of a picture she'd seen on a calendar of England. There were rolling fields and a castle. Her fingers had a life of their own as they danced over the material. Their fidgeting had woken her up last night as she slept on the sweatshop floor, sewing imaginary sequins on her blanket's scratchy surface.

When she got to the end of the scrolling leaves pattern she told her fingers to stop. She rubbed them warm and just above the cloth's selvedge she embroidered, with the smallest sequins she could find, a little star. Sitara's mother had promised that every night she would look up at the stars and if Sitara did too, they would stay connected.

***

Maude purchased nine yards of silky fabric from the man in the turban. He wobbled his head from side to side as he put the material into a plastic bag. Tooting Market was almost all Indian stallholders now, Maude reflected.

'She's going through with it, then?' Joe said as Maude ran up the garment on her ancient Singer.

'Yes, she heard this morning. She's got the job. Professional dancer on a cruise ship. She's over the moon, Joe. Try and be pleased for her.' Maude pushed her glasses back up the bridge of her nose.

'What's the point of going to university if she's going to throw it all away and become a stripper.' Joe lit his cigarette.

'I heard that, Dad.' Lynne came in, flopped down on the armchair and crossed her Ugged-feet over the pouffe. 'I'm a professional dancer on a cruise ship! The tips alone will keep you in fags and beer for a year.' She admired her just-manicured nails.

'Love that colour, Gran.'

Maude didn't look up as she rattled the machine along the hem, close to the sequinned edge. Holding it up to the light she said, 'This shade will suit you down to the ground.' She tossed the finished skirt to her granddaughter.

Lynne stood up and wriggled the skirt over her skinny jeans. Getting up onto the largest of the nesting tables she twirled on the spot. The sequinned, circular hem spun out, flashing back the light, Sitara's star subsumed in a kaleidoscope of colour.

Maude folded her arms and smiled. 'You'll knock 'em dead in that, love. I've always said there's nothing like a bit of sparkle.'

THORNS AND THISTLES SHALL IT BRING FORTH

BOB CARLTON

Every day, acres at a time, they are tearing Eden away. The land is left flat and unnaturally barren. There once were trees, prairie gourds, prickly pears without number, wildflowers whose colors were nuanced beyond naming. Now, here will be streets. There will be houses.

We moved here less than two months ago, believing in the power of our own volition, but what appeared a free choice now seems little more than a statistical trend toward regional growth. Our neighborhood, connected to the interstate by a dozen miles of winding asphalt two cars wide, had the appeal of a small human space fashioned out of, and integrated back into, surrounding wilderness. It was, in short, the country dream of suburbia. And now everyone wants to share in that dream. We must have places to live, places to shop, and roads wide enough to accommodate our insatiable need for convenience, as well as the urban necessities that claim the greater part of our days. The gods of gridlock and exhaust clamor for sacrifice and appeasement. We offer them homeless songbirds and cactus pulp.

The rumble and whine of heavy machinery begins and ends in darkness, continuing uninterrupted throughout the daylight hours. Gaps are appearing in the tree line, and I get glimpses of them rumbling past: bulldozers, front-end loaders, enormous vehicles whose technical names I do not know, but whose function is to scrape and flatten. It was the constant sound of laboring engines, punctuated by the intermittent beeping of their reversals, that drove the children from the park that bordered the fence that had once stood as a boundary beyond which lay the mystery of the untamed. Forced indoors, whole families began to implode under the pressure of constant presence. Divorce rates rose, and the sullen and defeated faces of children stared back at me as I drove past the school bus stop each morning.

We live in a cul-de-sac, second home in on the east side. Eight houses in all, the two that sit closest to the boundary fence were the first to experience the changes. Though all our children play together constantly, no one knows their neighbors' names, the rootless nature of the middle-class adult manifesting disinterest and distrust. I will call one couple Bert and Francine, the other Arnold and Michelle. Though I give them names here to bring coherence to the events, all of us are essentially interchangeable.

Bert and Francine's yard was the paragon of order and demarcation. Grass, uniform in color and height, grew to the edge of the property line and no farther, as if aware of the invisible lines plotted and plumbed by surveyors. Shrubbery and trees stood, trimmed and groomed, at strict attention, unmoved by the fiercest winds, and dropping leaves only as scheduled. One might fairly assume that the interior of the house was attractively regimented as well. Mice were the first invaders to disturb this strict tranquility, followed quickly by rattlesnakes. Once the mice were exterminated, whether through natural predation or Bert's chemical exertions, the snakes, aggressive with hunger, struck at anything moving. One day, a 'For Sale' sign appeared on the front lawn amidst dandelions and dollar weed.

Arnold and Michelle were the type of people who lavished their capacity for love and compassion on their pets. They could watch the evening news with indifference when the stories were of famine in refugee camps, epidemics in quaintly primitive countries, the collateral damage of wars fought by proximate despots in distant lands, but they could not restrain tears when viewing footage of a puppy mill in the Ukraine. Imagine their terror and grief when confronted with the evidence of the first visit of starving coyotes to the doghouse of their beloved Pomeranian and her new litter. Of course, the coyotes, and the foxes who followed, would have contented themselves with feeding on the squirrels had they been able to reach them. The squirrels, however, busied themselves in the attic of the house, causing roof leaks and electrical shorts. The grand hopes for their home that Arnold and Michelle once harbored were reduced to the continuation of return on investment implied by putting the house up for rent.

     Now, the chaos has become general. For every garden there are rabbits, for every new kitten there is a hawk. Even the plants, their wild, untamed forms further twisted by diesel and steel, are making their way here, driven by inscrutable vegetable need. The entire subdivision is being rapidly abandoned now that one child has had a fatal encounter with migrating fire ants and another has been victimized by the temptation of fruiting nightshade. Like diseases once thought eradicated will sometimes reappear in a neglected corner of some impoverished nation, plagues I had thought relegated to Biblical stories occur on an almost daily basis. Lines once drawn are being erased, and every day they are tearing Eden away.

THE OLD CHAPEL ROAD STORY

STEVE CARR

This story actually begins in Farmville, Virginia which is a little over a thousand miles from the Old Chapel Road and a farm in rural Missouri about fifteen miles from the town of Cameron. It was in Farmville that a completely black long haired feral cat was rescued from wandering the back yards and streets in Farmville in search of food and water. At approximately a year old he had learned to fend for himself, but he was a sweet natured cat that liked affection from humans, and in particular a couple who fed and petted him whenever he came around. They named him Sweety and while his journey wouldn't have happened without the couple or other humans, this is his story.

In December, the couple was leaving Farmville to move to Oregon and not wishing to leave Sweety behind to an uncertain fate, the couple decided to rescue him and put him in a cat carrier and drove with him in the back seat to the farm. After being an orphan, Sweety finally had a family, they had become his humans, and he rode the entire way without complaining, as if he had been brought up used to traveling as a passenger in a vehicle.

The one hundred and ten-acre Harms farm was located along a road named Old Chapel Road which had been the county road at one point but was now only used by a couple of farms on both sides of it. The Harms farm had fields of hay, a small pond full of trout, a large wooded area and a small creek with a footbridge that crossed over it. There was also a trailer and a pole barn, both located fairly close to the Old Chapel Road. At the Harms farm, Sweety was let out of the carrier and allowed to roam around in the field next to the house and in and out of the pole barn. Because of the time of year, the grass was dead and the trees bare of leaves, but none of that mattered to Sweety, of course. After scouting out the area for hours he always returned to his humans and spent the night in the warmth of the home with them.

This respite from being a cat without a family came to a quick end when visitors who came to visit Sweety's humans brought their three, large rambunctious German Shepherds with them. Sweety was out in the yard by the trailer when the dogs were allowed out of the car and as soon as they saw him they ran his direction, barking excitedly. Sweety was so alarmed by the dogs that he ran into the field and out of sight of his humans. When Sweety couldn't be found and after three days and lots of searching, his humans were forced to abandon him, believing because he had grown up feral he would know how to survive on his own or find someone to take him in at one of the nearby farms.

Sweety watched his humans drive off down the Old Chapel Road and found himself once again alone but this time there were no backyards or homes to visit in search of food. He wandered through the fields sniffing the holes of field mice, rabbits and moles and then circled the pond and watched the trout as they occasionally came to the surface for air. He crossed the bridge over the creek and wandered among the tall cedar trees and foraged for food among the fallen leaves. Those first few nights he slept under the trailer then found a hole in a wall in the pole barn large enough for him to get through; and there he established his new home, alone but safe.

Winter weather turned harsh quickly, bringing freezing rain and frost. As he wandered the fields in search of food, the ground beneath his paws was frozen hard. A thin sheet of ice covered the pond. He brought all of his natural instincts to the fore and quickly learned how to track and kill field mice, moles and small rabbits and an occasional squirrel, then became an expert hunter of small birds, catching them as they also were searching for food in the fields. Water was easy to get, thanks to the pond, even when it was frozen. At night or during the day when he needed comfort, he returned to the pole barn, which also provided an easy place to catch field mice seeking the same warmth he was.

Occasionally, Sweety would wander onto the Old Chapel Road and sit and watch for the car that had taken his new-found family away. There was another farm nearby that he thought about visiting but they raised border collies and their constant barking kept him from it. He had already decided he wanted nothing to do with dogs.

When snow began to fall, Sweety retreated to the pole barn, catching what few field mice he could inside it, and venturing out only when he had to in hopes of catching a bird. The snow became deep and lay on the ground until late February. He became thinner but the less he exerted himself, the less food he needed, and in the pole barn there were numerous places where he could just wait for better weather. He enjoyed sleeping anyway and what better place to do it then on an old burlap bag on a shelf? Even in the deepest snow he took time to wander up to the Old Chapel Road and look for his humans.

March brought an unusually warm reprieve from the frost and snow, and as the sun warmed the fields and water in the pond, and the snow and ice melted, Sweety returned to his original hunting grounds and found plenty of food and water. He also found a spot on Old Chapel Road where he could lie in the warmth of the sun and groom himself. It was there that he was lying when up the road came his humans. They jumped out of the car and ran to him as he ran to them, and after getting all the attention from them he had craved and missed, he took one last trip through the field and around the pond, with his humans following close behind.

Nineteen years later, being an old cat, Sweety sits on the arm of the La Z Boy chair his human sits in and enjoys having his thick fur combed and his head rubbed and reflects back on his life of adventure and comfort.

MURAL MAN
PATRICIA CARRAGON

No one could figure out why Debbie Weinstein hid behind the question mark. At thirty-one, she had no social life or marriage prospects. She drifted from one career to another. During the day, she taught fifth grade at P.S. 11. At night, she stayed home with her parents. Her good times were reading novels, listening to classical music, or watching The Ed Sullivan Show on the new Admiral television. For a change of pace, she would gaze out her bedroom window, letting her mind wander the streets below. Sometimes, she would help out with the holiday cooking. Being nondescript, Debbie was invisible at brises, bar and bat mitzvahs, and weddings —dwarfed by her younger and more successful siblings. Some yentas would whisper behind her back, "Plain and studious, cold like gefilte fish without the chrain."

Last weekend, Aunt Sophie, the local shadchan, insisted on fixing up her fledging niece with Manny Horowitz's son, a CPA accountant. Debbie protested and won. Her blind date with Zack Rosen, the fish-lipped salesman from Howard's, proved to be worse than being transformed into one of the "pod people" from the "Invasion of the Body Snatchers." As the fake stars of the Loew's Paradise Theater twinkled above, Zack's clammy hands crept underneath her skirt. No matter how many times she resisted, he wanted more. She excused herself and left the theater. Never again would she submit to Aunt Sophie's services. Debbie figured that she wasn't destined for love. She felt safer "wearing blinders" until she walked into the school auditorium for the Wednesday morning assembly.

The Francis Costa WPA murals flanked both sides of the auditorium's stage. On the left, "The Old Bronx" —the Dutch settlers and Native Americans preparing a meal. On the right, "The Bronx Today" —the apartment buildings, the Macomb's

Dam Bridge, the Hall of Fame, a classroom scene at P.S. 11, Yankee Stadium, the El, a construction site, and the Hunts Point Market. Debbie usually sat with her class on the left. But this Wednesday, the principal switched the order.

The fourth grade performed "Snow White and the Seven Dwarfs." Debbie preferred exploring the right-sided Bronx mural instead. In the Hunts Point section, a dark-haired fellow carried a cedar barrel on his shoulder. Studying his well-defined arms moistened her private parts. He was probably a goy in his mid-twenties, perpetually frozen in his alluring charm. Nice Jewish guys wouldn't dare schlep barrels or dirty their hands. They carried documents and pushed pencils. Being semi-Kosher didn't deter her from staring at her fictitious interest born from oil paint.

After assembly, it was back to class, the Louisiana Purchase, and the disorderly conduct from the last row. She hated 5-3—the class of misfits who were either too stupid or disruptive for the 5-1 or 5-2 levels. Being new to teaching, she lacked seniority for the better classes. She bit her lip, wishing for the clock to strike three. She regretted her move from the Madison Avenue secretarial pool, except for the groping hands of her ex-boss. Selling at S. Klein's and Ohrbach's killed her feet and self-esteem. Nevertheless, Debbie couldn't figure out what she wanted to do with her life. Like the hands of the clock above the blackboard, her life moved at a rigid pace.

The school bell rang at three. Time for her to grab her pocketbook and satchel, and lead her screaming brats out the door. Debbie didn't notice the knife-gray eyes of the assistant principal following her down the stairwell. Before Debbie reached the exit, Miss Donovan's haughty voice halted her. "Miss Weinstein, step into my office! You seem to forget that you're on a warning."

Miss Donovan served her her "walking papers." Debbie had to leave by the end of the term. Her reaction ping-ponged from relief to despair and back. The airless classroom and the assistant principal's scathing dismissal magnified the June heat wave. Fatigue trailed her to the bus stop. The bus arrived eighteen minutes later. Once in her seat, dizziness took over. Although the windows were open, the bus was like an oven. She closed her eyes and fell asleep.

She didn't remember getting off at 161st street and Jerome Avenue. Debbie walked east toward the bakery for her favorite cake, similar to the one Larsen's would sell. Bubbe also loved that confection and jokingly called it the "cockroach cake." A perfect solution to sooth her mood—rich milk chocolate icing covered with chocolate sprinkles over yellow cake. Before leaving the bakery, she overheard someone say "Excuse me, Miss. You forgot something."

A dark-haired man handed Debbie her cake box. From his clothes, face, and physique, he looked exactly like the man from the mural. Her mind questioned, *How could this be?* She stammered an inaudible "thank you."

He smiled and asked if she was in a hurry. She shook her head from side to side. He queried if she wanted to join him for a hamburger and coke. Debbie couldn't refuse.

This encounter could only occur in a dream. She pinched her arm to make sure. And it was a dream. The pinch came from someone else.

"Excuse me, Miss. Are you okay?"

Debbie wasn't in her seat. She was lying on the floor of the bus. To her surprise, the concerned person was her "Mural Man." Her eyes couldn't stray from his.

"Are you okay?" he repeated.

"Yes, I was asleep. The heat, you know . . ."

He picked her up. The sympathetic looks and comments from the passengers and driver embarrassed Debbie. Even worse was the wedding band on the "Mural Man's" hand.

As she departed the bus, he asked again if she was okay. Debbie lied when she said yes. He offered to buy her a hamburger and coke. She refused, preferring to go home. Noticing that she was unstable on her feet, the man brought her inside a nearby luncheonette. He ordered two medium-rare hamburgers and two cokes. Debbie thanked him for the meal. As she sipped her soda, his wedding band gleamed under the light. A piece of her hamburger dropped from her mouth, landing on his pants. She apologized. He said not to worry.

Debbie had no appetite and left most of her hamburger untouched. She hardly spoke at all. The man assumed it was because of the heat. He almost made conversation, but backed off. He paid for their meals and escorted her outside. He said goodbye and wished her well. The "Mural Man" left to take the uptown train home. Debbie continued walking toward the Concourse. She passed the bakery and Bubbe's "cockroach cake." Her favorite cake sickened her that day and the days that followed.

PRECIOUS MEMORIES
JEAN M. COGDELL

I watched as Dr. Cynthia Morris scratched copious notes with her fancy Mont Blanc. From this side of the large imposing desk, I couldn't decipher her scrawl. A shiny laptop on her left looked brand new. Odd she preferred scribbling on paper, must be a doctor thing. Other than my statistics, Jane Bristol, age 25, what could she write? She didn't know me. Didn't know him.

Her pen paused, she looked up, meeting my gaze, she acknowledged my presence with a condescending smile. I could spot a fake a mile away, and she was a phony.

"Jane, how are you doing today?"

She was kidding, right? What a dumb question. Words stuck in my throat.

"I can't help if you won't talk to me. Don't you want my help?"

Of course, I wanted help, but there was nothing she could do. No one could help, not now. Unless she had the power to turn back time and alter the course of my future. Nothing I said mattered. She knew I was beyond help, and so did I.

Head high, I sat silent, ankles crossed and feet tucked under the chair. Mama's etiquette 101 burned in my brain. Circumstances don't define the lady. Hands folded, I waited.

"All right, let's try something different this morning. It's called word association. I'll say a word, and you answer with a word. Say the first word that pops into your mind. Don't think, just respond." Dr. Morris flipped through the file; I assumed mine. "Understand?"

"Sure," I said.

I could think of worse ways to spend the next hour than playing a child's game. But, she could forget about me not thinking, not remembering, because that was not possible. That was asking too much. I leaned back and willed myself to relax. To humor the good doctor.

Pen poised, she tossed out the first word. "Time."

"Waste."

This was a total waste of mine, but it didn't matter, I had lots to waste now.

"Hand."

My reply escaped with a soft sigh. "Touch."

His— gentle and demanding as he caressed my body, lips teasing...

See, couldn't shut down my thoughts. Not sure I wanted to forget, at least not everything. Touch and kisses were worth remembering. Certain memories kept me warm at night. I squirmed in the hard chair as I crossed and uncrossed my legs. Dr. Morris peered over tortoise shell glasses her dark eyes boring into mine. I dropped my gaze.

"Memories." Each syllable enunciated as if spoken to a child.

"Precious. Precious memories, how they linger, how they—"

I clamped my lips and swallowed. The words of the old hymn from my childhood stuck in my throat. The song had bubbled uninvited to the surface of my mind. I wished all memories were precious. They weren't.

Dr. Morris scribbled on another page, looked up and frowned.

"Stick to a one-word response. Okay?"

She waited for my nod and then continued. "House."

"Fashion."

We'd met at a fashion house in New York. He'd worked magic draping my skin in silk, transforming the soft fabric and me into a thing of beauty. I'd fallen hard.

A shiver hardened my breasts. They strained against the rough, cotton tee-shirt. No more silk for me. I missed the silk. I missed Mark.

"Love."

"Hate."

Those two words represented two sides of a double-edged knife. Don't go there, Jane. Don't go to that dark place. Focus on the good, not the bad.

"Truth."

"Lie," I said.

All lies. I didn't know about Amanda, not for six blissful, ignorant months, and then I did. Sometimes a lie is easier to live with than the truth.

"Right." Dr. Morris mouth pursed, tapped her pen against the file as if making a point.

"Wrong," I said.

Wrong and criminal, him not me. He lied. Love doesn't cheat, lie, or hide a wife. Breathe, Jane. Focus. Remember the good. Forget the rest.

The steel bracelets jangled as I clenched my fists and watched the doctor scribble another page with more judgmental nonsense.

"That'll be enough for today," she said.

Her tone, clipped and professional, she dismissed me with a plastic smile. A soft buzzing interrupted the silence as she pressed a small round button embedded in the rich mahogany of her desk. Behind me, the door clicked. I stood and brushed at the wrinkles on my thin, cheap pants. My escort had arrived. I turned and walked toward the open door. At the threshold, I paused.

My voice firm and strong as steel. "He should've loved me."

"Jane?" Dr. Morris looked up, raised her hand, and nodded for my companion to wait.

I squared my shoulders and through gritted teeth replied, "Love doesn't lie. He really should've loved me."

Memories of cool silk, naked skin, and sweet, deep kisses filled my mind, crowding out the dark thoughts of blood and death. Humming, I stepped through the door and left with the white-coated orderly. As we walked, I set free the words from my past, letting them echo through the long sterile halls.

Precious memories how they linger, how they ever flood my soul...

WANING RIPPLES
BRETT CULLEN

They gave me this medal for "bravery." But it's too heavy for my chest and too painful in my palm.

I ignored Bill when he pointed at a high flock of swallows. The air pressed me down. With my skin sticking to itself, it took effort just to amble homewards. I dreaded another day at the factory, worrying summer was slipping away. My summer. I said, "We should go swimming first thing tomorrow." He preferred sleep and his mum's bacon sandwiches. But I said May bathed in the river before work (because I knew that would get to him).

After dawn, Bill and I undressed on the silt riverbank, scarred with footprints from yesterday's bathers. I rushed out of my braces, trousers and underwear and skipped into the treacle-brown water. The cold stabbed me in the chest; I panted just treading water. Bill was wading in, pale and arms up, like he was mimicking a ghost. "My," I teased him, "asthma." I was just joking. And I heard something behind the reeds – I really did – so I shouted, "The girls are here. Don't let May catch you shaking like a lily." His face twisted as he splashed into the water; I was already racing away. But when I turned back – gone. He didn't reappear, as I drifted with his waning ripples, so I ducked under and snatched at the passing murk.

Nothing.

I came back up to breathe.

I ducked again and touched something wispy, slipping away.

I grabbed and kicked and yanked against the sucking current.

I gasped and opened my fist above the water - Bill's hair.

I dived, grasped again.

Nothing.

Now, my knuckles wrap and whiten around the medal. I kept it to remember him; I never want to open my fist.

OCEAN'S ELEVEN
DAVE D'ALLESSIO

We met in the back room of Sergei's Starfall, a dump of a bar on the far side of the Moon. Farside's a good place to make plans. It feels like no one's watching.

Everyone was there, the ones that knew each other exchanging knowing nods and silent acknowledgements. I'd gotten Duvalier for the cybernetics, and Maria Lleshdedaj had brought three of her gunsels for muscle. Ishikawa was handling the explosives; I'd asked if he wanted an assistant but he'd just sneered at me. Mario Fela and Lim Po were going to roughneck the grav carts. If you want a long criminal career with minimum time served, learn to wrangle a grav cart and leave your blasters at home.

There were two I didn't know personally: Sandy Gonsalves was the yegg. I'd heard she was good, very good, the best on Mars. She was tiny, less able to handle mass than the rest of us, but cracking locks is brains and touch, not muscle. And the getaway pilot, Adam X. He'd been booted from the Space Patrol for having a "relaxed" attitude about safety regs. Word was he could fly a gnat up an elephant's trunk.

I should have seen the way he sailed into the seat next to hers, eyes locked on her baby blues. It would have tipped me off that he was gaga for her on first sight. I should have seen the tiny smile on her face that said she felt the same. I would have broken that up, pronto. We had a job to pull.

If I'd seen, you wouldn't know my name. Hi. I'm Murray Ocean. That's why the newsies called us "Ocean's Eleven." I won't say I'm pleased to meet you, under the circumstances.

The rest of the room was empty and Duvalier gave me the thumbs up: no bugs. "All right," I said. "This is simple. We're hitting the Bank of Hong Kong in Port Luna."

If anyone had looked shocked I'd have fired them on the spot. The Port Luna HKB holds the interplanetary exchange currency for the entire inner Solar System. On a good day, there's over a million Yuan in gold in its vaults. Anyone intimidated by that was on the wrong team.

"Here's the plan," I told them, and we went over it in detail. It was simple enough. Lleshdedaj and her boys would secure the corridor in front of the bank. Duvalier would scramble the security cameras and systems. Adam X would keep the getaway rocket hot.

The rest of us were going in from behind, through the maintenance tube. Ishikawa would blow the back of the vault, Gonsalves would hit the safe deposit boxes, and Fela and Lim Po would haul off the gold. Simple. Easy as pi.

We checked our watches and I told them, "Okay, beat it. Don't be seen together."

It was Adam X that started the trouble, and even if I hadn't seen it before I should have caught it then. "Hey," he said. He jerked a thumb toward Gonsalves. "It wouldn't look right, a classy dame like this walking around Farside all alone."

"Right," I said. Maria's boys had already melted away, so I told him, "Take care of it."

I should have known better, pairing our pale Martian queen with the green-eyed devil. You can't plan for everything, but you damned well ought to try.

It was all going well. Duvalier had cracked CloudWeb so many times he could do it in his sleep. In seconds, the guards were watching scenes from the week before on their surveillance monitors. We sealed up our nano suits and hit the tube while it was still in vacuum. No one would look for us there, and in space no one can hear explosions. It was perfect.

Four shaped charges later we were inside the vault. Fela and Po had the carts out, and we were stacking them with gold bars as fast as we could wrangle the shiny stuff. The three of us were all from Earth or Venus, so Luna's one-sixth gee made the gold seem light.

Gonsalves was rifling the boxes. She had the touch, all right. Locks practically melted away if she looked at them sideways. A pile of loot started to accumulate.

"Look," she said. "Diamonds."

She held one up to the light for me. "That'd make one hell of an engagement ring," I said, and got back to business.

The next time I looked she was gone. Damn! "Leave what's left and let's get out of here," I told the boys, and we wrestled the loaded carts into the tube. They didn't weigh anything – that's what a grav cart does – but they still had plenty of mass and they resisted force plenty.

We met Ishikawa on the launch pad. "They're gone," he said.

"What? Who?" I was barely listening. I was looking for the getaway ship.

"The pilot and the yegg." Ishikawa was ronin samurai, and anger beneath him. He was simply pointing out that conditions had changed. "They have left together."

It made no sense. "But we have the gold," I said.

Ishikawa patiently pointed out, "But they have each other."

You read the rest off CloudWeb, except for the names, and I changed those to protect the guilty. You know I was found alone, sitting on a grav cart piled high with gold, just waiting for the police. The others got away. I'm not a rat, so they're still out there. Still working, too, I think; just a couple days ago I heard about a payroll heist on Ceres that sounded like it had Lleshdedaj's fingerprints on it.

But I'm telling you this story for two reasons. First, because I want Gonsalves and Adam X to know I wish them all the luck in the Solar System. They're going to need it. It's never easy to make one life together out of two.

And so they know that someday I'm going to kick their asses.

THE THREE CHAMBERS
PRADYUMNA N. CHAUDHURI

The iron foundry was working overtime.

Whispered messages travelled across the huge setup atop the hill. The Fort was awaiting orders.

The Mughals had decided that war was inevitable. But who will fight the war? The Mughals were too powerful to fight directly. They had allies like us to fight on their behalf.

Kabul and Khandahar were actively planning a direct attack to take over the Mughal Empire from their cousins ruling this side of the Indus!

And my Kingdom was the ally that was the last bastion before reaching the Mughal Empire.

Active for over a hundred years, this foundry had cast some of the most famous cannons known to man.

We were preparing for war for almost a decade now.

The Fort was ancient and existed for a few centuries. This Fort was in ruins for most of the last fifty years. More recent restoration ensured the protection of the older Fort just below.

The work was on. The number of logs consumed was never shared. But huge trees felled from the nearby dense forest remained stacked and regularly replenished within the sprawling Fort.

A hundred cannons were readied. And delivered across all my forts.

Our family and the Emperor were related. But with the current Emperor, things were not so good. We had lost favour. I was waiting for an opportunity to restore our family's pre-eminence.

"I want our family and Kingdom's position restored.

The only way to do so is to be of use when the Emperor needs help. We should be useful when the great Empire is exposed to an external attack. He has already ruled for forty years. His age is catching up. We need to be on high alert at all times."

The foundry was part of that strategy.

A clear day was a giveaway. The smoke from the foundry could be seen across the plains.

We received a message from the Emperor.

"O King! How are you doing? We are related as all know. I know your famous foundry is active. Are you planning a gift for me? A large cannon for the great Mughal army? Let me know when should I come to inspect the cannon!"

And I was angry. How did the Emperor know of my plans?

I had to play on.

I replied to the royal summons…

"O Emperor, we are grateful that you remembered us and our old relationship. We hold our relationship with pride and dignity. Related to the mighty Mughals is by itself a blessing. The foundry is working to keep the great Mughal Empire strong and protected. We will be delighted to welcome you – always. It's your family and you need no invite. Our hospitality will welcome you, my Emperor!"

With this message, the immediate political escalations were calmed.

The work continued in full steam. Ore reached the foundry and the best alloys were researched and subsequently used for the casting of the latest cannons.

And the Emperor's words continued to ring in my mind. The biggest cannon for him! The biggest cannon in the world?

The northern border was under ferment. Advance battalions were attacking the fortifications. They were attacking and then suddenly withdrawing. This was a confusing tactic. Either attack or don't – why attack and then withdraw?

I seemed to know. They were testing our fortifications. We were careful not to share all our aces.

How strong? How much will it take to seize the forts?

Our Kingdom was a buffer state between external attacks and the capital province of the Mughal Empire. The huge Afghan army planned to overrun our Kingdom on their way to attack the heart of the Mughal Empire.

After months of short incursions, suddenly there was a full-blown attack!

We were prepared.

All our border forts were ready to repel the attack. Our new cannons were positioned and boomed across the rugged terrain.

Simultaneously, several outposts were attacked. And I knew we could hold off the attack without help from the Mughal army. We had prepared for this.

The great Mughal Emperor was watching how long I could hold off the attack.

I had other plans.

We repelled the attack comprehensively. The Afghan army retreated – bruised and defeated. But we didn't relent.

We continued attacking and taking over parts of their Kingdom and ransacked their forts and treasury.

Kabul was only a day away now!

We captured over thirty forts and confiscated their gold and inventory. We had become slow laden with carts full of gold, jewellery, precious stones and silver!

Then suddenly, we retreated and returned all captured lands.

Why?

I was supposed to defend only. And I attacked! And how!

I didn't want to antagonize the Mughal Emperor for attacking without his permission. He might feel that I am rebelling against the great Mughal Empire.

He might feel I am trying to build a parallel centre of power independent of the Mughals.

I was taking what was due to me and my Kingdom. My Kingdom was denied its due share of revenues for decades thanks to the Emperor's insular policies.

And within a week I was leading a triumphant army back to my fabled old capital.

And when I returned, I had a message awaiting me from the great Mughal.

"I knew why the foundry was working overtime. I knew you were ready and your army was prepared. The great Mughal army was ready too but on standby. You are loyal, my friend and my relative! I have no doubts in restoring all that was denied to you all these years. You are truly one and half times anyone I know! You are the new governor of the great Deccan now."

And I was overjoyed!

The honor of my family, the honor of my Kingdom, my honor – was finally restored! Restored to the previous levels of my ancestors! But should I have got more?

A few centuries later…

My wife, my son and I were visiting an ancient city.

And we were visiting a huge Fort on a hilltop. The ramparts and the fortification spread across hills, as far as the eyes could see. We walked on the wall and bowed in front of the largest cannon ever cast. We visited a foundry – the likes of which were never seen or known before to man.

Finally, we visited the subterranean triple water tanks. Each tank was designed to hold rainwater. Each drop of rainwater that fell on the walls of the fort was harvested into one of the three tanks. Each tank had enough water to maintain an army – a hundred thousand standing – for a month.

And beneath the tanks were the chambers – three waterproof chambers filled with all the gold and jewellery surreptitiously won by me!

A PIG IN COURT

C.J. COLE

I cannot believe he pulled it off. Strudwick is a genius! Of course, we already knew that. Why else would he be in charge of the Memory Visualizer program? Of course, none of us believed Farmer Longfellow had murdered Dr. Cerenkov, the Head of the Department of Visual Dynamics. He had no motive.

Detritus, Inc. hired Douglas Longfellow, a farmer from Arkansas, because of his dedication to animals. His twelve-acre farm was home to one-hundred-and-ten animals, plus the twelve members of his family.

When it was time for Detritus, Inc. to put all of its recycled space junk to good use in the newly-named Department of Visual Dynamics, the execs got all the right permissions to start the animal testing for its electronic devices. The company geniuses foresaw a bright future for memory visualization technology in the fields of Law Enforcement, National Security, and Justice.

Longfellow was made a company employee in charge of caring for the lab animals: mice, chickens, Guinea pigs, sheep, pigs, and chimpanzees. He worked alongside a zoo veterinarian named Keith Jenkins, who watched over the animal's health.

Different sizes of Visualizers were made to fit the different animals.

The Memory Visualizer for mice shows images of each mouse's memories of the maze, and the location of the cheese treat, as the mouse last saw it. As the maze is always the same, each mouse not only follows its nose, but also relies on its memories to find the treat.

Chickens have a clear memory of what the processing machine looks like and the sound it makes. Their stress levels go up every time they hear the sounds of machinery, making them produce less eggs. When they cannot hear machines, chickens are more productive.

Sheep, it turns out, never really get lost. They create maps of the landscape in their minds and have an excellent sense of direction. They just enjoy playing hide-and-seek with the farmers. It is nothing but a game.

Chimps have mostly visual minds, same as humans. They can recall memories of visual cues they saw months before with the same ease as four-year-old human children.

The long-term memory tests for the pigs started when the murder happened.

The security officer making the morning rounds found Dr. Cerenkov dead, next to the pigpen. The only personnel with access to the animal testing labs after hours are the Head of the Department, Farmer Longfellow and the vet, Dr. Jenkins. Security access cards are demagnetized by a machine when each scientist leaves the premises, but as anything could happen to the animals during the night, both Farmer Longfellow and Dr. Jenkins have their living quarters inside the facilities. Unfortunately for Farmer Longfellow, Dr. Jenkins had been absent for the past three days due to the flu. Douglas Longfellow had been alone with Dr. Cerenkov that night.

A strand of his hair had been found next to the dead body. His prints were on the syringe containing the poison that killed Dr. Cerenkov, found in one of the garbage containers under the lab garbage shoots. The trial was considered a mere formality given the overwhelming evidence against poor Longfellow.

It was Dr. Nick Strudwick who saved the day by taking a chance and yelling out, "Wait! I have one last witness!" just as the judge was about to send the jury to deliberate in the next room.

By pure miracle—and curiosity, suppose—the judge let the last witness give its testimony in visual form, with the Visualizer strapped on its head, the electrodes in place, and an HDMI cable attached from the back of the Visualizer helmet to Dr. Strudwick's tablet.

The witness snorted when it was given Dr. Cerenkov's shirt to smell. The image of the doctor taking notes and instructing Farmer Longfellow to give the pig a treat while a technician listened to its heartbeat appeared on the table in the form of an amateur video.

Next, pictures of the staff who worked in the Memory Visualizer program were passed for the porcine witness to look at. The pig snorted and gave a happy squeal when it was shown the photo of Farmer Longfellow, who the pig knew as "the man with the treats." The video that came up when the witness was shown Dr. Jenkins, showed the doctor just a couple of inches from the camera (the pig's eyes) whispering, ordering the pig to be quiet. Then the doctor pulled a black ski mask over his face. The figure clad in black dragged something big and heavy in what at first seemed to be a laundry bag, but turned out to be a lab coat. With a swift movement, the man unrolled the heavy object onto the floor. It was the lifeless body of Dr. Cerenkov. Since it was close to the pigpen, the pig saw the doctor's face clearly.

Dr. Jenkins had taken the mask off to sooth and quiet the animals that knew him well, to avoid alarming Longfellow with the ruckus. Neither Farmer Longfellow nor Dr. Jenkins was informed of the kind of testing being conducted. They only took care of the lab animals, and information was provided on a need-to-know basis. If Jenkins had known about the Memory Visualizer program, he would have never taken off that mask.

The judge's shout of "Seize that man!" filled the courtroom when Jenkins—who had attended the trial as to not look suspicious—tried to flee. He later confessed to having a duplicate of his ID card, and having been paid by the execs of a competing electronics company to kill the Head of the

Department as to the competitors more time to come up with a similar device. Obviously, Jenkins was not the only employee working in Detritus, Inc. as a double agent.

This was the first time in history that a pig testified in court, and saved its farmer from life in prison.

* * *

By pure miracle—and curiosity, I suppose—the judge let the last witness give its testimony in visual form, with the Visualizer strapped on its head, the electrodes in place, and an HDMI cable attached from the back of the Visualizer helmet to Dr. Strudwick's tablet.

The witness snorted when it was given Dr. Cerenkov's shirt to smell. The image of the doctor taking notes and instructing Farmer Longfellow to give the pig a treat while a technician listened to its heartbeat appeared on the tablet in the form of an amateur video.

Next, pictures of the staff who worked in the Memory Visualizer program were passed for the porcine witness to look at. The pig snorted and gave a happy squeal when it was shown the photo of Farmer Longfellow, who the pig knew as "the man with the treats." The video that came up when the witness was shown Dr. Jenkins, showed the doctor just a couple of inches from the camera (the pig's eyes) whispering, ordering the pig to be quiet. Then the doctor pulled a black ski mask over his face. The figure clad in black dragged something big and heavy in what at first seemed to be a laundry bag, but turned out to be a lab coat. With a swift movement, the man unrolled the heavy object onto the floor. It was the lifeless body of Dr. Cerenkov. Since it was close to the pigpen, the pig saw the doctor's face clearly.

Dr. Jenkins had taken the mask off to sooth and quiet the animals that knew him well, to avoid alarming Longfellow with the ruckus. Neither Farmer Longfellow nor Dr. Jenkins was informed of the kind of testing being conducted. They only took care of the lab animals, and information was provided on a need-to-know basis. If Jenkins had known about the Memory Visualizer program, he would have never taken off that mask.

The judge's shout of "Seize that man!" filled the courtroom when Jenkins—who had attended the trial as to not look suspicious—tried to flee. He later confessed to having a duplicate of his ID card, and having been paid by the execs of a competing electronics company to kill the Head of the

Department as to buy the competitors more time to come up with a similar device first. Obviously, Jenkins was not the only employee working in Detritus, Inc. as a double agent.

This was the first time in history that a pig testified in court, and saved its farmer from life in prison.

THE DAY THE PONY WENT
JEANNE DAVIES

Liz heard the tinkering of cups downstairs and guessed Roger was making early morning tea. The faint sounds of morning drifted in from the farmyard as she rolled over, basking in the spring sunlight shining through yellow curtains. Then a sadness came over her; today was the day Scrumpy was going. She reflected on all the fun they'd had with the little pony over the past 15 years … although she'd always been a naughty horse.

"What time are they arriving?" Roger asked as he juggled with a tray at the half open door.

"Not 'til 4."

"Does Sophie know it's today?"

"I think she's hoping it won't happen; she tried to persuade me to hold on to her until grandchildren arrive!"

"Well, that won't happen for a few years yet; Martin's got his career to think about," muttered Roger, clumsily landing the tray on the dresser.

Liz glared at the spilt liquid in the saucers.

"We can't go on like this, Roger; she's having a terrible influence on Fred … she must go today!"

After breakfast, Liz fed the chickens and goats and then went to clean out the stables. Fred seemed subdued and didn't protest whilst she brushed him down. She stood back, admiring his deep mahogany coat. Ir gleamed in the sunshine.

"You really *are* a handsome fellow!" she affirmed.

Fred gazed ahead solemnly; his dark framed eyes made him seem sad and seal-like.

Liz cantered Fred around the field several times. It was always a pleasure to ride this big powerful Bay as he'd once been a top Eventer and was all of 16.3 hands tall. It seemed a shame to stable him again, but she needed to focus her attention on the pony.

Scrumpy, a New Forest Bay, was shorter and stouter than Fred, especially in her winter coat. Her flaxen mane and tail stood out against her chestnut coat. She dumped everyone who rode her except for Sophie, but adults she scorned the most, deserting Liz on a road once.

"I know you're a wicked horse, yet still I shall be sorry to see you go," whispered Liz.

The pony whinnied and peeled back her lips to reveal yellow tombstone teeth. Liz ignored the devilish look in Scrumpy's eye and allowed her to nuzzle her jacket to find the usual hidden apple.

Scrumpy had been great fun over the years despite her behaviour at children's' parties when she flatly refused certain kids to mount her. She had a deep hatred for their grounds-man and often took it upon herself to destroy items of his equipment. She'd once eaten the padding of his car seat when he left the door open.

Roger was busy cleaning up Scrumpy's horse box for the new owners. He carefully polished the plaque that Sophie had made with Scrumpy's name on it. Fred was watching Roger intently with his head leaning over his stable door.

If Scrumpy hadn't been so risky, Liz would have taken her for a final canter, but she decided to play it safe and lead-walk her to nearby water meadows at Churchy Meads before returning her for grooming. She carefully put on her brightly coloured headcollar and lead-rope and nostalgically took one last photograph for Sophie. She called Emma the Collie and their young Dalmatian, Humphrey, to join them.

They crunched over puddles turned overnight into bewitched glass; baubles of snow perched precariously on naked trees threatened to drop in any whisper of wind. Emma, being a very sensitive animal, walked close to heel but Humphrey streaked through mushy snow causing a blizzard with his long whipping tail.

Sun pierced through a crack in the powdery cloud like a torch from heaven and the light changed to a haunting silver hue, which bounced off a silver Mercedes abandoned by walkers. Curiously there was a pile of clothes on the bonnet – perhaps someone had bravely taken an icy dip nearby, Liz thought.

Before she could stop him, Humphrey dashed over to the car and began dragging the clothing to the floor. Emma ran over to rescue them but instead the Dalmatian and Collie picked up an arm each of a man's tweed sports jacket and danced across the meadow in a tug of war.

Dropping the pony's leading reign, Liz tore after them only to find the Saville Row jacket had two gaping holes beneath each armpit. She scolded them both and quickly put Humphrey on lead. As she turned back towards the car she saw to her horror that the pony had foraged through the pile of soggy clothes and found a rather smart broad-rimmed ladies country hat. Made by Burberry, Scrumpy was lovingly creating a fringe around the brim, whilst the bow dangled limply in shredded tatters. Liz tried to grab the hat, but Scrumpy's jaw clamped down tight on her prized possession.

Liz peered through the car windows but they were steamed up. Seeing nobody was about, she carefully rearranged the clothes back on the bonnet of the car, hiding the sports jacket at the bottom of the pile. To make a quick getaway, Liz realised they'd have to take the hat with them.

As they hurried home, a huge sash of rainbow arched over the farm cottage, its windows peeping shyly above the hawthorn hedgerows.

Scolding her again, Liz put Scrumpy into the paddock for her last afternoon at Thurlestone farm … hat still in mouth. She headed to the kitchen to put the kettle on and put a few crumpets on the top of the Aga before sinking into the chair. Her heart rate had just begun to calm when Roger burst into the kitchen looking ashen.

"You didn't put the extra chain on Fred's stable door, Liz!" he said.

Fred had used his teeth many times to open the door but Liz had been so preoccupied with the pony leaving, she'd forgotten to chain it. They rushed outside in time to witness Fred clearing the fence effortlessly, galloping around Scrumpy's paddock and then trotting grandly over to the pony. She seemed delighted and they nuzzled each other's manes. As soon as Liz and Roger went over they both began to tear around the paddock together in a frenzied race.

"She's responsible for this!" bellowed Liz, pointing her finger at Scrumpy. "We must get Fred stabled again."

Eventually Fred sauntered over to Liz to accept a carrot.

"I'm surprised at you, Fred," Liz chastised as she secured the extra chain on the stable door.

The smell of burning crumpets radiated from the kitchen.

"You go, Liz, I'll see to Scrumpy," shouted Roger.

As Liz entered the smoke-filled kitchen, the cat dashed passed her, nearly tripping her over. She soon realised he'd knocked a whole churn of buttermilk over whilst trying to escape.

It took some while for Liz to calm down. Roger came in from grooming Scrumpy and put a hand on her shoulder.

"She's groomed and ready, dear. Butter wouldn't melt in her mouth."

They heard a car making progress along the bumpy gravel drive. Liz regarded herself in the mirror before fixing on a fake smile and going out to greet Scrumpy's buyers. The silver Mercedes looked very familiar and she soon realised to her horror that it was the one parked at the water meadows. A short, well dressed, blonde woman in her mid forties walked towards Liz, followed by a man of a similar age wearing a dishevelled tweed jacket. Liz felt the colour rise to her cheeks.

"Hello," said the woman. "We've come to buy your pony."

Liz was stunned and glued to the spot. The woman looked over Liz's shoulder in disbelief. Roger was leading Scrumpy out to greet the new owners ... with the hat still firmly gripped and dangling from her mouth.

"Is this some sort of joke?" the woman asked through thin lips, her face turning bright pink.

After the couple left, Liz and Roger sat in the pantry with a glass of wine and laughed about it all ... the day the pony went ... although it didn't actually go because the buyers stormed off and sped down the driveway as though the car wheels might catch fire.

A week later, two girls arrived with their parents and took a great shine to Scrumpy. Liz watched in amazement as the pony trotted amiably around the compound with the eldest on her back; Sophie had been about that age when she'd first ridden Scrumpy. Memories came flooding back and Liz felt a tear trickle onto her cheek. This stubborn horse had waited for these girls, and she was in her element with them; she had chosen them just like she did Sophie all those years ago.

"Would you believe it, Liz! They were so pleased, they paid the whole amount in cash!" Roger beamed.

"Just as well, they don't know what they're letting themselves in for!" sighed Liz.

A SURPRISE FIND
PAT JEANNE DAVIS

Laura put on a white T-shirt with the words "Adopt A Pet" written in dark blue letters across the front, twisted her long hair up and clipped it under a barrette. She'd promised to help out at Aunt Peg's yard sale. Laura grabbed her keys. There'd be no time to look over the pieces being sold. If anyone had told her she'd be able to buy a house, she'd have said impossible. That was until Aunt Peg put the semi-detached up for sale at a price she could afford. Soon Lucy, her golden retriever, would have a yard to run around in.

When Laura pulled up at her soon-to-be home, Aunt Peg was talking to a man. She positioned herself behind a table ready to go to work. A surge of nostalgia gripped her as she gazed at an untagged Victorian Cameo music box nestled between knick knacks. It couldn't be her grandmother's. She'd always wondered what became of this hand-crafted piece. Laura was about to claim the music box when the man approached.

"Beautiful," he said, lifting the lid. Gran's favorite song came drifting out. Laura's eyes filled as the familiar melody with the words, "I can't help falling in love with you . . ." ran through her mind. It was the song Gran and Grandad danced to the night he proposed.

"Beautiful," he repeated after the music stopped. "How much?"

It was her own fault. If only she'd remembered to set the alarm for this morning. "Well. Um."

Before she could say any more, her aunt stood at her side. "If you're interested in that, it'll be thirty dollars."

He reached for his wallet. "It's a bargain."

Laura moved closer to Aunt Peg and whispered, "Could I speak to you?"

"Sure," she said, a quizzical look on her face. Then turning to the customer, "This is my niece Laura. Laura, Mike. She'll be your new neighbor."

Mike, who was probably in his late twenties, like herself, smiled broadly, revealing perfect white teeth and a small scar at the corner of his lip. He shifted his feet. "Your aunt's been a great neighbor, not to mention a great teacher way back when."

Laura managed a smile. "Nice to meet you." Her gaze shifted from his warm brown eyes to the box in his hand. Hadn't he noticed her interest in it too? Grandad gave this gift to Gran the day Laura's mother was born.

"My sister collects these."

Laura carefully wrapped the piece in bubble wrap. "All proceeds go toward pet rescue and adoption," she said, looking up.

He gazed into her eyes. "A cause close to my heart."

As she handed the prized piece over, their hands touched. Laura's face grew warm.

He grinned. "Maybe we'll run into each other soon."
"I'll be moving in two weeks," she said, hoping they'd do more than bump into one another.

Aunt Peg put an arm around her shoulder. "You wanted to say something?"

Laura smiled, attempting to hid her disappointment. "That's okay."

"Then I'll go for one last look around and say my farewells."

Laura squeezed her hand. "No buying. Remember, you're downsizing."

"You never know what you'll find," her aunt called out over her shoulder.

After Aunt Peg left, she studied the intent expressions on the faces of shoppers searching for a bargain, still regretting the loss of Gran's music box. A vivid picture of her grandmother's sweet smile

flashed before her. Laura remembered her words, "Find someone kind and gentle like your Granddad." She longed to find her "Mr. Right" and have the enduring kind of love that her grandparents had experienced.

"You should have this." Before her stood Mike—one hand holding a leash with a black Labrador dancing around his feet, while the other held out the music box.

She shook her head. "I don't understand."

He flashed that captivating smile. "Your aunt knocked on my door—all apologies. It seems she'd forgotten the history behind this treasure."

"That won't be necessary."

"Why not?" He placed the piece in her hand. "Don't worry. Sis doesn't need another."

"Okay, thank you. But you have nothing to show for your contribution." She regretted not having fixed her hair or put on makeup.

He bent down and stroked his dog's coat. "You did say all money raised goes to finding homes for animals. I got Boss from a shelter."

"I found my Lucy at one too."

He winked. "Tell you what. When you've settled in, invite me over for a meal."

"It's a deal."

From the corner of her eye, Laura saw Aunt Peg looking in their direction, smiling. Was she playing the matchmaker?

Mike reached down and gently lifted the lid. "These yard sales always seem to hide a surprise or two."

Laura's heart sang as Gran's special song floated out. "You never know what treasures you'll find."

BIRD'S EYE VIEW
ALANA GUY DILL

10/7/16, Mapleton, WA

Grick the crow perched in a scarlet-leafed maple, his sharp black eyes fixed on the picnic table below.

A youngish man named Liam sat writing and eating a burrito. He tossed the last bite to the pigeons, who mobbed it, cooing.

Grick liked tortillas, but he waited, head bobbing, tail feathers flexing.

Liam stood and produced some coins from his pocket, stacking them on the table.

Grick cawed a challenge and swooped down on the table. He tilted his head to examine the coins, and toppled the stack, bypassing pennies and dimes for the large, shiny quarter.

Liam looked up, chuckling as Grick flapped away with his prize. "Don't spend it all in one place." Every summer and autumn, this was an almost daily routine for them.

After years of not having a dime to spare, Liam enjoyed paying it forward. He re-stacked the remaining coins, disposed of his lunch litter, and went back to writing his novel. When the sun moved behind a tree, Liam closed his laptop, heading home. Behind him, a homeless man shambled up to the stack of coins, gathered them into his pockets, and stumbled on, mumbling "Thanks, Dude."

•••

In the woods north of town, Grick had a tumbledown nest that had been his parents'. Most of his local flock had found mates, so Grick was sadly alone. But HA! If he did find a mate, would she be thrilled! Grick had beads, a watch, $12.52 in change (mostly Liam's), three pull tabs, pieces of foil gum wrapper, and his prized possession, a gold necklace with a sparkly rock hanging from it, plucked from a girl he'd caught sleeping in a hammock.

Grick concealed his trove with leaves and old bits of down, then pooped on it, for that lived-in look. Then, obeying an irresistible restlessness, he took off south for his winter roost near Fremont.

•••

2/15/17, Fremont, CA

In a muddy fallow field, a quarter-mile from Grick's winter roost, a graduate ornithology student named Alyssa crouched in a blind, watching, waiting, and cursing under her visible breath. She had set a trap designed to capture crows unharmed for banding and measurement, alongside other bait trays around the area to acclimate the birds. Of course, there was food: nuts, acorns, corn, seeds, raisins, and roadkill. And treasure: new pennies, bottlecaps, clear glass marbles, 9mm plastic rhinestones, bits of foil, beads. Alyssa had been observing the winter roost at Fremont Marsh for twenty days, and only banded seven birds.

"You're all so smart. But you can't tell our funding's running out?" she gritted, shivering.

Grick noticed she was playing hide-and-seek again, and flew over the blind, to drop a bottle cap on Alyssa, then returned to a cottonwood branch, jeering from a safe distance.

She chuckled bitterly. *"Corvus caurinus.* Northwestern Crow. Come to Mama."

Grick returned to the bait station, pecked at fly-ridden possum belly, preened some feathers, then returned to the pennies, deliberately stacking them five high before they fell over. He repeated that, watching the blind, knowing Alyssa was there.

Emerging from the useless blind, the crow flapped to another tray and observed Alyssa stacking the pennies ten high. "Your turn."

Grick hopped impatiently, swept the pennies to the ground, and glared.

"You think I'm cheap?" she smirked. "Big spender here, Buster." She reached into her pocket for coins and stacked them, heaviest on the bottom. The other crows jabbered warning calls; her atypical behavior made them nervous. She stepped back. Grick returned to Alyssa's coin stack. He triumphantly knocked the other coins clear and flew off with her quarter.

"Whoa." She made a note in her field book. "Picky."

Three days later, Alyssa caught Grick, named him F8 in the database, and put four bands on his legs. Once in place, they didn't bother him. A side benefit: a crow hen named Auk considered banding a status symbol.

•••

Winter, 2017; West Coast

As storm after storm turned Mapleton bleak and gray, Liam brightened his mood by stacking coins at the library, at bus stops, atop newspaper vending boxes, on store counters, in tip jars, busker's hats or open instrument cases, and at bookstores. Sometimes he'd hang around to watch a finder's reaction, but not often. On his book tour, he left little stacks in bookstores and cafes all over the West Coast. His manager thought he was weird. It made him feel like part of something.

4/2/17, Woodglen, WA

Grick and Auk flew north together. Auk loved Grick's nest high in the sycamore. Grick's 'nest egg' was worth $583.97, but Auk couldn't count past four. Coins wasted valuable space. When Grick wasn't looking, she'd drop a piece out of the nest. They squabbled, feathers flew, and then— she laid an egg! Three more came along. When they hatched, the proud and devoted daddy was too busy shoving food into hungry beaks. He barely missed his hobby.

5/11/17, UO, Portland

Alyssa learned that, due to the effects of climate change on bird populations, her funding had been not just extended, but *increased*. She went to Powell's bookstore to celebrate, checking the biology shelves for new titles. The store was busy. She had just missed a semi-famous author on book tour. Someone had been examining *Field Guid to Crows and Ravens*, and stacked twelve quarters beside it. Alyssa smiled.

5/14/17, Mapleton

The book tour completed, Liam returned to his lunch routine, but was saddened not to see Grick. After four days, he spotted a dark flutter among the leaves.

"Welcome back." Liam stacked his coins.

Grick hopped down. "Caw."

Noticing Grick's banding, Liam murmured, "That's new."

Grick flew off, taking nothing.

The next day, Liam lightly taped down a 50-cent piece. The coin caught Grick's fancy, resisting long enough for a good video of his banding. Grick shot a sour look at Liam, yanked hard, and flew off.

Liam anonymously posted the clip online, titled *"Crow Behaving Badly."* It went viral. 38 comments ranged from *"Squee!"* to *"Shoot it!"*

•••

5/20/17, University of Oregon, Portland

Alyssa stared at the anonymized video. It was definitely F8. She commented, *"Banded that crow Feb 2017. Where was video shot?"*

Liam soon typed back, *"Let's not go public. DM me?"*

They direct-messaged: *"Video Mapleton Civic Park, WA"*

"I'm from Woodglen!"

After mutual sanity assessment, frequent messaging evolved to video chats.

Alyssa liked Liam's kind eyes and sharp wit. Liam thought Alyssa's smile could illuminate hell on a cloudy night.

•••

6/2/17, Video Feed

"How did you choose ornithology?"

"It chose me." She mimed while speaking. "I'm sixteen, summer vacation, napping in a hammock. This crow flies down and steals my sweet-16 pendant right off my chest. I'm so mad."

"Your career's rooted in vengeful fantasies?"

"No grudges. That was ten years ago. Best thing that ever happened to me."

"So far?"

"Yeah."

•••

6/29/17, Mapleton

Alyssa and Liam bypassed handshakes and went straight to a hug. They talked over lunch, voices low, then stacked some coins, and stepped away to watch.

Grick perched high overhead, baffled by seeing CoinMan with LegBandLady. But... *quarters!*

They hid behind a beech tree, peeking out. F8 cawed and landed, snatched his quarter, and rocketed away.

Alyssa grinned, "Cowardice *and* greed."

"That's him."

•••

6/30/17, Woodglen

They met for lunch. Alyssa stopped to buy a newspaper and stacked her extra coins atop the vending box.

Liam smiled. "Paying it forward?"

"What? You're afraid F8's gonna steal them?"

He patted his chest. "No. But it seems someone's stolen my heart. Can you check your pocket?"

Laughing, she swatted him gently with the newspaper. "You're sweet, for a cheeseball."

He leaned in and kissed her. "Yes," he said. "Sweet."

•••

Summer 2017, Woodglen

Alyssa tracked and recorded corvid movements around Woodglen and Mapleton.

Hiking with Liam, she pointed up into a sycamore. "That's F8's nest."

Liam peered through his binoculars. "You sure?"

"Just watch."

There was a flash in the air beneath the nest. Something bounced off a twig then plummeted to the ground. Alyssa and Liam stepped under the tree. The ground was littered with coins and bits of foil, half-concealed in the duff. Above them they heard the scuffle and squawk of tightly-packed nestlings.

Alyssa was absorbed in watching the nest. "Almost ready to fly."

Auk flew in, fed a nestling, and touched up her housekeeping. Below, Liam saw a tiny flash as something fell. He tracked it and knelt to collect a broken section of fine golden chain jump-ringed to a heart-shaped "*Sweet 16*". It was set with a tiny diamond, caked with guano and tufts of black down.

Above, Grick was feeding the babies half a lizard. Auk threw another coin over the side. Grick flapped and scolded, then noticed their visitors below and stopped, dumbfounded.

Liam found himself on one knee, smiling up at Alyssa. "Excuse me," he grinned. "Is this yours?"

She gasped. "Whoa!"

E TRAIN: JAMAICA TO WTC

RACHEL DOHERTY

"Stand clear of the closing doors."

I hear the familiar announcement and am relieved that we will finally be pulling out of Jamaica station. Sometimes you have to sit there so long before the train gets going. The good thing about getting on at the first stop is you pretty much always get a seat, which is a true luxury anywhere in the New York City subway system. The bad thing is that you have a seemingly endless trip into Manhattan. I ride the whole length of the E line every day from Jamaica to World Trade Center and home again. It always feels strange taking the train to a non-existent building. There is lots of talk of rebuilding the towers, but for now it is just a ruin, a carcass.

Before that awful day, the turnstile at the WTC stop led to the basement of the towers. I used to love getting off at that station: an underground, temperature-controlled, bustling indoor metropolis. Men and women in sharp business suits would rush past, briefcases in tow. The loudspeaker would announce New Jersey Transit trains departing to exotic destinations like Hoboken and Weehawken. Merchants would lure shoppers with bold signs boasting unbeatable deals. Then one day it was all just gone. Except for the subway stop.

The Jamaica station is a bit rough, but I have gradually gotten used to it: the blaring music, the aggressive panhandlers, and the rowdy teenagers that always seem to find their way into the nearly empty cars at that first stop. I try not to look at anyone and just look down at my book, but I am so on edge I cannot concentrate on the words on the page in front of me. I am bristling, aware of every person in the car and what their proximity is to me. Despite having been at the site of a horrible terror attack near my place of employment just a few years ago, I am still more worried about getting mugged than anything else.

Probably much of my trepidation stems from the fact that I grew up in the segregated suburbs of Long Island. We all have an inherent fear the unknown. People who act different, look different, sound different. We do not know much about them, so we rely on stereotypes to fill in the blanks. By the time we pull into the Forest Hills stop, a lot more people who are just heading into work (people who look more like me) get on, and I relax a bit.

One of the people boarding at Forest Hills is a man who looks to be in his sixties with unkempt white hair and strikingly pale blue eyes like my own. His ruddy, leathery face has seen its share of the elements and substances, and I am guessing he looks older than he really is. As he enters the train, I detect a hint of recognition when his gaze crosses my face. Looking up from my book a few minutes later, I notice his eyes trained on my face and quickly look away. Another weirdo, I think to myself.

I try to ignore him, but at the next stop - Jackson Heights - the rotund lady (who was practically sitting on top of me) with the smelly bag of food thankfully gets off and the seat next to me opens up. Sure enough, the old lush rushes to grab the seat next to me. I try to stick my nose further into my book, but the weight of his stare is too much. I turn to him and my eyes meet his. They are haunted, and he looks as if he wants to reach out and touch my face.

Suddenly, the man starts repeating, "It can't be. It just can't." He looks bewildered, as if he just watched a magic show and he is trying to figure out how the right cards got in the magician's hand. As his mind puts together the puzzle he becomes more agitated. He shouts, "I was there. So were you. I made it out. You didn't." People are beginning to notice us, some looking amused, others worried.

"Calm down," I tell this disturbed man. "Take a deep breath."

"I saw it happen. You can't be here. You died."

"Sir, you've made a big mistake," I tell him, attempting to soothe him. He is really starting to freak me out.

"No. It's no mistake. I will never forget that face. Those pale blue eyes. I watched the life leave those eyes." His voice is shaking. He truly believes what he is saying. "The subway car we were in caught fire and filled with thick smoke. I tried to save you. I pulled you out, but you died there on the platform. I know you died. I must be going crazy. I told myself I would never ride the subway again since that day. Now I finally do and this happens? I must be hallucinating."

I don't remember much about that day. I remember getting up and getting ready for work. I remember running to catch the train and being so relieved that I just made the train the second the doors were closing. The rest is a blur. I always just figured I blocked it out. I read all the horror stories of people jumping from the towers. I saw the signs people put up in the subway cars looking for missing loved ones who would never be found. I heard other subway riders talk to each other about their harrowing experiences that day or detail elaborate conspiracy theories about why it happened. I always told myself I was better off not remembering the details. Better to leave the past in the past.

"Sir, you must have me mixed up with someone else. I ride this train to work every day," I tell him gently. In that moment, I come to a realization: I do ride the train, end to end, every single day. I read the newspapers left behind on the seats. I watch the all types of people ride with me. I sit next to them. Sometimes I smile and nod. Sometimes the train is empty. Sometimes we are packed in like sardines. But I never get off. I just ride the E train. End to end. From Jamaica to World Trade Center. From World Trade Center to Jamaica. And back again and again.

I see the surly teenaged girl sitting across from us nudge her friend, motion towards the man I am talking to, and whisper, "Well shit…There goes another crazy on the train talking to himself."

DOG ON A HOT TIN ROOF
GLEN DONALDSON

Utterly spellbound, I watched in disbelief from behind the drapes of my bedroom window the scene unfold in dream-like slow motion before me. The lady from the devil house across the road was in the throes of unknowingly confirming herself to be what we local kids had suspected all along; here lived our very own neighbourhood witch. To usual passers-by she would grin and nod, flashing what was left of her yellow and black teeth, hitting people with her fermented fish-gut fragranced breath but taking care to remain polite and neighbourly. The adults may have been taken in by the thin veil of accepted elderly eccentricity, compelled as they were to respond kindly to a spinster living alone in their midst, but we younger folk knew better.

Standing on the front lawn bordered on either side by a garden under orders not to grow, the old woman was draped in a gypsy-like shawl and pointing her bony finger like it was some kind of divining rod, compelling with an unseen force her pet Chihuahua (whom we had named 'Devil') to come down from its position atop of her roof. The coal-black little beast with eyes in its head as wide as a baby's was known to be possessed of a particularly quarrelsome and hostile nature but on this occasion I witnessed it transform into a cowering servant commanded by the ghoulish woman's raspy voice (one that my friend Bobby said sounded like jagged rocks grinding against each other in a hessian sack) as well as that ominously directed finger.

With a final desperate leap, the animal launched itself off the roof and into her waiting arms below. After a reflexive side to side movement of its head and wag of its tail, I saw the animal submit and come to rest in complete stillness while buried in her old woolen sweater. This was a proper witch's dog to be proud of. Fanning out a last cursory glance in all directions to check if she'd been observed – including a randomly flung look at my concealed position behind the curtains in my parents' house opposite – causing my heart to skip several beats and my eyes to involuntarily snap shut for a brief moment – she retreated from the front lawn and dissolved back inside her gloomy, ivy-draped cottage, the weathered door proverbially creaking shut behind her. "Back to cooking her owl stew'', I thought aloud to myself while noticing that my left calf was now without sensation due to the state of suspended animation I had maintained while on terror watch.

    Now for the fun part. Finally freed from the constraints of concealing myself, I tried opening with my teeth the bag of pretzels I had been holding all the while and began planning exactly how I would tell my friends the next day of the decidedly unnatural scene I had just glimpsed. In the next moment the bag burst forth, spilling most of its contents on the floor. I laughed, relieving some of the tension that had been allowed to build in the minutes before. Appropriately, come to think of it, it was more of a cackle than a laugh.

BONSAI

LORETTA A. FOLZ

You are curious to learn about the day it happened. It is what drew you here. I will tell you, Dear One. First, you must know something of my past, for the past informs the future.

Nearly four hundred years ago, I was a tiny, white pine seedling sprouted amidst the ferns of the high mountain forest. Rooted there, I might have achieved full growth. Doing so would have limited my life, for the distance between crown and root becomes harder to sustain as a tree reaches for the sky. The man who gently lifted me from the earth intended a greater destiny for me than height. I was to become *bonsai*, a carefully tended tree in a pot, meant to evoke the scenery of harsh mountain tops where trees dwarf and bend to the wind.

In the garden, I submitted to the precise technique of my caretakers, who wielded small tools, sharp as *tanto* knives. Responding to their painful encouragement, I pushed vigor to my roots and greened up my pine needles with a flourish. Though *bonsai* share a gnarled, diminutive beauty, I was not pruned to bow or twist like the others. I rise nearly four feet and stand as straight as the *samurai* once did. My stout trunk of rough bark holds a weighty cloud of fragrant, emerald-green needles in its dense branches.

My first visitors were of gentle nobility; emperors and lords in subtle dark *kimonos*, trailed by women in silk, lovely as butterflies. One never forgets such attentions. Delighted by my appearance, they drew close. I inhaled the soft breath of their admiration and returned it, clean and pure, to the air. For three centuries, I beheld them as they passed through the garden, their beauty softening with age. But, my life was not all grandeur. I endured typhoons and winters of bitter snow. Yet, every spring the promise of cherry blossoms was fulfilled. Soft pink and white petals blanketed any footprints of misfortune lingering on the garden path, renewing the season of mutual esteem.

Change came slowly to my country, then more rapidly, fueled by the opening of Japanese shores to trade. In the street, the steady clomp of horses' hooves faded, replaced by the chuffing and screeching of modern machines and cars. Visitors to the garden no longer wore traditional robes. They donned the clothing of Westerners—men in shirts and pants, women in simple dresses.

I was moved to Hiroshima, two miles from the city center, to a walled retreat behind a fine residence. There, generations of gardeners—father, son, then grandson—tended to me. August 6, 1945, began like many summer mornings in Japan, bright and warm. With no warning, an explosion brighter than a thousand red suns lit the sky. A violent tremor shook me to the roots. Daggers of flying window glass drew blood inside the house. An angry, invisible hand struck water from the garden pond, flinging orange and silver koi helplessly to the stone path. Little Boy, an atom bomb delivered from the United States, had reduced more than eighty thousand citizens to dust. But, the wave of death did not take us. Shielded by the wall, everything held.

Dear One, my canopy of needles quivers at your emotions. You held your breath in distress as I told of the apocalypse, and exhaled in relief at my survival. I, too, feel enormous gratitude for my continued existence. My story does not end there. Please stay and hear the rest.

The devastation was of a magnitude never before witnessed by humankind. Hunger, lack, sickness, and pain were our cruel companions. Many fell like trees after a fire, yet some remained standing. From the ashes of suffering, we began anew. With the help of our former mortal enemy, we rebuilt Japan and entered an era of plenty. Our two countries became enduring friends. In 1976, my people chose me as a gift of great importance for the celebration of the United States bicentennial—a nation born when I was already one-hundred-fifty years old. With preparation and fanfare, I, with fifty-two other bonsai, were carefully transported across the ocean to a shining city of marble and placed in a beautiful garden with a high wall.

In my new home, I was protected, honored, sought. But, I did not have my caretaker, and I was lonely. Some who came to the garden bore a familial resemblance to him—their glossy black hair and creamy skin a poignant reminder of my early life across the ocean. I waited for five years, my branches heavy with atomic significance, my appearance resolute. I could do so because the art of *bonsai* teaches patience to all—to the tree, the gardener, the beholder. When he came, I knew him, though age had faded his features. His hair was muted silver, his countenance stooped. *Yamaki!* A rush of gratitude rose from my gnarled roots and intertwined in my branches. My caretaker wept with happiness at seeing me, and with sorrow, for the time we had spent apart. Twenty-five years later, his descendants came, and there was joy on their young faces. They stood beside me for photographs, smiling, as I proudly showed my *samurai* stance. I captured their breath in my emerald cloud of needles and released it, making a true gift to them. We regarded each other with respect, and in their shining dark eyes, I saw my eager youth reflected.

Dear One, as to your question: Would I trade my fame for the anonymity of a quiet retreat once more, with gentle company and a pond of quicksilver koi? Truthfully, there is a longing in me. Reminders of a simpler life reside within my heartwood, a time when capable hands tended me, quenched my thirst, and moved me to capture the sun. My only concern was to grow stout in the trunk and lofty in branches. Alas, one can never go backward.

Through fate, I have become more than a tree, more than *bonsai*. I am a symbol of what endures. Like the exchange of breath into air, we are *otagai no tame ni*—with and for each other. Even an atomic blast cannot change this.

When I have attained more than five hundred years, I will again consider my longevity. One can age, and still be young in the garden of memories. It is an open secret—a life of beauty and significance arrives through patience. Patience is how a student becomes a master. How a mere *bonsai* becomes a tree of wisdom. As long as they come to me, visitors seeking peace, I will be there with branches outstretched.

ORANGE BLOSSOMS AND TELESCOPES

JOANNA FRIEDMAN

Ellie rocked on Greg's porch swing. The bittersweet haze of the sun cast a farewell orange glow onto the observatory dome. The shriveled cacti fell into shadow. They reminded her of the Old Man cactus Greg gave her the night she told him she'd cheated with their neighbor. The smile faded from his eyes that night and his mouth settled into a flat line.

She watched crows fly down the mountain, blown off course by the wind. The swirl of orange blossom pollen pulled her toward the mountain. The nostalgic scent of it made her want to try once more to explain something, although she wasn't sure what, about the one night. She wanted his smile to return, even if it was no longer for her.

True to routine, Greg emerged from the cabin at 7:30 pm, ready to begin his observations at the telescope. His long hair was past his shoulders and his lips hidden among stubble.

"When are you leaving?" he asked.

She followed him off the porch. "My plane leaves tomorrow. I wanted to talk before - "

Her skirt caught on the spines of a barrel cactus and he stopped to watch. Something scurried past her foot. A rattle snake, she thought. She yelled out, "Oh - " and hoped he hadn't noticed the loss of control in her voice.

"It's just a spiny lizard," he said and continued toward the telescope.

It took a few tugs at her skirt and several long steps before she caught up again.

"Can I watch you at the telescope?"

"What's the point in that?" he asked.

"I'll read my book and listen to music." She popped her gum, but Greg's sour look told her that was another mistake. In fact, the whole trip was a mistake.

A sliver of moon rose just above the horizon by the time they arrived at the white observatory. The scent of orange blossoms was stronger up here, so was the wind. Greg struggled with the door, and it took both of their pulling to open it wide enough to enter. The four-meter telescope sat at the center of the cavernous dome room. Greg pulled a lever and the opening on the ceiling clattered open.

"The stars are right there just past the opening, aren't they?" she asked.

"Or the rain." He put his hand on her shoulder, more from habit than anything, and guided her toward the control room. They sat on stools in front of a computer. He pulled a manual from the shelf.

"You still look at the checklist?" she asked.

"I like the ritual of it." He read aloud. "Step one - turn on the power, step two - open the dome, step three - check the weather, step four - eject any unauthorized persons."

He typed in the coordinates and the telescope creaked as it moved into position. A star appeared on the screen.

"Step five - don't sleep with the neighbor when the boyfriend's away," she said.

He stared woodenly at the screen. He clicked the same button a few times.

Ellie leaned toward him. "What's the name of that star?" Her face was an inch away from his hair. He smelled like campfire.

"No name, just coordinates. What do you care?"

She put her hand on his shoulder and heard the tension in his throat as he swallowed.

"I like the dark blue and orange flecks on it." Ellie felt his shoulders against her body.

"Nothing special about it."

"Until we look up close," she whispered in his ear. "I'm so sorry."

He sat stone - faced. The star on the screen flickered.

"I wish you'd said that a long time ago." He lifted his hand and placed it on her arm, held it there for a breath.

They heard the wind crash against the dome.

"I have to check for rain." He stood and walked outside and Ellie followed him.

The Milky Way arched above them and the red light of a plane blinked through it on its northern flight. An owl's screech cut through the wind. Ellie took his hand, but he let go and studied the clouds instead. She took it again and pulled him onto West Side trail, toward the scent of the blossoms.

"I can't wander up the mountain with you, Ellie. I have a job to do." He moved toward the telescope door.

"Let's go to our spot, one last time." She walked backwards, a few steps up the trail.

He looked toward the clouds and she could see him calculating time until the rain. She turned and ran.

"Ellie - "

A gust of wind pushed her further on. Scrub brush and cacti scratched at her ankles. A scorpion darted across the path. She ran to the clearing where the orange tree's branches caught her in their tangle of flowers and fruit. She leaned her cheek against the rough bark and listened to its inner quiet.

Rocks crunched and Greg skidded down the trail toward her. An orange thumped on the ground as he pushed through the branches. The petals flew around them like shooting stars. Time ticked back to their first kiss under this tree. She felt the wet of his tears and his rough stubble against her neck. He sounded like he was laughing but it came out hoarse and dense and strange.

      She leaned down to kiss his eyes and then his mouth, which had curved up into a reluctant smile.

THE SUITCASE
SHARYL FULLER

She bought the antique leather suitcase at a weekend auction. Joe had collected old things all her life. Now that she was old ... old things seem to find her without even trying.

Tired from a long day of fighting the other deal stealers, Joe decided to unload her truck tomorrow. Now was time to relax, eat a light supper, catch up on emails and messages, write about her day for an upcoming magazine deadline and settle in a hot bath with a glass of wine and a book she had been trying to read for days.

Joe woke up when the water turned cold and chilled her to the bone ... damn ... napping in the tub again. Soggy paperback on her chest at least the empty wine glass was safe on the rug beside the tub. A quick hot shower to chase the chill and she was down for the count.

Sunday morning was sunny, and the air had that October crispness that demanded jeans, boots, and her favorite flannel shirt ... the one Micah left hanging in her closet, the one that held his scent ... his soul after that tragic accident. There were old things of his still where he left them waiting for him to return because she couldn't stand to move them. Wearing his flannel shirt was like being hugged again every time she slipped it on. Smiling, she went downstairs for coffee and her favorite breakfast.

Draining the last sip of coffee from her mug, Joe decided dishes could wait until the truck was unloaded. She had scored two vintage linen tablecloths that made her smile. One with cherries on a field of white trimmed in green. The other, robin's egg blue with a tiny double white line border that created a checkerboard effect on each corner. She also brought inside to be displayed on her bed for pictures later two fussy antique aprons to add to her collection, a red fiesta pitcher, and a set of multi-colored aluminum tumblers that would keep sweet tea cold for hours.

That task done, Joe went back for the suitcase … or it really should be called a valise because of its vintage and size. It was a smooth oxblood worn leather valise with brass fittings that would make a stunning piece to round out an arrangement atop her black leather steamer trunk in the sitting room. One inside, Joe searched under the kitchen sink for a tin of leather polish. She would leave the brass as it was since the patina was perfect.

Cleaning the leather took a while, and every time she turned the suitcase around to get to the next section, Joe felt rather than heard something inside. Curious, she waited to unbuckle the straps until each section of leather had a warm glow and smelled like her favorite boots.

The ping of a new email landing brought her back to reality. Checking, Joe saw it was from her editor wondering what goodies she found at the auction to be featured in her article due next week. Pouring another cup of coffee, she read the other details and requests, quickly took snap shots of her goodies, attached them to her email response to Emily. That done, it was time to tackle the dishes before the remainder of her sunny side up egg sat too long before being washed … 'damn, that plate will have to be buried in the backyard for a week to get it clean'. As a child, Joe didn't understand what her mother meant when she said that, but it made perfect sense now. So many things she didn't understand as a child made perfect sense the older she became.

Now was the time to open the suitcase and see what was moving around inside. Antique leather straps slipped from their bindings smooth as butter. Using the leather tables on each side, Joe began the unveiling. Carefully she eased the suitcase open. A flicker of sunlight hit the opening and revealed a sealed envelope lying upside down on the bottom. With a shaking hand she lifted it out, looked at it for a few minutes before turning it to the other side. Joe nearly fainted when she saw the writing on the outside.

The envelope was addressed to her with Micah's return address, his address before he died. The envelope had no postage, no cancellation date, just her name and address written in Micah's distinctive hand.

With trembling fingers, she eased open the flap ...

FARMER'S MARKET DAY
JONI GARDNER

I loved Saturday because it was Farmer's Market Day. My friends and I called it Triple F Day (Fun, Friends, and Food). We must be going because she didn't fix my breakfast or hers. She was all dressed up and carefully putting her lipstick on at the mirror by the front door. I couldn't contain myself, I was so excited.

Not soon enough, she grabbed her big tote bag and looked down at me. "Remember, if you embarrass me with your inappropriate behavior, we can just forget about Farmer's Market Day next week."

I tipped my head humbly. It always made her smile. She knew my friends and I only got to see each other on Triple F Day.

I got in the car before her, and she stopped to talk to our neighbor. I resisted telling her she was on my time today, and to make it short. We pulled into layered parking in downtown Sarasota, and I ducked in the front seat as the low cement beams seemed to brush the roof of our car.

"Level 3, space 14, help me remember that, would you?" she asked.

I tilted my head at her, and we walked out of the parking structure. I could already smell the breakfast sausages, onions and bacon smoking on the grills. I began salivating.

We entered the market near the guitar player who was singing and playing songs from years ago. The smoke from the grills stirred among the seated people enjoying their morning coffee and tasty treasures so different from their cold cereal on the other days of the week.

The first friend I saw was Harley, and, of course, he had his red, white and blue Harley jacket on. He always made me feel so undressed. We got to spend some time together while the women chatted.

We couldn't believe it when we saw our other friend coming toward us with a hat and sunglasses. Harley and I jumped up to greet her.

"Oh, how embarrassing for you. What was she thinking? Can you see out of those things?"

Harley said, "Does the hat hurt your ears?"

Princess's gaze went down, and we knew she was mortified.

"Hey, I have an idea," I said.

Harley and I put our heads together, and then started barking at absolutely nothing. The people around us froze as he grabbed the hat, I grabbed the sunglasses, and we tore the leashes out the women's hands and took off running. We left Princess standing there absolutely naked, but no longer devastated.

Harley and I knew we were in trouble, but we didn't care because that's what friends do for each other. We chewed up the costume so it was useless and slowly walked back to the two startled women. We hung our heads and returned to the scene of the crime.

The ride home was quiet, but I knew we'd still be going to the Farmer's Market next Saturday. We always went.

THE KITTEN IN THE RYE BREAD

T.C. GARDSTEIN

If you really want to hear about it, I may decide not to tell you, so it's best that you pretend not to care too much. It's caring too much that drives you crazy, plus telling anybody anything, especially that David Catterfield kind of crap. You just wind up missing everybody.

I'm a cat, so you don't have to be a goddamned genius to figure out that I had brothers and sisters, whom I had to share the teat with and all. But in my case, it was further complicated by the fact that both of my sisters were evil. I managed to come out first despite being the smallest one, but Cookie Puss and Pookie Cuss were right behind me and I didn't have a chance against them—so much for sisterhood! —plus my three brothers, one bigger and meaner than the next. I never bothered to learn *their* names because those bastard brothers never cared to learn mine, which is Meow-Meow. All my siblings cared about was hogging the teat. There were more than enough nipples to go around, but I kept getting bounced. That's part of the reason I stayed so goddamned small. Not like I would've been a *basketball* player or anything.

Never met my daddy, but I bet he was the king of the phonies, probably trying to get in good with the guy at the corner bodega for free cold cuts he had no intention of sharing with his family, while my mommy was left alone to deal with us kittens in an abandoned house in Ditmas Park, Brooklyn, that looked like something out of a horror movie, with boarded-up windows and rotting floorboards. Local kids called it haunted, but it was really just an eyesore shack that somehow never got knocked down even as the rest of the hood improved.

Mommy told me once, since I was the only one of her litter who ever listened to a word she said, that she couldn't even tell me who my daddy was for sure because she had been gangbanged by six toms in the parking lot of the Foodtown on Coney Island Avenue. I made the mistake of asking if that meant each of us had a different daddy. I didn't mean anything disrespectful, for Christsake, I was just a kitten, but my mommy's response was to bitch-slap me and send me out into the goddamned drizzle for provisions. She said that since I was the smallest and most pathetic of the litter, with ribs sticking out and all, I would have better luck than my bigger, nastier sisters and brothers. I believed her, and let me tell you—that was the last time I *ever* believed my own kind. Never trust cats, even if one happens to be your mommy. She'll just wind up sending you out for provisions one gray, rainy day in September when you're only six months old, and you'll never get to go home again.

I mean, if I were you, I wouldn't even trust *me* to tell you the truth, because I'm just as likely to make up some goddamned fish tale. It's awful. Like when some cat once asked me about my kittenhood, I spun some fairy tale about being born into New Orleans aristocracy—yeah, I was an aristocat—and my people served me gumbo, jambalaya, and baked oysters with spaghetti Bordelaise. My sisters were all soft-spoken belles (in this version, I had no brothers). My mommy, a seal-point Siamese with violet eyes, was a show cat. My daddy, a silver tabby whom everyone said I was the spitting image of, was a hero who singlepawedly fought off two burglars from swiping the Meowiental rugs, the Meowgritte painting, and the family baby. How I wound up in Brooklyn was because of Hurricane Katrina. I was two years old at the time and had the misfortune of being in the goddamned backyard when it hit. I was swept away, eventually landing miles away from my home near a freeway with other lost pets of the Crescent City. An animal rescue squad picked me and other cats and d-o-g-s up, put us in a van, and drove us to New York City. My people must have been absolutely devastated, along with my biological family, but they'd never gotten around to putting a goddamned tracking chip in the back of my neck, and no matter how much I meowed, the rescue squad couldn't understand the information I was giving them.

The cat actually believed that crazy story I spun, which got me so depressed I slept for the rest of the day. Of course, I also sleep a lot when I am not depressed. I'm a cat, for Christsake, not a goddamned worker bee.

So, what really happened was that I got bounced from three bodegas. Almost got my scrawny butt kicked by a huge bodega cat that unfortunately was not asleep when I wandered in. I didn't want to go home to face the meowsic and get my butt kicked for real by my bastard brothers and sisters, and bitch-slapped by my mommy, but it was raining, I was cold, and at least that shack would keep me dry if not safe. Trudging along the wet sidewalk with my eyes scanning for unleashed pit bulls and kids on Ritalin riding out-of-control scooters, I heard the loud crashing noises and smelled the rot before I saw what was going on: the only home I ever knew being demolished by a wrecking ball.

I screamed, not like anyone standing around watching the spectacle heard me or cared. I was convinced that my mommy and brothers and sisters were trapped in the rubble, ribs and necks broken, suffocating from the dust, maybe already dead. Not that I cared so much about my brothers and sisters, though I surprised myself by caring at all, but I did love my mommy even though she hadn't kept my siblings in line when they bounced me from the teat and she was impatient with me when she should've been more understanding that I was just a kitten.

The truth turned out to be far worse. This is what I get for sheltering in a garbage can, covering myself with newspapers to keep dry, until the shack was totally demolished and the wrecking crew departed. The news stories were all so depressing I was really sorry that I was able to read. When I crawled out of the can to explore the wreckage, it was dusk and it had finally stopped raining. My sharp cat eyes along with superfine cat nose soon determined that my family had not died: they had had escaped! That's a fine goddamned how-you-do—they'd all managed to jump out the south-facing window and high-tail it out of there without waiting for me to get back. I followed their scent two blocks before I lost it, probably thanks to the rain.

I was only six months old and on my own, with nobody to love me or take care of me. Still, I refused to cry just yet. My goddamned belly was grumbling. I knew there was a Dumpster by the McDonald's, but the idea of jumping up into that huge thing scared the hell out of me, and it would be just my luck to get food poisoning then wind up at the bottom of a garbage truck. I squared my puny shoulders and decided that I was going to find work as a mouser, and it wasn't going to be at a small-time bodega with a deli counter that stocked crappy Boar's Head cold cuts. As crazy as it sounded, I planned to cross the Brooklyn Bridge into Manhattan and throw myself on the mercy of what was supposedly the best and most famous deli in the world, the gold standard of pawstrami: Katz's. I was a cat, after all. I figured there would be goddamned nepotism and all regarding who they hired—probably a bunch of phony poseur cats who didn't even need to work for a living would get dibs over a pathetic, scrawny southpaw like me—but I told myself what the hell, I would be working under the table anyway. It was a huge gamble, yet I knew that I had to give it a shot.

So, you are probably wondering whether I got to be the kitten in the rye bread, but I am so goddamned tired telling the story of my life that I can't see straight. I really need to take a nap now. If I feel like it, maybe I'll tell you when I wake up. Maybe I'll even tell you the version that really happened.

MAGGIE'S NEW BEGINNING

SHEILA M. GOOD

"I'll be Goddamned." Maggie's head fell against the pillow. Her chest burned from the effort of pounding her fists on the sweaty mass pinning her to the bed. "Dammit, dammit, dammit." She'd heard of dead weight, but this was ridiculous. *What the hell had she been thinking? Oh yeah, her new beginning-fuck!*

Thanks to *Mr. fat-ass*, her dreams of wallowing in a bed filled with money disappeared with a grunt and a snort. She squirmed but went nowhere. The weight of his bulk was making it difficult to breathe. She sank further into the plush mattress and felt the stones of the coveted diamond necklace press into her neck.

His arm flopped over the side of the bed giving Maggie a glance of the room and a teasing chance to breathe. She maneuvered a leg free, dug her heel into the side of the mattress, and pulled. The muscles in her calf screamed. She tucked her head underneath his flaccid arm and clawed for the edge, her whole body shaking with the effort. The pungent odor of his armpit struck Maggie across the face like a brick, and she fell back gasping for air. "Jesus Fred, ever heard of deodorant?"

Earlier in the evening, he'd taken her to one of the finest and most exclusive restaurants in the city. The food and atmosphere were more exquisite than she imagined. She reached across the table and stroked his hand. Her new beginning was at her fingertips.

Within the hour, Maggie stepped through the doorway of her dream into the biggest and most magnificent house she'd ever seen. Fred made a quick, one-sided introduction to the housekeeper, Juanita. Maggie muttered a polite "Hello."

Fred took the woman's elbow and step aside. Speaking to her in Spanish, he peeled several bills from his money clip and extended them to her. Maggie wished she understood their chatter. Maybe Juanita could teach her later.

Stealing a glance at Maggie, the woman slipped the money into her apron pocket and hurried from the room.

Fred reached for Maggie's coat. "Would you like a drink, my love?"

"What about Juanita?"

He took her hand and kissed it. "Not a problem; she has the weekend with her family and we, my dear, have our privacy. Shall we?" He asked, leading her up the massive staircase.

She met Fred at work when he came into the jewelry store looking for an anniversary gift for his wife. Maggie noticed his Armani suit, the Rolex watch glinting from underneath monogrammed, starched cuffs, and nudged her co-worker out of the way. "I'll take this one."

Maggie gave him her most winning smile. "May I help you, sir?"

Round and soft, he looked like *just the ticket* for her way out, a way up, and a new beginning. An hour later, he walked out of the store with a $10,000 diamond necklace and a hankering for Maggie.

The wife didn't concern Maggie or the less than desirable physique hiding underneath the Armani suit. She could deal with short, soft, and pudgy - *been there, done that*. All she saw were dollar signs and a new future.

Maggie played him hard, reeling him in like a flopping fish on a taut line. Her commission check grew with each visit, and she wondered if the shower of glittering gifts surprised his wife or made her suspicious.

It took Maggie two months to land her fish. Over dinner and a bottle of wine, costing more than her monthly salary, Maggie discovered he'd given his wife a trip to Europe for their anniversary. The jewels he saved for her.

Later, Fred slipped the necklace around her neck. The beauty of the stones took her breath away. "They're beautiful."

He nibbled her ear and whispered, "You'll get the others later."

Ribboned boxes taunted her from across the room, where they sat unopened on his wife's dressing table. She let his hands roam as visions of fur coats, diamonds, and exotic trips filled her mind. Her dress slipped to the floor. Maggie closed her eyes and imagined the body pressing into hers belonged to Brad Pitt. Her mom always told her, *"Maggie, you can do anything for a short time; as long as the payoff's worth the pain."*

Maggie adopted it as her motto, but when Fred's fat, soft, sweaty body crawled on top, she almost balked. The precious stones adorning her neck and the promise of more to come kept her in place. She fantasized about Brad, the Caribbean Islands, and waited for it to be over. She figured it wouldn't take long, and it didn't.

A loud, painful sounding grunt snapped her back to reality. A swoosh of sour, alcohol-laced breath escaped from Fred's mouth like hot air from a balloon, and he collapsed pinning her to the bed. A deadly silence descended. Maggie waited for him to say something, whisper sweet nothings, tell her how *great* is was, or for God's sake move.

"Fred? Fred?" Ignoring her rising panic, Maggie eased her fingers to the side of his neck, *nothing, nada, zilch.* "Goddamnit Fred!"

She pushed, punched, and cursed. The sweat from their naked bodies had turned to super glue. Maggie wasn't going anywhere.

Panic turned to anger and anger to horror. Minutes ticked by, then hours as the situation sunk in and Maggie realized her fate. The joke was on her

Come Monday, Juanita would be in for one helluva of a surprise and Maggie, nothing more than an afterthought - a greasy spot underneath some rich, hairy ass, cheating bastard.

How the hell did she end up here?

Exhausted with each breath growing more shallow, Maggie let her head fall back into the pillow. She grasped the cherished stones in her hand and closed her eyes. Not exactly, the new beginning she had in mind.

LOVE BY A SKY-BLUE THREAD

E. MARGARETA GRIFFITH

Buh-mi-dow wriggled his claws along the branch. He shook out his wings, looked around for danger, and saw none. Barely turning his head, he made sure Pab still perched on their acacia branch. She had her tail turned to him, but Buh-mi-dow had seen his mother do the same to his father and did not worry.

He glanced down at his chest, back under his wings to his tail. His feathers lay exactly right. He chirped once to clear his throat.

"Buh-mi-dow," he sang, two matching calls and then a solid, dependable deeper note. Buh-mi-dow was faithful. Buh-mi-dow would bring the prettiest grasses and leaves to his mate for her nest. He would guard the nest while Pab foraged and always come home on time from his own outings.

"Buh-mi-dow, Buh-mi-dow, Buh-mi," he sang.

Hens did not sing, so Pab would call him Buh. If she answered him, Pab-Buh, the next step would be to offer her some grass toward a nest.

"Buh-mi-dow, Buh-mi-dow, Buh-mi," he sang.

From the pavement under the acacia, a voice. "Oh, how pretty!"

Buh-mi-dow had attracted a lady, but very much the wrong one. Large and wingless, she had coated herself in bright dirt and nesting material. So unsightly next to Pab's neat gray wings and subtle black and white bars. But of course, this lady was not a hen, and in her kind, the females wore the colors.

Sometimes her kind scattered seeds on the ground or left them in containers. They were often good to have around, but some would stomp their feet, or yell, or even throw things right at you. He did not like to let them get too close. This one was just far enough away he did not think he had to move.

He sang again. "Buh-mi-dow, Buh-mi."

"Thank you, Mr. Bird" said the wrong female. "I'm on my way to ask for a modeling job. Maybe a song from something as pretty as you will bring me luck."

Buh-mi-dow wished she would go away. She might scare Pab! Pab was brave, often the first to return to a feeding spot when a hawk or cat had moved on, but she was not foolish. If the large creature stayed close, Pab would not chirp back to him.

"Buh-mi-dow, Buh-mi-dow, bap, bap, bap!" He let lose with the song he used to warn off other birds.

Her wrap of sky-colored nesting scraps swaying and sunset-colored crest bouncing, the intruder left.

"Pab-Buh." Pab had turned one bright eye on him.

Buh-mi-dow swooped to the patch beside the pavement for a particularly green and delicate grass leaf. Making sure the sunlight hit his orange cheek patches just so, he presented the prize to Pab.

She tilted her head, considering his offering.

Pab was particular. He liked that.

Buh-mi-dow saw a thread on the pavement. It looked like a blue feather of sky had fallen just to help him win Pab. He swooped down for the thread and offered it to Pab.

She accepted it. Turning her tail again, she found a little hole in the acacia and began their nest.

* * *

Pab's perfect nest had a patina of excrement. Neither she nor Buh-mi-dow minded a bit. They were too delighted and busy with the three featherless birds, two hens and one cock, who had soiled the nest.

It was Buh-mi-dow's turn to get some seeds and stretch his wings, but he waited near the nest. There were too many large, two-legged wingless ones around for his liking.

One, he almost recognized. She walked by the tree often and her red crest was both bright and unusual. One of the other creatures seemed to be grooming her. The groomer said something, and another creature, this one holding a long limb with something propped up on it, answered.

The creature with sunset hair walked away from the rest, then turned to face them.

Clicks. Brightlights. And then they all climbed into a moving box, chattering as if pleased with themselves. Buh-mi-dow could finally take his break.

LAST CALL

ERIK HIRSCHER

Ugh, what I would not give to be in a quiet place to drown my sorrows, Jason thought. He came to this establishment, Big Wang's the sign above the door read, prepared to get sloppy drunk. He did a marvelous job despite the raucous roar of male's yelling at TV screens ruining the effect. Jason resorted to laying his head on the countertop hoping the firm, solid surface might ease the throbbing behind his eyes. It did not. Through squinty eyes, Jason stared at the remaining amber liquid in the glass he almost drained dry. He wondered if his stomach could take more.

Movement nearby drew his attention to the left toward a man wearing a dark green Russian Greatcoat that had seen better days. His appearance was haggard and his raven black hair was matted, the front long enough to obscure his eyes. When the man pushed it aside giving Jason a clear view of his eyes – they were grey like a storm sky promising to soak anything in that dreary gaze.

Sensing something was amiss, the man glance at Jason, offering a sterile smile.

"Hello, friend. Hope you don't mind my sitting here."

Jason blinked, determining the man was friendly. His voice had a deep, rumbling tone that reminded Jason of his father. Then again, it could be the whiskey he had consumed doing the talking.

Offering what he hoped looked like an agreeable smile, Jason said, "No, I don't. I can see you have had a rough day, something I know all too well."

"Oh? Rough day at the office?" The man signaled for the bartender, even snapped his fingers to get the man's attention.

After delivering his order of a frosty, tap beer and paying for it, he slipped a white piece of paper toward the man behind the counter. Glancing at it, the bartender warily picked it up and read the contents. Seconds later his eyes, wide with either shock or surprise, shifted from the man to Jason and back. Offering a subtle nod, the bartender moved down the counter to serve a newly arrived customer.

While curious, Jason asked no questions.

He said instead, "Yeah, my day sucked. I graduated from a University with a degree as worthless as tits on a bull. My job description requires doing tasks no one appreciates. Today was especially awful. And after I get home to relax, maybe have a smoosh or two, you know what happened?" Jason picked up the whiskey shot to down it and partially missed, decorating his tie and sweaty white shirt with splatters. Ignoring it, he slammed the glass on the counter while a sizable belch ripped from his throat.

"Oh, that hit the spot." He swallowed what little had hit his mouth. "So, going home where I wanted to rest, but instead I had to deal with an ungrateful, miserable woman and a neighbor who served me with divorce papers on my wife's behalf! If I had larger balls I would have …" Jason gritted his teeth, backhanding air before his head crash-landed on the wood counter of the bar.

"I loved her; I did," he mumbled. "I thought we would be there for each other. I took serious, that it was death do us part. I don't understand why she did this." Sitting upright, Jason grabbed his empty glass, signaling for a refill. The bartender was nowhere to be found. Swiveling around in his chair, Jason noted the room had emptied. Turning forward, he wondered where the barkeep vanished to.

"Christ, what does a guy have to do to get a refill around here?" Jason gazed at the stranger. The man shrugged. Squinting, he asked, "So what's your story? What kind of 'miserable' day did you have?"

The entire time Jason talked the man listened without interrupting. Instead, he sat with his fingers laced together on the countertop. He had not touched the beer before him. The look on his face was contemplative. Now it held surprise at having been asked about his day. That smoothed out as the man let out a rumbling chuckle.

"My day?" he reflected, "Well, let's see…I was called to work, same ol same ol. I'm a detective who does specialized assignments, tasked with examining things that don't fit within a mundane portfolio. So, I head in and get thrown right into the shit. There's a body in a home, a concerned neighbor who called it in and when I arrived I discovered a pool of blood by the front door."

The man paused as if reliving that scene and seemed to shudder, "That," he continued, "was one of the worst scenes I've ever walked into. Upon further investigation, we discovered the woman had been dismembered. We also found chunks of undigested food beneath a coffee table. We had it analyzed, used the latest in techno-sorcery from the boys and girls of RnD. You know what we found?"

Struggling to comprehend the tale, Jason shook his head. His thought locked upon a cut up woman, RnD and techno-sorcery. It sounded like something from a horror film.

The man's next few words, however, chilled Jason to his soul.

"The puke," the man went on to say, "was a mixture of human flesh, pasta, and Ghoul powder, which we believe was cooked up by a necromancer. When the stuff is consumed, it induces rage in the victim that can only be waylaid by consuming human flesh, albeit temporarily."

Reaching into a left coat pocket, the stranger pulled a piece of cloth out and unraveled it, flattening it on the counter. A myriad of symbols and sigils adorn the cloth, inside and out, which continued to peel apart revealing the inner contents. To the uneducated, the scribblings appeared to be of a foreign language. The man added a few stones from his pocket, seemed to stare thoughtfully while shuffling them around. He pulled out a stark white stone affixed to a copper ring that had threaded leather cord attached to the sides. Holding it up, he dangled the object between them.

After hearing the story Jason felt the urge to distance himself from the stranger. He felt alarmed at the idea of Ghoul powder. At the mention of 'necromancer' Jason became creeped out, wanting to leave. Clearly this man had a few screws loose and being close to him felt hazardous to his well-being. But, despite that assertion, Jason found he was unable to get up. He just sat, staring at the stranger.

In that moment, he realized the bar where they sat, hell the entire establishment, had emptied completely. There was not a soul in sight while the televisions continued spewing boisterous commentary of sports including thuds from body's crashing into each other.

The stranger cleared his throat. Jason looked at him in surprise.

"Now, before we get ahead of ourselves, I must make sure of one thing." He held up the necklace, moving it in front of Jason's eyes, "This might get a little, well … weird."

The sound of chanting filled Jason's ears, a strange lilting sound with occasional words. Initially, nothing seemed out of place. Then the stone glowed. A moan escaped from between Jason's lips as he drifted within himself. The stone shined brighter, becoming brilliant white. That low moan emitting from Jason's throat erupted into a gaudy scream.

As sudden as the glow appeared, it vanished.

Jason took a deep breath, blinked in an attempt to clear the bright spots blinding his vision. He noted the stone the man continued to hold up between them. Instead of its former color, the thing was now crimson red, just like blood.

The strange man sighed, shook his head in disappointment while packing away the items on the countertop. Shoving it back in his pocket, the man produced a large pair of manacles. Giving Jason a sad look, he said, "Jason Cutler, you are under arrest for the murder of Madeline Cutler, a death that occurred two months ago. I, Joshua Grishoff, must inform you that you will be tried by the Court of Night and upon confirmation of guilt, be sentenced to Eternal Damnation."

Eyes clouding with sorrow, the man finished with, "Because of the circumstances around Madeline Cutler's demise, may your end be unmerciful."

LOVE ETERNAL

TIMOTHY C. HOBBS

The aged car coughed and sputtered as it climbed the hill and passed through the cemetery gates. Headlight beams flowed eerily over rising ground fog and the well-kept headstones.

The car continued forward until it reached the cemetery's older section where the graves were no longer well attended; the families of those buried there long gone themselves.

The gravel paths once present for visitors were overgrown by grass and weeds. The car navigated down a trail it had traveled for many years, and when that path ended, the car stopped, the headlights extinguished. An elderly woman opened the car door and got out.

The woman was bent by age and walked to her destination in the grip of pain but paid it no mind. In the distance, the sound of thunder rode across the sky. It would not be long until clouds obscured what moonlight existed.

The woman came to a grave marker that was completely snared in the arms of a wild rose bush. She slowly sat down in front of it, took a candle and a box of matches from her purse, struck a match and lit the candle. After the flame had a firm hold on the wick, she held the candle above the grave marker, letting wax puddle on what stone was still exposed until there was enough hot paraffin to secure the candle's base. Yellow light danced across her wrinkled face in weird shadows as fog swirled and ascended.

The woman hesitated and then reached forward and pricked her finger on one of the rose thorns. In the candlelight, many scars from previous encounters with the thorns were evident on her fingers and palm. She held her finger above the grave's mound and allowed blood to drop on its earth.

"Arise, my love," she whispered. "By my blood I conjure thee."

The wind rose and teased the flickering candle flame. A low groan came from under the grave mound. Fog swirled and joined a rising cloud of vapor from the moldy soil. The mist elongated into a shape stretching across the length of the grave. The figure throbbed in an unearthly blue glow, its features constantly writhing in turmoil as they formed and reformed, never able to completely coalesce.

A voice rose as if from a well of despair. "Agnes, let me rest. Leave me in peace."

The woman placed a hand tenderly on the mound. "Uncle Martin, I love you."

"Agnes, what I did was wrong, perverse," the figure moaned. "Please, let me go."

"I can never let you go. You were my teacher, my lover. I can have no one but you."

The thunder moved closer. Veins of lightning appeared momentarily and revealed rolling storm clouds.

"Agnes, I abused you for my own pleasure. Hate me, Agnes, for what I did."

The woman's eyes glittered with melancholy. "I cannot hate my lover. I exposed your crime because you spurned me when I was turning into a woman. I was angry, but I should never have betrayed you."

"It was a sickness, Agnes. A wickedness. I could not see you lose your innocence, your purity to maturation. I wanted you to remain a child."

"Mother said you were a pedophile. I didn't understand the word. I kept saying *pedalphile* by mistake. You know I had trouble pronouncing words. I had a speech impediment. You tried to help me with it, remember?"

"I did that to make you think I was kind, Agnes. To gain your trust so I could . . ."

The figure wailed, "Oh, the pain! The torment of being brought back from eternal rest! Agnes, please!"

"I came to visit you in prison, Uncle Martin, and you would not see me. I was so hurt. I felt abandoned." She bent over and laid her cheek on the form floating above the grave. A feeling like an electric current rushed through her. "You were the first, my love. You are the last," she whispered.

"No, Agnes, no. Have mercy."

"After you died in prison, I had you buried here. That was thirty years ago. I've come every night. Every night, my love."

The wails increased. The form thrashed in agony. "Let me go back, Agnes! For pity's sake, let me go back!"

Intermittent drops of rain began to fall. The wind rose and threatened the candle's flame.

The woman sighed. "Very well, Uncle Martin. You may return to your rest."

The glowing figure broke apart, dissipated, and streamed into the mound of earth in front of the headstone.

The intensity of rain increased. The candle was extinguished. The woman started to rise and then hesitated and placed her hand back on the grave mound.

"The doctor said my cancer has metastasized. It will only be a matter of months now." She tilted her head slightly and whispered, "I purchased the plot next to this one years ago, my love. Soon we'll be together night and day, until the end of time."

A cry of grief escalated from below the mound and was soon obscured by a deafening peal of thunder.

A MOCKERY OF TEARS
CHARLOTTE HOLLOWAY

Grass, grown tall, cuts at his arms. He swipes back, but blade after blade they fight him, drawing lines of blood that serve only to feed the gasping soil. Poppies parade past as he runs. Their stems erect, heads tilted back, they watch him leap and fly, tearing through the endless green.

A shout: *Captain! Captain!* The call twists around him, dizzying in its antiphony. Pulled forwards and then back by the words, he stumbles in confusion, then rights himself and continues to trample through the virgin field. Decapitating poppies as he passes, petals dance like the damned around him, fluttering to the ground to form a blood red pool. Black seeds scatter across the mass of petals, only to be crushed beneath the Captain's feet as he pounds on and on.

Again, there is the call. This time closer, but he doesn't hesitate. On he runs; faster and faster, until he trips. There is the sensation of falling, a velvet thud resounds as he hits the ground, then everything goes black. How long he lay there he isn't sure, but when he opens his eyes those broken petals have fallen upon and around him. A reassuring blanket, they act as his own personal shroud, protecting him from what lies beyond.

Men next to women and children; they reach out around him. Legs lean on heads. Torsos stretch out across arms. Innocents that beseech him; a saviour who has arrived too late. Gazing down, he sees the single gunshot wound to each head, the stream of dried blood that lines each face in a mockery of tears.

He crouches beside a young girl who clutches at a bed sheet as though to protect her. He strokes her cheek then wipes away that bloody tear. Beside her, a baby lies in his mother's arms, his head buried between her small breasts so he won't see the bullet coming. In death his mother rests her head on his, forevermore kissing his limp, greasy hair.

"Captain, Captain!" The call is almost on top of him now and he no longer resists the cries of his men.

"Here," he shouts. Within seconds he and his discovery are surrounded. Moments pass, then a young Private steps forward. As he reaches his arm down, the Captain notices a white flower attached to the young officer's lapel. *Anemone*, he thinks; *daughter of the wind*. Extending his hand upwards, the Captain reaches past the proffered arm and instead touches the flower. A bloody tear sinks into the virgin petal and feeds the dying flower.

CRAZY COMES FIRST

SUSAN IMBODEN

Coyote was a spirited animal. I wouldn't call him a pleasure horse by any stretch; he was a cow horse and a good one. Tall and lanky with a stilt-walker stride, he had quick reflexes, but he also had a hair-trigger panic button behind those alert brown eyes—not a good combination for a family horse. That's why no one except Dad had been allowed to ride him.

Then one Saturday morning, just into my twelfth year, my time arrived. It wasn't roundup day, so I wasn't sure what had prompted Dad's decision or what we were going to do. What I did know was that he always had a plan.

I imagined we would wind our way along the road into the hills, look at the water level in the lake, check the cattle and be home for lunch. An easy ride, only this time I would be on his horse. Not on Pal, whose arthritic shoulders made him slow. Or the young, mischievous Chipmunk, our two-year-old floppy puppy of a horse who wandered about, head swaying from side to side as though smelling the California poppies along the way. I would be on a grown-up's horse for the first time, and the importance of the occasion—like finally being allowed to wear lipstick—didn't escape me. It was a rite of passage, and I was excited.

Coyote and Chipmunk grazed in the morning sun as we approached, their red-brown coats still wooly from winter's cold. Steam rose from their nostrils in the brisk air as we slipped the bridles over their ears and led them to the barn. Handing me Coyote's reins, Dad shook the dust from the red and gray saddle blanket and threw it over his horse's back. Coyote spooked and the muscles in his neck jerked the reins tight in my grip. I flinched but dug my heels into the dirt and held on. Shying away from anything was not in Dad's playbook.

Not only was I going to ride his horse, I was going to ride with a saddle. This, too, would be a first. I was accustomed to climbing on bareback and holding on with my legs. No saddles had been allowed because a foot caught in a stirrup could end in disaster. And Coyote liked to crow hop when he got excited, which was often. Though he never would have said it, maybe Dad thought I would need something to hang onto.

Lifting a stirrup and laying it over the seat, he tightened the cinch and gave it a yank. Coyote snorted and waved his head in Dad's direction, as if to say, "That's tight enough!" The next thing I knew, I was stepping into the stirrup, swinging into the saddle and taking the reins.

Right away, this horse felt different from the other two. Unlike our old Eeyore, Pal, Coyote stood high-headed and tall, his ears searching like radar antennae in all directions. He was all business without even trying. It could have been his thoroughbred nerves ready for the starting bell, or his quarter horse genes on alert for a cow busting loose from the herd. It was who he was. And, now that I think of it, he and Dad were a lot alike: muscular and smart and high-strung. I think that's why Dad respected him more than most people he knew, maybe even loved him more. That's why it was such an honor to be on his back. And that's why, when Coyote died in an accident three years later, it broke my father's heart.

Dad saddled Chipmunk and off we went toward the hills. But when we got to the gate, he turned south along the fence instead of heading up the road to the lake. Where were we going? I had no idea what he had in mind, but Dad was my Roy Rogers, and back then I would follow him anywhere.

Travelling the fence line beneath a canopy of moss-covered oaks and pungent bays, we crossed the lazy, cobbled creek where I caught pollywogs, passed my grandfather's barn and stepped into the sun at the far side of the ranch. The air buzzed with newly hatched flies and I waved them from my face. Looking up, I could see our two tall peaks. One overlooked the road to the lake. I'd never seen the other from this vantage point.

We were at its foot, and looking up I saw deer trails crisscrossing its slope like light strings on a Christmas tree. A bald, clay-faced rock crowned the summit, its dense chemise beard a protective moat into which the trails disappeared. This was rugged country––a scrubby safe haven where deer escaped hunters not ambitious enough to follow.

I took pride in knowing every meadow and ridge, every boulder and tree of our ranch. But this was foreign. I had seen this peak from a distance, had even ridden the trail along its spine. But the rocky face staring down at me was daunting.

"Are we going up that?" I asked, incredulous.

These were horses, not mountain goats.

"Sure, why not?" Dad said, tugging on the brim of his crumpled cowboy hat to secure it tightly to his head. And it seemed that a smile almost parted his lips as he leaned forward and rested an arm on his saddle horn. He didn't smile often, and maybe now, remembering his love for adventure, I'm just imagining it. But from where I sat, the fatherly Roy Rogers had morphed into Matt Dillon, and I was about to be his posse. Together, we would charge the hill and bring in the bad guys.

Setting out on the first leg of the trail, we switched back on the next, skirting the slope and rising as we went. Coyote's breathing picked up, and I settled in, saddle horn in one hand, reins in the other. We were about to be rock climbers on horseback and I was excited but scared. I hadn't even climbed the face of this peak on foot where I could wedge my fingers into crevices to get a grip. How were these half-ton animals going to do it on hooves?

Had I been with anyone else, I would have balked at something so crazy. Horses aren't meant to climb rocks. But Dad liked crazy. It fed something in him—the hunger for a challenge, the need to face danger. To plan and prevail. And I think for him there was romance in that quest. Romance and power and some sort of validation. He was an engineer by trade, and engineering is all about whittling risk to its finest point. But crazy always comes first. Crazy opens the gate and lets the cows stampede to see if you can round them up before they plunge off the cliff. Dad was my hero, but also his own. He needed his challenges, and the ranch was alive with them.

Deep down, I relished them, too. I once swam Chipmunk through Josephine's Hole—rode him in deeper and deeper until he lifted off the bottom and swam to the other side—just to see if we could do it. Just like on Saturday morning when the *vaqueros* swam the *Rio Grande* on our black and white TV. It was a hot day, and the cold water felt good. Thus far, I'd returned from this and other adventures mostly unscathed. But this new one looked huge and was just beginning.

Chipmunk carried Dad steadily up the trail ahead of us. He was heavy and strong, built more like a Budweiser horse than Coyote and not as agile. But if you gave him a job and kept a firm grip on his reins, you could keep him on course. Following his swaying rump, I knew that if we fell, we'd fall a long way before hitting the ground and tumbling to the creek. I was teetering on the outer edge of what nerve I'd mustered, wondering what possible test of grit could be worth this risk.

There was nothing to do but trust.

The sun was high and the slope steep as we pivoted onto the final leg of the trail. White sweat lathered Coyote's shoulders, and my saddle squeaked with each step that pulled us higher. Though my eyes were on the patch of trail between his ears, my body could feel the view of the orchards widening below. I was grateful for the tight cinch.

Chipmunk's hindquarters flexed and trembled up ahead as he struggled over the loose pebbles that had fallen from above, harbingers of what awaited. Trusting Dad was no longer the issue. My safety was now in the care of this hair-triggered horse—my horse—as he picked his way along a path carved by the tiny hooves of deer.

We were almost to the peak. So close I could see the crevices that etched it like wrinkles on the weathered face of an old man. Coyote's head bobbed up and down, and he breathed hard and fast, nostrils wide open as he pawed and slipped and pawed some more. Beneath me, his blood raged like a river, and I knew I was no longer in control. Loosening my grip on his reins, I gave him his head. He would have to make it on his own.

I leaned to the high side and hung on.

TIC

KILMO

They'd made for the woods first, looking for shelter amongst trees the colour of iron until the Enemy brought axes to stop the disease. Maybe they thought the steaming bodies that had crawled from the pit would burn quicker that way. But what the Foxes had was too thin for light to find. It slipped through them like a knife, and cut them to ribbons inside until all that was left was their smile. What was left kept to the furnace now.

Toc took a gulp of the charcoal drifting from its chimneys.

'Enemy can't have found all; rest will be here.'

They'd all heard the noise as the Foxes had fought their way back with the sun burning the howls from their flesh.

Brindle's laugh was the same as the chain grinding its way through the Furnace. 'Maybe they hide too well for me now.' Metal glinted as the silver in his sockets caught the light. He wouldn't be caught out twice. When the pit wanted paying, every part of you had a price.

'We find you new ones.'

'I like these fine.'

Toc's spit hissed through the ashes.

'Wait…there.'

A nearby dune crawled as something moved beneath it.

'Clever.'

The Foxes industry hadn't yet blotted the light from the sky, for that it would need more fuel. And with the Cats that had been forced onto the chain at liberty, they could only use their own. The Enemy's favourites hadn't foreseen the rebellion, and the result lapped the furnace sides deep enough to drown the Styx.

Toc hadn't seen one of the Foxes since he'd crawled from the pits threshold stinking of grave shit and the dead. He bared his teeth.

'Is coming closer. When it gets here, stay out of my way.'

Brindles limbs rattled, he was getting worse any of the tribe could see that.

'I join them soon anyway.' The Cat kicked at the powder, 'Better than being owned again.'

Shadows leaked between his teeth, and Toc wondered how much he'd dragged from above world to the Enemy's trap. Those who worked the hardest went first when the disease came calling.

'Then we must win. Let it out. Take light from the sky.'

Toc watched the chain's rust-pocked metal wind across the pits brim until his eyes ached. He wondered how long they'd last up here. He wanted to drown in the darkness, let the night cool them.

'I know what you are thinking. Don't.'

Brindle pointed to the stumps where they'd been stitched in place. Cog teeth and torque grind hadn't sliced all of them away. He was surprised there was that much left; the pits machines pared what the Cats stole faster than knives.

'What if Fox make us worse?'

'Cut deep. Cut till you hear the bone scratch. You've seen why the Enemy chucked them back in.'

Toc fingered the stump of his tail. He could still taste iron from the chains links.

'You think rest still alive down there?'

'No.'

He weaved its head down low like a snake and flicked his eyes towards the treeline, as Brindle continued.

'It could have been worse.'

'How?'

It grinned, 'Pit could have taken our feet.'

'Taken plenty already.'

They'd worked till their backs broke and wrinkles crawled across their skin. It was why the Foxes had had to stitch their tales in place.

'Enemies here, maybe they want to talk.'

Toc's voice showed how likely it thought that was as the eyes amongst the trees got closer. He yowled a challenge as a champion split from their ranks; gleaming skin stained to mark old kill's. It moved slowly; like the ash at its feet burned.

'You know why we've come. Get below, or we throw in ourselves.'

'Chain drags nothing empty. Foxes can't do it on their own; not now they're sick.' Toc barked a laugh, and winced as he sank further into the muck, 'Your problem not ours.'

'We fill pit with your bodies. Not take darkness from the land like agreed. Better this way, quicker. Shouldn't have tried to make bargain with Foxes. Now, we wait, we watch. Come dawn still shadows here we kill you instead.'

Toc watches it retreat, slipping through the dead forest like it's being eaten.

'Bring help?'

'From where?' The Brindle's silver eyes are full of scorn. 'The pit. I've listened. Know what it says?'

'Tell me.'

'We die if we go back. Not long till no choice anyway. We slide down with Foxes on our backs.'

'They won't throw us back. Too useful. Maybe this time Foxes burn enough the sky goes black. War's won then.'

'In a night? Not possible.'

As Toc watches, something pale twists through Brindle's fur. He doesn't see the Fox rearing through the ashes until it's too late. It's got the same problem as Brindle; worse in fact. Its teeth are buried in itself, gnawing, and nipping as it chases the scurrying things hidden there. It's lucky it's still got flesh on its back.

'You've been talking to them. No more time, not for them, not for us.'

Toc's, uneasy, there's something in its eyes that tells of worse behind them. It's not the first he's seen like that either.

'Follow, and listen, listen good. If you come with empty hands, maybe there's an answer there.'

Toc glances at Brindle and what's left of the Cats before he wades toward the furnace entrance. The wind's pulling ash off the stones buried there. Stone backs arch into the storm as the pack passes by.

'Where is everyone?'

Silence fills their ears, and Toc can feel eyes stare back although he can't see his whiskers.

'Gone. They drowned themselves in it. Let them lick it clean if they could. They were lucky.'

The Fox gestures at the hole torn through the furnace where the chain leaves it. It's like looking at a mirror. Lips curl from Toc's teeth, as it sings butcher shop songs in praise of the dead.

He stops and stares. Something's listening.

'Feel it?' A shudder wracks the overseer, and liver spots dance across its skin as it tries not to scream. 'We had to work for them, understand?'

Toc steps away; its spittle stinks.

'Of course.'

Light flares in the darkness as though someone's put fire to a torch. Fat's sloughing off the Fox's bones faster than water in a desert, and its eyes sink following tidelines and cataracts into oblivion. Soon the only water in them is like looking at the bottom of a well. Whispers kiss the hairs on his cheek, and he steps a little further.

'The dead approach.'

He wondered how long the Fox will be able to talk, but he doesn't need its permission. Ghosts don't need to unlock doors; they're already claimed. The Styx's water is in his fur, every circle of it, and he's seen what the chain's clad in: Cats. The chain was sewn with them, every scalp a gravestone.

His haunches stiffen and hairs along his neck ruff.

'Sorry.'

The Fox won't look at him; it's not the Cat it's interested in. It stretches out its arm and watches darkness eat its paw, oiling its way up thin veins on the way to where it's warm. Toc's thirsty. Thirstier than he's ever been in his life.

The chain rattles loud enough to wake him, steam reek, and cinders dropping though the screams from the pit. He can't look away.

'Toc?'

It's too late to dodge the blow, but that doesn't stop Toc's claws slicing back as he's pulled close enough to throttle. There's metal against his neck before he can do any harm. Brindle's teeth might not do much, not with so much rot in them, but the slice of pain at his throat certainly will.

'You think you can give me to it? You never learn. It was with me since the beginning.' Toc holds himself still as he listens. 'What was the bargain this time? That you'd keep your fingers? Your toes? You don't have much left.'

Brindle drops the act; Toc had been wondering when he'd do that, as Cat skin slips to the floor and one of the Enemy's grins stares back at him.

'We have you.'

Toc has time to think; they've short memories traitors. He jumps, listening to the clank of iron rattling past his ears.

THE WEIGHT OF FICTION

E.E. KING

My friend says I write light fiction---and it's true I guess. He said, "It's not like you're Hemingway or something...." Well that's certainly true! For one thing, I'm alive. And female....and a vegetarian. Definitely -not - Hemingway. I do like short sentences though.

Thoughtfully I hefted a Hemingway, then balanced Sylvia Plath on one hand, but they were paperbacks, so I guess my judgment was skewed by material things (another problem of mine according to my friend.)

The hard-backed collection of Danielle Steele was considerably weightier. And when I attempted to heft the complete works of Nora Roberts, I could barely lift them. (Maybe I need to work out more.)

My friend is reading Nietzsche. When he wasn't looking I cautiously hoisted it. It was hardly heavier than a feather. The same was true of Sartre. In fact, it was even lighter, barely weighing more than a thought.

I snuck off to the bathroom, surreptitiously concealing Sartre beneath my sweater. Once inside, door locked, I greedily browsed through the pages. The sentences were brisk and clipped. The words were sparser, less rich and velvet than Nora or Danielle.

"Three o'clock is always too late or too early for anything you want to do." I read. Well that's true enough... I never have been a morning person. But heavy?

I reached for Nora, which I had wheeled in, concealing it inside a carry-on bag.

"She had large doe eyes…"

Now that was a disturbing image!

I pictured huge liquid brown eyes, lacking whites, black horizontal pupils spread wide on either side of a small human face, like some alien monster or cubist nightmare.

I couldn't sleep that night.

The next day, sleep deprived and haunted, I returned to my friend. I once again slunk into the bathroom with Sartre.

"If I became a philosopher… it's all been to seduce women." And so??? Like this is news? Sounds like every guy I know. I read another …. "We do not judge the people we love." Humm…maybe I was missing something? I hurried home to Nora…. (She'd been too heavy to keep lugging around. Although to be honest it gave me the heebie-jeebies to have the doe-eyed woman lurking inside the pages of my room at night.)

"When we grow up, we lose the talent for loving without restrictions." I tried hefting the volume again… I had been working out, but even so I could raise it only an inch off the ground.

Maybe I should try Nietzsche and Danielle?

"He who would learn to fly one day must first learn to stand and walk and run and climb and dance; one cannot fly into flying." Nietzsche.

"Sometimes, if you aren't sure about something, you have to just jump off the bridge and grow wings on your way down." Danielle.

"Invisible threads are the strongest ties." Nietzsche.

"It's hard being visible, so I've made myself invisible." Danielle.

My friend has become lachrymose. He hardly looks at me when I enter his home. His eyes follow me morosely as I scuttle in to use his bathroom, trying to discover the secret of profundity.

I am haunted by the doe-faced woman. She creeps into my dreams upon those rare nights when I am able to sleep. Her face talks wordlessly of predation and fear.

Nietzsche though… he speaks to me of dancing and laughter… "We should consider every day lost on which we have not danced at least once. And we should call every truth false which was not accompanied by at least one laugh."

Ha, Ha. I try to laugh. But somewhere out there I see a doe-eyed woman, running through the snow, beset by predators, threatened by famine, her child's head framed in the scope of a rifle.

POP IT

CASS SIMS KNIGHT

The encircled triangle looms in the middle of a black screen. Along the bottom the phrase *Rosie – Pop It* identifies this video among all others. You look at the views: 3 billion. It was all over the news, breaking records and such. It is why you are here.

A woman with her black hair tied up in a red kerchief with an old timey mask you don't recognize fades into view. She wears a denim shirt and behind her the backdrop is bathed in yellow light with the words, *If you don't stand for something you will fall for anything* plastered above it. Her painted-on smirk gives her voice modifier a playful tone as she begins to speak.

"For eons mankind has built a house of inequity," she interrupts herself with laughter. "Nah, good buddies, I'm just messin' with ya. We all know that tired old rhetoric don't play today. Not in the world of digital over-sharing. Instead, I bring you a bedtime story and, as y'all know, bedtime stories always have happy endings."

As the screen fades to black, she proselytizes over the transition. "Once upon a time, in world not unlike our own, lived a girl who dreamed of the future." A puerile cartoon replaces the black screen and pantomimes her voice. "Like all girls her age, Kitty dreamed someday her prince would wrap his arms around her and whisper, '*The black hole information paradox can only be resolved by the holographic principle within the framework of string theory.*'" This is naturally paired with a Hubble photo mashup that could have been in a Hollywood blockbuster. You wonder how they had funds for such swank production.

"Naturally this would be followed by the sweet secret nothings of the universe, life, and everything. There may also have been a puppy involved. Or, hell, a whole bunch of puppies, crawling all over her." You love pictures of puppies, you are human, after all. "Well, some would nap, naturally, as the future professional cuddlers that they are. But her principle dreamboat was not to be. Not for lack of looking, mind you, but chasing a fairytale is always a cursed act."

The screen snaps back to the brunette bombshell rolling up her denim sleeves to reveal artistic sleeves of individual American traditional tattoos covering her skin. "It's a good racket, after all. Convince a whole population that no matter what boat you want—dingy, sailboat, yacht, or spaceship—yours will come and find you like a bloodhound on the hunt. You don't got to do diddly. Of course, hope is the best way to control the populace. They feed it to you like good ol' American pie, although you just don't care for apples. Instead of romance, Kitty woke up with her panties around her ankles and pine needles in her hair."

You grimace at this accompanying image.

"Kitty knew when someone did something wrong, especially when evidence of it was still trickling down her leg, they got punished. Home of the free, land of the brave. So, she took the guy's ass to court." The screen fades to a claymation courthouse with an angry lady lawyer whose clay bosoms line her chin. "But it becomes less like justice and more like your typical American date: one way or another, it's the lady who gets screwed. There was plenty of evidence to convict, but the judge dismissed the sentence. But, I promised you a happy ending."

Returning to the room bathed in yellow light, our faithful hostess is joined by two other women in identical uniforms: suicide rolls and denim. "The answer is always accessible if you know where to look. And, in fact, girls can code. But let Rosie tell you, she was the one clever enough to figure it out."

The blonde to her left steps forward. "Thank you, Rosie. You are too kind. I was able to switch his identity with a meth cooker who had killed two cops in a shootout a month prior. Being a hothead that likes to rape people, he resisted arrest and they tazed him in the babymaker long enough to cause permanent damage."

The brunette continues, "So, like the OG justice we got for Kitty, we can also taze your rapist's testicles until they pop..."

"Excuse me, Rosie?" The ginger doppelgänger on the right steps forward to tap her on the shoulder.

"Yes, Rosie?"

"That's actually a misconception. The taser really just damages nerves that render the genital area useless."

"Shit, Rosie. It's metaphor." Turning back to the screen, "There are two schools of thought on how to most quickly remove that blemish from your face: apply ointment and hope for the best or pop it like the boil it is. Like the zit on the face of humanity, we will pop it."

"But shouldn't we…"

"Stop being so literal, Rosie. While we at the Riveters aim to be informed—we are, after all, women of science. We don't actually expect testes to burst like tiny supernovas of the pants. We aim only to take away their weapon, as you would a shooter on a rampage."

The original Rosie returns her gaze toward the viewer. "You see, good buddies, after a millennium of asking and not getting the respect we deserve, we got a clue from the playbook of men and taking it." By some chicanery, her porcelain mask winks at you. All three turning back to the camera in eerie unison, the expressions on their masks look altered, menacing in a gentle way. "What you, good buddies, must know is when the cops fail you, as they fail 97% of all rape cases, you have other options. Got a rape kit shelved in the basement of some jelly-filled precinct?"

"We can do it!" chant the doppelgängers.

"Did the judge ignore the sentencing recommendations because the man who raped you was 'a good kid whose life would be adversely affected by a prison sentence?'"

"We can do it!" chant the doppelgängers.

"Did the law fail you? Well, fuck the law. Justice and the law are not synonymous. You don't need one to find the other. So, get out there and get yours. But dogs only get their day when everyone else is watching. Tweet your story with #PopIt and we can award your rapist with a Darwin Award of his very own."

"We can do it!" chant the doppelgängers.

"Live in America?"

"We can do it!" chant the doppelgängers.

"Live in China?"

"We can do it!" chant the doppelgängers.

"Live in India?"

"We can do it!" chant the doppelgängers.

"Live in North Korea?"

"Wait, we don't have anyone in North Korea yet," The blonde doppelgänger interjects.

The ginger doppelgänger jumps in, "No, remember Kim Jon Un just kidnapped an agent in order to teach his children English."

"Oh, right. Brain fart," Blondie apologizes.

"The point is, good buddies, we are here to help. Let's trend this bitch."

The screen abruptly asks if you would like to replay the video or watch related videos. You'd rather see what's trending on Twitter.

THE COOT POND

DARIN Z. KROGH

A flock of coots dropped in on our farm every spring. The low end of the pasture next to the highway would flood and create a large shallow pond. Coots would gather on water, grazing on bugs and other floating edibles.

My black lab, Jake, used to wait by the coot pond for cars to come down the highway. As a car neared the pond, Jake would jump into the middle of the birds, which caused them to fly across to the other side of the highway. A few coots would get picked off by the cars. Birds sometimes died in the stampede, and cars often wound up in the ditch.

My neighbor down the road, Smitty, owned a tow truck business. We worked out a deal. The lucrative arrangement lasted for several years. I thought about taking pictures of Jake's coot stampedes, but I wasn't sure if they were legal or not.

The good deal ended one day early in 1996 when a red Buick got blinded by Jake's flying coots and drove off the road into our shallow pond.

I was out back of the barn, busting up a bale of hay for the horses when a gunshot and a squeal got my attention.

I trotted to the front of the barn where I could see the coot pond. A red Buick was lying with the passenger side up in the water. A man was running across the highway toward the trees.

Jake was down in the water near the car. He was jerking as he struggled to right himself onto his feet. I ran into the pond, but by the time I got to him, Jake was mostly dead, leaking brains out of a bullet hole above his right eye. "Sorry boy," I sobbed and pushed his head under the water to shorten his dying time. Hardest thing I ever did.

I pulled Jake's body up on dry ground and went into the house to call the county sheriff. It wouldn't be long before a deputy would show up. We lived in a rural area, but the highway was good. A skilled driver could travel a hundred miles an hour and be safe if the coots weren't spooked. I ran back outside hoping to see where the driver had gone across the highway.

The culprit was out of sight. He must have slipped into the timber. There were a couple of logging roads in that area, but most of it was virgin forest with thick brush.

I waded back out into the coot pond. When I got near the car, some of Jake's blood was floating on top of the water. My eyes blinded with tears.

Jake lived with us for all his life, from when he was a pup. I never saw another dog as smart as him. Jake could judge the speed of an oncoming car and synchronize that with his own jumping into the flock of coots. It took a sense of timing. He could do other amazing things. Jake could keep a frantic calf in a corner while the mother cow was having her nails trimmed. He was like border collie. That kind of dog doesn't come along every day.

I peered into the open window on the upside of the Buick. Apparently, the driver had crawled out that window. The car was sitting in about eight inches of muddy water which was leaking into the vehicle. A few things were floating around the inflated airbag, a pack of cigarettes, food wrappers and a map. Some clothing was piled up in the back seat.

When the Sheriff's deputy arrived, he asked me if I had a farm tractor that could upright the Buick. I did. But no way was I going to use it for that. Smitty was five minutes down the road with the tow truck made for the job. This would be the last towing of our partnership. Smitty answered my call and showed up shortly with the truck. He ran a hook line from his truck to the car and righted vehicle. Then he locked on to the bumper and pulled the Buick out of the pond onto dry land.

The Deputy opened the driver's door and punctured the airbag with a knife so he could get around inside the car.

The map I had seen floating was actually a car-rental contract. The sheriff scoured the paperwork then turned his attention to the pile of clothes in the back seat.

I had been wrong again. There was more than fabric in the back seat. The pile of clothing contained a corpse, huddled up in a fetal position. It was smallish female adult; the side of her skull had been smashed with something heavy.

The Sheriff's Deputy told Smitty and me to leave the pasture. He radioed in for assistance and strung crime tape around the area.

He asked me to describe the man who had fled the scene. I did and pointed to where the man had gone across the highway. The deputy listened but ignored my suggestion that he chase after the criminal before the dog killer got deeper into the woods. I told him that forest was thick with brush and the suspect's progress would be slow.

The deputy said, "We've got our own dogs for this kind of situation." He looked over at my Jake lying on the grass. "Sorry about yours."

Jake was territorial, especially when fast moving events occurred on our property. He must have come at the man crawling out of the Buick and got shot in the head for his trouble.

The Sheriff's Deputy and I agreed that shooting Jake added to the evidence that the driver was someone other than an honest citizen in the ditch. The guy didn't want to be there when the police arrived.

My front pasture began to fill with marked and unmarked police cars. Most stayed until nightfall.

Several armed men in fatigues followed a police dog across the highway into the woods. I had given them my best directions.

The woman's body was placed in a white van.

After the medical examiner shut the door on the van, he told us the bullet had to be removed from Jake's skull. After he finished, I wrapped Jake in a blanket. We dug a hole on the back side of our acreage and laid him to rest. Jake loved the pond, but I figured the coots would drive him nuts if he were buried anywhere near the water.

A deputy stayed all night until an impound truck came in the morning and hauled the rented red Buick away.

The trackers never found the guy who shot Jake. The man I described was suspected of hi-jacking the woman and her rented Buick in the parking lot after robbing a bank. His get-away driver heard cop sirens and ran off so the woman became his involuntary. He ended up driving down our highway and meeting up with the coot stampede. The whole story was big news for a few days but then blew over. Somehow the suspect got away, probably made it to the interstate and hitched a ride.

Smitty and I didn't have a connection other than his tow truck. Our business arrangement was necessarily dissolved due to the demise of our third partner, Jake. Smitty and I became distant neighbors again, just a wave when we drove by.

My wife and I let the sad episode slip out of our conversations although we still spoke of Jake now and then.

GOING UP

STEPHEN LANDRY

She fell. I couldn't believe it. I didn't want to believe. I ran up to the edge, but I was too late. She fell. I stood at the edge looking down. It was the closest I had ever felt to the world below. If I had lost my balance I surely would have followed her down into the clouds. I wish I knew why she fell. I can't stop thinking I could have done more. It wasn't fair. I wanted to do more. I wanted to *know* more. Why was she here in the kana district? It was the edge of the city. She didn't look like us, she didn't belong in our district. I only saw her for a second, but it was clear she came from the towers. Had things gotten so bad that even the high and mighty were jumping now?

The city sits on the top of a man-made mountain above the dust clouds and the dried-out ground. I remember once looking through old photography books, seeing pictures of the world below. It was a world full of life and dreams. The only thing we dream about now is our next meal, and maybe taking the free-fall elevator to the world below. Solar flares destroyed most of the world, several thousand years ago. Since then we became divided. The lower class like me live out on the edges, while the upper class thrive in the towers, watched over by their machines.

Some say the machines are the ones that saved us. They tell stories of a war between men from the ground and men from the stars. We made the machines to protect us, and when we lost the war they constructed this city as a shelter, high above the radiated Earth, far below the conquered stars, neither up nor down but trapped somewhere between.

In my hand was a small amulet. I'd snatched it from her hand as she fell. Snatched is the wrong word; in truth, I reached out for her and grabbed the amulet instead. For a second it connected us and I could have used it to pull her in, but she looked at me and let go.

I stayed up for several nights staring at the amulet, wondering what significance it held.

Was it an heirloom? A gift? I imagined stories as to why she stood on the edge, why she let go. I knew the amulet was important, and I got the feeling she wanted me to have it – or somebody at least.

Days turned to weeks. I thought about selling it. I even took it to an antiquities dealer. He had no idea what it was and couldn't price it. It was beautiful but worthless. So, I kept it. It was a reminder that no matter where we went we were all trapped. Prisoners of this precarious city.

Prisoners of the mountain and the sky, and of whatever actually happened in the distant past.

A small group of soldiers came looking for the girl not long after she fell. It wasn't uncommon for the poor to jump. No one thought anything of it, even if she was dressed in fine clothing. Nearly every morning I went to the ledge where she had fallen and looked at the birds flying below us. I thought somehow, I would see her again, or a vision of her ghost. The soldiers asked me about her, wondering if anyone had found anything strange.

I thought about asking them about the amulet. Perhaps it was the strange item they wanted. But I kept it close to my chest. I didn't want to give it back. I followed them back to the gates of the tower. I wanted to know more about their world. The walking machines scanned their wrists as they entered. That was when I saw it. On each and every soldier, wrapped around their wrists, was an amulet identical to the one she had. The amulet was their key to get inside the gates!

In the slums, we were free. Free to fall. To live our lives fighting for survival on the outskirts of the towers. We couldn't walk a single alley without feeling fear. The girl who fell gave me a way out. For years, the Kana district had been my home but now I held a way out.

It was time for a change, this world be damned...

There were two ways to leave - up or down and I was going up.

THE STATION

Q. LEI

She hasn't seen her father since her wedding last summer. She is waiting for him now at the station, watching strangers with umbrellas hurrying in and out, and her like a desolate guard of something precious and timeless. Her father is a pragmatic man. She respects him more than she respects anyone in the world. Especially after mother's death, he took up all the tedious work that followed the death of a family member. The funeral, the relatives, the insurance, the paperwork, all of that he managed by himself, so that his daughter—she was only eleven then, still full of dreams and easily impressed by both the happiness and the sadness in this world, would be saved from everything she didn't have to experience at her age. Sometimes the work deprived him of the time to mourn his lost wife with melancholy and romance. He would sit in front of the TV with a pen and a phone in his hands until morning. But still he finished the work alone. In her memory, he's always been a consistent man who enjoyed working on his own, mourning on his own, doing just about everything on his own so that people he cares for could be saved from what he had to go through alone.

He shows up at the station with only a canvas messenger bag, half soaked. It is raining heavily outside, and neither of them has an umbrella, so they will have to wait, he says. They stand at the exit behind glass windows. They can hear the sound of raindrops falling against the windows; they fall and fall, as if not able to help themselves. They start talking about grandfather's death while waiting for the rain to stop. Two months has past, and father didn't seem to her to be affected by the event anymore until this moment. He tells her that he and her uncle were the only family members there to watch the cremation. In the instant, just in the instant, the body was devoured by the fire and became ashes. Shocked, a bit fragile, he looks. It's the second time she sees this look on her father—the first time was when her mother passed away. It is not so different from his usual solemn look when he tries to solve a math problem, but slightly more tender, and more vulnerable, just like a newborn. He trusts her with his feelings, wholeheartedly and with nothing left for himself. She was going to tell him something about Matthew and her, but instead she decides to listen quietly.

    He says he parked a little too far. It would take about twenty minutes for them to walk to his car, and by the time they get there, they would both be soaked. There's no point that they should both get wet. After saying that, he tucks the messenger bag underneath his arm and departs into the rain. It is early autumn. He walks steadfastly in the rain without looking back. His shirt turns transparent, as he passes the corner and disappears into the grey mist. All she can do now is to wait for him to come back.

THE COLLECTOR

KARI LIVINGSTON

I collect things. Doesn't matter what, really. Just stuff that catches my eye. Some folks might call it junk, but it's not. If a body can find value, or usefulness, or beauty in something, then it ain't junk, is it? I kind of see myself like a treasure hunter, always on the lookout for a thing for my collection. Sometimes I find it on the clearance at the Wal-Marts. I've found some stuff at yard sales and some at Goodwill. I've even found some stuff on the side of the road next to folks' garbage cans on trash day. Just goes to show you what they say about trash and treasure is true.

That's where I found my latest treasure. A Fleetwood TV set. It looked just like the one me and Marjorie had when we first got married. What a find, and just sitting there on the side of Hickory Avenue, like it was waiting just for me. I lifted it in the bed of my truck and hauled it on home. It took some doing to clear out a spot for it in my living room, but boy, was it worth the work. It was beautiful! The screen was so shiny that I could see my reflection. Of course, it didn't work when I plugged it in, but that's alright. I didn't expect it to, but it sure did remind me of my Marjorie, when her hair was still thick and red, before the cancer came. Just looking at it, I could smell her meatloaf. I half expected her to come out of the kitchen and call me for supper.

She didn't, of course. I know she's gone. I sat right there in that hospital and held her hand as she breathed her last. At the funeral, I saw the sweetest little cherub figurine sitting next to a headstone a row over. It had red hair and looked so much like Marjorie that I knew it had to be a sign from her that she was alright. I probably shouldn't have, but I slipped it in my pocket and brought it home with me. I knew it would look just fine sitting on top of the bookcase in the living room. The next week, on my first trip out of the house since the funeral, I walked through the Salvation Army. I saw the nicest little wing chair, yellow and covered in pink roses. Pink roses were Marjorie's favorite. It looked really nice in the den. Sometimes I would look up from the paper and I would swear Marjorie was sitting in that yellow and pink rose throne and I would forget for a split second that she was dead.

Some people think I get kind of carried away with my little hobby, but I'm not crazy. I mean, my house is a mite cluttered, but if it makes me happy, what's the harm? Now Jennifer, she don't agree with me.

"Dad, your house is a hazard. You could trip and break a bone. What if the house caught on fire? We would never find you!"

Jenny's a worry wart. Always has been. She got it from her Momma, along with the red hair and a neat streak. But she loves her old man. She's taking me out for a catfish dinner tonight. Just me and her. She didn't even say anything about the TV. She saw it. I saw her eyes turn a little sad when she looked at it. I know how she feels. I know it reminded her of her Momma. We had that old Fleetwood until Jennifer was around 12 or so. It was so hard on her when Marjorie passed. They were always so close. I should give her the little cherub statue, or maybe that set of dishes I found at Goodwill, the ones that sort of look just like the dishes Marjorie's mother saved for special occasions. It's just so hard to decide what she would like, what I can let go of.

The catfish was good. Not as good as Marjorie's, but that's asking a lot. It had all the fixin's, and I ate so much I had to loosen my belt. And they had the neatest silverware! It was plastic, but all silver and shiny, like regular table silver. I wiped my fork off on my napkin so I wouldn't make a mess of my pants pocket. "Dad, what are you doing?" Jennifer reached out and tried to take the fork out of my hand. "You can't take this home."

"Well I don't see why not. They're going to throw them away! There's nothing wrong with them." That's the problem with young folks nowadays. They just throw every damn thing away. Nothing's worth saving any more.

"You have plenty of silverware." Her voice was soft and slow, like she was talking to a toddler or a retard. "You have plenty of everything. You've got to stop hoarding things. What would Mom say if she could see the house?"

The fork in my hand went all wavery through my tears. Marjorie would love it. She would understand. The house was so damn empty without her in it. And all of it, every last thing, reminded me of her. The Hula Girl bobble head reminded me of our trip to Hawaii. The elephant statue reminded me of our trip to the circus, when we took Jennifer but had to leave early because she was scared of the clowns. The stacks of cooking magazines reminded me of her recipes. She collected hundreds of recipes, and most of 'em she never got around to trying. No one said a damn thing to her about collecting too many recipes. They just let her carry on. It's not one little bit different than my collection. "I think I'm ready to go home." I dropped my napkin, but stuck the plastic silver fork in my pants pocket.

"Let's have dessert first." She gave me a smile that made her look so much like Marjorie that I had a hard time telling her no. I shook my head. "I've been away long enough. Time to get home. Tomorrow's Saturday. I want to get to the yard sales early. Never know what you might find when you get there before things are picked over. Last week I found an old ViewMaster that had a reel of pictures from the Grand Canyon. You know your mother and I went to the Grand Canyon on our 35th anniversary."

"I remember," Jennifer smiled. "That was right before Mom got sick." Was Marjorie sick? I seemed to remember her being in the hospital, but she was with me, and with all the things I bought for her. She always did like me to bring her little presents.

We drove the streets, past Jennifer's nice brick house. "You're welcome to stay the night with me." It was a nice, her asking, but I never really liked to stay away from the house too long.

As we got closer to the house, I fingered the fork in my pocket, feeling a little excited as I thought about finding just the perfect spot for it. Maybe with the souvenir spoon collection.

I smelled the smoke a block away. By the time we rolled up to the corner, and I saw the flashing lights, I already knew. As soon as Jennifer slowed down at the stop sign, I opened the car door and jumped out. I ran as fast as my old legs could carry me. I could hear Jennifer calling out to me, but Marjorie was calling to me too. I could hear her, trapped in the house, begging me to save her.

"I'm coming Marjorie!" I screamed. Jennifer caught up with me and wrapped her arms around me. "Dad, you can't."

"Your mother's in there!"

"Mom's dead!"

I slapped her then. "Don't you say that about your mother!"

I dodged the firefighter, their hoses, the neighbors who turned out to watch the show. Everyone who would stop me. My Marjorie was in the house. Trapped by flames that would eat her alive. I snuck in the back door.

"Marjorie!" I climbed over stacks of books and piles of furniture. I could hear her call my name. "Where are you? I can't find you in all this smoke!"

"I'm in the den, honey." I heard her sweet voice and my heart pounded in my chest with so much love I felt like I would bust open with it.

I pushed open the French doors that separated the den from the dining room, and there was my Marjorie, sitting in the yellow and pink rose chair. I knew she would love that chair. "What took you so long?" She smiled that smile that could stop my heart. "I brought you a gift," I said and put the plastic silver fork in her hand.

INVISIBILITY
CALLEY LUMAN

She was small. She was soft, pale, and polite. She delighted in laying on the ground, looking up at those above. They were above her. She hated the cold because they couldn't warm her. She loved the heat because she could show them she was happy. They talked about her hands, saying "Let me feel your hands in my hands. Your hands are so small. Your fist is the size of your heart. Your heart is so small.

She felt her heart was big. Most mornings it consumed her. During the day, she walked quickly. They liked when she walked quickly because they had long legs and didn't bother to call back to her if she fell behind. She never learned to shout so she had to work hard to be heard. She would whisper again and again until they finally noticed a buzzing in their ears. They swatted at imaginary flies as she tried to tell them her favorite color.

She used to pretend she was invisible as she walked through them. "Watch this," she whispered. "Watch this. I can become invisible."

She practiced being invisible. It was a superpower. She felt she had power and held all of the sacred knowledge of the universe. Even so young, so small, she recognized the universe lived inside of her.

One day I'll choose my religion, she thought. *I'll study them all and then I'll choose my religion.* She believed in crying. She cried a lot, like a helpless, pathetic baby. They didn't know how to help her when she cried because it was so consuming. They thought they would get sucked into the ether of her tears and drown. They didn't know she was crying for them. So they didn't have to. For it was her path to be a vessel for the universe of unwanted feeling. Her tiny, soft, pink little body held their sorrow. It held their love. Their embarrassment. Their giddiness. Their pride. But never their anger. No. That was the only one she refused. She was constantly pulling that sticky, gooey anger out of her heart and pasting it onto her shoulders. Her shoulders lived up by her ears so they could always whisper to her the temptation of anger.

She wished to be older. She wished to be somewhere else. She wished to be free from her body. She wanted to live with color, to live inside of forest green, slate grey, and lilac. She wanted to be the navy blue on the walls of some little boy's bedroom or a lime green notebook carried to class every day by a middle schooler. She wanted to be simply loved and to be shared. But trapped inside her body, she craved to be sensitively and carefully touched.

She pretended the boys from her class would sneak from their homes at night, coming into her backyard just to peer into her window and watch her sleep. She loved to sleep. It was the escape. The solace. Her dreams weren't always pleasant, but at least they weren't real. The best nights were when she didn't dream at all, when she ceased to exist completely. Then she didn't have to pretend to be invisible. Then she didn't have to walk quickly or use her small voice. Then she didn't have to feel for herself or for anyone else. Then her little body didn't ache from holding the entire universe inside of it. She didn't have to be anything.

***

When they asked her what she wanted to be when she grew up, she told them that she wanted to be a volcanologist because she liked the way molten lava looked before it hardened.

Calley Luman is from Yukon, Oklahoma, and has been secretly writing on PC's since she was at least seven.

A DOG'S TALE
BRIDGET MAGEE

When Gail appeared in front of Bowser's kennel, leash in hand, the dog's stubby tail wagged wildly. Despite his Bulldog girth, he managed to get his two front paws off the floor in a show of appreciation for his morning dog walker. Gail had been volunteering at the Humane Society since her husband passed away, but no other dog had touched her heart the way Bowser had.

"Come on, buddy, let's get you some exercise," she cooed affectionately to the burly dog as she clipped on his leash.

"Woof!"

After a leisurely walk through the neighborhood, Gail stopped at the park to play fetch with Bowser. She justified her detour by reasoning that a dog of his stature needed more exercise, but really, she was reluctant to return to her empty house.

An hour later, when Bowser was sprawled out in his kennel snoring softly, Gail went to check-out at the volunteer desk. The tall silver haired man she vaguely recognized was signing the volunteer log. When he was done, he smiled shyly at her on his way to the kennels.

"He's the afternoon dog walker," Connie, the Volunteer Coordinator, informed Gail with a wink.

Gail cheeks burned as she turned her attention to the volunteer log. The name on the bottom line was Mitch Brown. Could that be the same Mitch Brown that coached little Mike's baseball team all those years ago?

The next day when Gail appeared in front of Bowser's kennel, his tail nearly detached from his body from wiggling so much. Gail was flooded with affection for this portly pooch that was so happy to see her. It had been a while since she'd had such an enthusiastic greeting. She needed to rectify that.

"Let's skip the neighborhood walk, buddy, and head straight to the park."

"Woof-woof!"

At the park, Gail threw, and Bowser retrieved. Mostly. Every third or fourth throw, Bowser would simply plunk down on the grass to rest. When this happened, Gail would walk over to him, sit down, and scratch between his ears. Eventually, when Bowser was rested, he would get up and look at Gail expectantly, ball in mouth, ready to resume their game.

Gail was having so much fun, she lost track of time. When she finally glanced at her watch she realized she was late getting back to the Humane Society…and back to life.

She sighed as she gathered up Bowser's leash and ball. Suddenly, the Bulldog started barking wildly. A different ball went flying past Gail. Bowser took off after it.

"Bowser!" Startled Gail looked up. There stood Coach Brown. She was sure of it. "Coach Brown?"

"Mitch Brown. I haven't been called Coach in years." His voice was deep and kind, exactly how Gail remembered it from the ball field. "Connie from the volunteer desk said I might find you two here."

"Yes, we come here every day," Gail said flustered. "By the way, I'm…," she started to introduce herself, hand extended when Mitch interrupted her.

"Gail. Yes, I remember," he said as he squeezed her hand gently. "How could I forget little Mike's mother?" His blue eyes twinkled.

Gail's cheeks bloomed in return.

"How is little Mike?" Mitch continued.

"He's great, though he's not little anymore! In fact, he has a little Mike of his own now. How is your son Kyle? Our boys made quite the pitcher/catcher duo."

"Kyle is doing well, last one of my kids to move away."

As they held each other's gaze for a moment longer, Gail thought she saw a trace of loss in his eyes, too. Then Bowser came bounding up.

"Woof-woof!"

"You ready to go, buddy?" Mitch and Gail said at the exact same time. They both laughed.

"I'm sorry, this is your time with Bowser, my volunteer shift doesn't start for another…" Mitch looked at his watch. "…oh, a half an hour ago."

"I'm so sorry! I lose track of time when I am with this bundle of cute." Gail bent over and scratched between Bowser's ears again. "Spending time with him is the highlight of my day."

"Mine, too," said Mitch, "and seeing you."

For the second time that day, Gail was flooded with affection.

Together they walked Bowser back to the Humane Society. Mitch left Gail at the volunteer desk with Connie as he took Bowser to get some water.

When he returned with Bowser, he asked, "Has anyone applied to adopt Bowser, because I was thinking…"

Connie cut him off. "As a matter of fact, someone just completed the paperwork! Meet

Bowser's new owner." She motioned toward Gail.

"But only if you agree to come to the park to play ball with us every day," Gail said.

"I wouldn't want it any other way," said Mitch.

"Woof-woof!" Bowser's tail wagged his approval.

THE SUPPLEMENTAL TURTLE
JACKIE DAVIS MARTIN

"That turtle cage smelled all the time," Harry, my husband's son, says, "and so one day when Nora was at school—maybe second grade-- I tried to clean it out and then I couldn't find her turtle!" Harry reminds me disturbingly of my husband when I met him over twenty-five years before. Harry's big and sprawling and talks in exclamation points. I love him.

"So, I knew the kid would be broken-hearted over that turtle—over losing it—and was feeling so responsible, you know." Harry sits back in his chair—a new one he and his wife have just purchased for the holidays—and rubs his moustache thoughtfully. His dad still has a moustache, too. Nora is Harry's stepdaughter and is now twenty-nine. We're waiting for her and her husband and little girl to arrive. Harry and I have been talking about—of all things—pets of the past.

"So, what did I do?" Harry leans forward again—he loves being in control of a story—and knocks a Santa ornament off the tree. "I went out and bought another turtle and put *it* in the turtle box. And it looks like the first turtle—I mean, who can tell these things apart?" Harry takes the slender hook between finger and thumb and carefully re-hangs the Santa.

My husband, Harry's dad, leans into the room and asks me where my purse is so he can get his hearing aid batteries from it. His presence startles me, as though Harry himself had suddenly transformed, aged, in front of me. Harry watches his dad retreat and is silent for a moment. "It's great to have you guys visiting," he says. We have flown in and are staying at a local motel. "It's great to see you and Dad."

I agree with him, the usual exchange: yes, yes, good to see each other again.

"Oh, the turtle," he says, resuming. His face too is becoming lined. "I was telling you about Nora's turtle. So she came home and was happy with what she thought was her turtle. But the next day I saw the first turtle on the doorstep, you know, the one she originally had, and so now I had this supplemental turtle." Harry laughs his large laugh and I laugh, too, at his sense of fun.

"Yeah" he agrees, as though I've said something, "and I can't stand turtles. Now I had this supplemental one and so I had to tell Nora I liked her first turtle so much I went out and got her another one!"

Harry's laughter subsides into thoughtfulness, as is often the case with him. "They should be here soon," he says, pulling the new curtains aside and glancing at the road. "She probably doesn't even remember the turtles."

They do arrive, and we all fuss over the child, and Harry is proud and shows me pictures he takes each minute of me with the child, of the child opening each of our gifts. "Look," he says. "Look how much she likes you."

I bask in it all. I love being around Harry, who is my stepson by definition, although I never raised him and so don't feel that ownership immediately. In a way, he compensates for losing my daughter—she died four years ago—and no one talks about it any more, not in this joyful setting, not even me who feels joy in the presence of family, even with our step-relationships.

At the dinner table, later—a dinner which Harry has helped his wife to assemble—we fill each other in on holiday plans—events that will occur after we separate tomorrow, and Harry says how he will get his Mom at the airport and bring her back for Christmas Eve and Christmas, which it is not, not quite yet. We tell Harry that we have tickets for the Botanical Gardens the next day and will visit them before we fly back, and he says that's great. He took his Mom and Nora and her family last year, he says, and they all had a great time. "There are hills," he warns, eying his Dad. "Just a reminder—there are hills to think about. Mom got exhausted with the hills."

Mom. Mom is returning. We'll take it easy, I assure him, regarding my husband, his hair white and sparse on his scalp—a large scalp, these are big men. Harry sports a still dark crew cut. He smiles in my direction, but his smile makes me sad. I feel I'm losing something beyond our being gone.

I turn to Nora. "Do you remember turtles when you were little? Didn't you have pet turtles?"

She straightens up from giving her child a cracker and the child runs off again. "Turtles? I think I had one, in a plastic cage. Oh—I think Harry got me another one. So, yeah." She laughs, "For some reason I had two."

Harry rubs his moustache and nods his head knowingly. "The supplemental turtle," he says, just to me.

SWIFTLY THE SWIFT

PAUL MCDONALD

If you could see me beneath this Walsall Football Club 'Swifty the Swift' costume you may be surprised. You might assume that a football club mascot called Swifty would be young - a drama student, perhaps, funding their way through college; or someone on a work experience scheme; or an apprentice at the club looking to learn all about it from the bottom up. The fact that I'm a fifty-five-year-old with three grandchildren might shock you. It wouldn't surprise you so much if I were playing the part of a sloth, or an elephant, perhaps, but swifts connote rapidity of movement, vigour, and a certain instinctive oneness with the capricious elements: not the stuff of late middle-age.

I don't blame you; I myself have expectations. Before I meet them, I always try to imagine who might be beneath the costumes of the various mascots I meet when travelling with the club. For instance, Sheffield Wednesday's mascot, 'Barney the Owl,' I assumed was a retired male history teacher; Norwich City's 'Camilla the Canary' a female vocalist down on her luck; and Southend United's 'Elvis the Eel' a forty two year old man, destined to die on the lavatory. In each case I was well wide of the mark. Indeed, I am *always* wrong, and it is always a shock. They may be female rather than male, clean shaven rather than bearded, older than I imagined, younger, fatter, thinner, darker, lighter, etc., etc. I am often wrong even after I have actually met the person beneath the costume. That is the most unsettling: when I assume I know who they are, and the person I was expecting has moved on, to be replaced by someone completely different! I'll be expecting a tattooed, shaven-headed ex-bricklayer from Burnley, and I will get a willowy blonde acting student from the Royal Academy of Dramatic Arts. You can only have faith in the costume, not in the performer. It is an important life lesson.

When I tell you that I'm an actor, you may also assume that I am a failure who's lived an unfulfilled life. You can imagine me performing as an extra, or in corporate videos, or provincial amateur dramatics, while my actual ambitions go unrealised. Wrong again. As it happens, I am a brilliant and hugely successful actor, and if you could see beneath the costume you would recognise me. I perform as 'Swifty the Swift' because I enjoy it, and one of the stipulations in my contract is that the club keeps my identity a secret.

Of course, because this foam 'Swifty the Swift'suit could contain anyone, you may think that I'm lying. But judge for yourself: next time you see me at football game, contemptuously lifting my tail feathers at the opposing supporters, or rallying home fans from the touchline with frantic wing-flapping, take a hard look: notice the conviction I bring to the performance; witness my oneness with the moment. If you're not impressed, don't worry: it may not be me after all.

PUSH THE LOBSTER
ANNE MCGRATH

The summer of my junior year of college I lived on Cape Cod with three girlfriends in a tiny no-bedroom house that used to be a fruit stand. We shared meals and bicycles, clothes and secrets. We housed a pet bunny that ate our underwear and we had epically bad jobs as waitresses at the fledgling Smith House; a seafood place run by high-strung people with zero restaurant management experience.

We were smart and saw the work as beneath us, but that did not prevent us from being terrified of messing up. Claire used to walk in her sleep, taking orders from whoever was still awake, so consumed was she by her food serving ineptitude. She later became a partner in a top law firm, making private jet money.

Julie somehow got a tampon stuck inside her and couldn't wait for her shift to end so we could escort her to the emergency room to have it removed. We told her she should leave early, but none of us was brave enough to offer to leave early with her, so she finished the shift.

Our deranged boss, Frank, set a tone of fear as the restaurant owner and chef. He was in a perpetual state of panic over the money he was losing. Ee suspected he had a meth addiction, or something worse that caused him to lose all his front teeth and swing into cycles of screaming rage.

We'd go back to the kitchen to pick up an order and find him wielding a ten-inch butcher knife over his head, yelling at us to: "get out on that floor and push the f-cking lobster." His face contorted and certain sounds made him lisp, because, as I've said, he was missing his front teeth. We tried, seriously *tried* to push the shellfish, but people are selfish; mostly ordering what *they* want to eat. Frank would have none of it when we returned to the kitchen with an order for say, a hamburger. "Lame-ass kids couldn't sell ice to Eskimos," he'd hiss.

Mary Jo cried when he insulted her and we offered behind the scenes support, but never stood up to Fred directly. Two of our original group of six had already left, returning home to their parents. I was determined never to let him see me sweat. I refused to give him the satisfaction. *He messed with the wrong girl. Just wait until the end of the summer when I can give him a piece of my mind,* I thought, at some point during every shift.

We made almost nothing in tips, out on the floor, which is what we called the dining room, for reasons I can't explain. It was as if we were stepping onto a stage when we exited the aluminum kitchen swing-doors. One reason the tips were so horrific was because the average customer was of an age they could remember a time when a quarter could actually buy something. They thought they were being kind when they gave us a wink and left their odd spare change under the plate.

But, that wasn't the worst of it. Worse than the fear of getting killed by Frank or not making enough money to feed ourselves, were the hideous uniforms. Pale blue and white gingham tops with big poofy sleeves, white peter-pan color, thick apron tied with a giant bow, and a baby blue skirt that fell to an unflattering spot mid-shin. This was all topped off with a sheer-white, shower-cap style bonnet. No one looks good in a shower cap. Our hair had to be pulled back in a bun, leaving us looking more Mrs. Santa Clause than hot college students. Besides being ridiculously unfashionable, the uniforms were filthy because we didn't have a washing machine. We'd just iron the food into the apron, because Frank would not tolerate wrinkles, although it seemed he couldn't see the food stains.

Despite the hundred-degree temperatures, we had to wear panty hose, which were ripped to shreds by the end of the summer.

We had a pact: if a cute guy ever came in, which was highly unlikely given the uncool vibe of the restaurant exterior of a wooden sailor in a yellow raincoat perched beside the road: but if a miracle occurred and one should walk through the front door, we vowed to signal each other, and leaved though the back-kitchen exit, telling Frank what we really thought of him on our way. We talked about telling him off more than once, going in a blaze of glory. It got us through many a long and lonely shift.

At the end of the summer with less than a week to go, one of our last shifts, and I saw my friend Claire point her bonneted head toward the front door. There stood a small group of young, good-looking, long-haired guys. The four of us who worked that day gathered together with an excitement beyond anything we'd experienced all summer. Boys were in our midst. They were adorably tanned and scruffy. We looked like we belonged in the Disney parade. We knew this was it, time to enact our dramatic quitting plan. In a flurry of lip-gloss application and bonnet hiding, we prepared our version of Brexit. We gathered ourselves.

"Let's roll," someone squealed, and we stormed the kitchen like an incoming tide, whipping off our aprons and bonnets as we went, nearly naked by the time we reached Marvin the dishwasher, whom we all had crushes on.

We marched through the kitchen, our long hair streaming behind us like victory flags. I saw Frank peer over the counter, eyes popping out of his head, and *I* knew that *he* knew, the gig was up. Then for a millisecond, I saw a look I never expected to see on his toothless face. Hurt. Quickly followed by fury.

He gathered his composure and screamed, "Get your scrawny white butts back out there on that goddamned floor." I started to say, *not this time Buster*... but the words caught in my throat. I suddenly saw Frank not as a crazy chef, but as *our* crazy chef. Part of our gingham-wearing summer family. The others must have felt it too. Without a word, we slowly turned around one-by-one, picking up our aprons and blowing kisses at

Marvin-the-dishwasher. We pushed through the swinging metal doors, returned to the floor, cute guys notwithstanding, and pushed the lobster. One last time.

THE EYES HAVE IT

JOANNE JAKLE MCKINNIS

The moment Tom entered the storeroom of the town hall, he knew that this time the rag picker had found something really special. The hide of the animal was shaggy and ragged, but the enormous head was magnificent, the glass eyes bright and oddly knowing, the mouth in a perpetual snarl. You were almost afraid to get too close to the tiger, lest he bite you and carry you off to his long-gone lair.

What really surprised him, however, was that the head had been transformed into a kind of crystal ball via coins fed it. There was a slot right over what would have been its brain, and each time you put money in it, you were not only saving it, but if you asked a question aloud, an answer would appear in each of those all-knowing eyes.

At first the constable had asked only trivial things, just to test it. "What will the weather be like tomorrow?" "Should I wear a coat or just a sweater?" Each time both eyes lit up with what proved to be a correct prediction. Of course, the response could just be the result of a random-event generator powered by carbon dating. Tom had seen an explanation of this on a sci-fi program on the telly, not so long ago.

However, the answers were invariably true, and, addicted to this game, he accelerated to more meaningful questions. "Will I get promoted and a salary raise?" was his latest question, but he wasn't satisfied with the tiger's answer this time. Up popped: "Heaven only knows." What could *that* mean? Was he supposed to *pray* for such good fortune? He hadn't been on his knees since he'd been bullied as a schoolboy.

He tried a question that didn't require a yes/no answer. "What good fortune lies in store for me?" Up popped: "Your treasure is where your heart is."

A *treasure*? He had always been a skeptic, but now he was as excited as when, as a boy, he'd played his own version of Stevenson's Treasure Island. Could the former owner of the tiger skin, perhaps an Anglo-Indian, have hidden a precious jewel like the Koh-I-Noor diamond somewhere in his home?

"Home is where the heart is," came instantly to his mind. He must find the rag picker who'd put the skin into the town hall in the first place!

It took him a while to locate the man, as the nature of his job was to be out and about, in all kinds of weather. Today was unusually cold, wet, and windy for the first of April, but Tom found his quarry shambling along a nearby street, whistling a cheerful tune.

"Jack, come have a warm drink on me, at that pub over there. I have an urgent question to put to you!" The elderly man, as ragged as the rags and other trash he'd been shoving into his sack, looked surprised, but then his seamed, grey face struggled into a sly smile. "Sure, guvnor, and let's make it two?"

The pub, only just opened, was warm and welcoming, but the publican motioned Jack's burden disdainfully to the umbrella tree. When the two men had settled into their warm seats, sipping their comforting grogs, the constable felt his way slowly and cautiously to his reason for this unexpected invitation.

The minute he mentioned the animal skin, a shield seemed to slide over the rag picker's face. "I don't know what you're talking about, sir, as I never did steal any such thing in my life!"

"Nobody's saying that, my dear man, but you obviously *found* the thing *somewhere*?" "What's it to you, sir? Why ever should you care about that mangy hide?"

"It's just an unusual thing to find in a small English town, very far from any jungle. Have you been to any abandoned homes on High Street, perhaps? I seem to recall that, a few days ago, an eccentric old man passed away, without any survivors or heirs. Could you have found some of his possessions in the alley behind his now empty house? I'd share anything we'd find there, no questions asked!"

A cunning smile, like a furtive animal, crept over the older man's face. "You know how honest I've always been, sir, and everything that isn't outright trash can be found in the town hall storeroom!"

Tom couldn't let go of his prey. "Let's just visit that dead man's house in case you overlooked something important? It couldn't hurt just to make sure? Anything worth something would be split fifty-fifty, no questions asked! No one else need know!"

After a third drink, Jack let himself be persuaded, and the unlikely pair walked arm in arm the few blocks to High Street. In back of a crumbling relic of a bungalow, the rag picker pointed to a large bin filled with odds and ends. "The only thing that looked worth picking up for the monthly town auction was that animal hide," he said. "I didn't want to keep it for myself, the way that face was snarling at me, but maybe some gent with a nostalgia for by-gone Imperial England will bid on it."

"You mean you didn't ask the tiger's head any questions?" Tom demanded suspiciously.

"Of course, I saw the slot in its great head, but that's only a piggy bank, or should I say, 'feed-the-kitty,' right?" Jack replied in an attempt at humor.

"I'm sure that the head knows more than it's telling us," Tom insisted. When the old man looked bewildered, Tom felt a strangely murderous urge to fasten his hands around Jack's scrawny neck and shake him as a tiger would its victim.

Then, unexpectedly, the words of the tiger echoed in his ears: "Your treasure is where your heart is." He grabbed hold of the shirt of the dumbfounded man, ripping it down, off his chest, exposing a no less ragged undershirt. There, instead of any jewel, was a small saint's medal. "That's my only treasure, my patron, St. John, so please don't take it from me, sir!" the old man cried.

Tom's own eyes were finally opened, and now he knew what the true treasure was, and the secret of happiness, and why Jack actually whistled while he worked at his menial, seemingly unrewarding job.

THE CHRISTMAS ORNAMENT
C. J, MCPHERSON HEANEY

The blast of hot air assaulted my face. I backed off briefly, then reached into the dark abyss with gloved hands and grabbed the thin, metal handles. The telephone rang and the doorbell chimed simultaneously.

"Someone answer those!" I called over my shoulder as I heaved the roaster onto the counter and kicked the oven door closed with my foot. Suddenly, my 8-year old identical twin granddaughters burst into the kitchen through the cafe doors, proclaiming, "Great Grandma's here!" and stormed back out, the doors swinging wildly. Greetings could be heard coming from the entryway. My widowed mother had arrived. How was she going to get through this Christmas season? My parents had been married for 63 years, and they weren't going to celebrate 64. I began basting the large turkey.

"So what smells so good in here?"

I looked up to see my mother's wonderful face as she slowly pushed through the cafe doors.

"The house looks so nice, Carol..."

Putting down the baster, I gave my mom a hug. "How're you doing, Mama?" I looked into her hazel eyes – the eyes that hadn't changed since I first felt her love as a little girl. I was grateful she was still in my life.

"Oh, I'm doing... you know..." She patted my shoulder. "How are you?"

"Ha! Well, just look!" I spread my arms in mock triumph. "I'm relegated to the kitchen per usual." Laughing, I returned to basting.

From the corner of my eye, I noticed my mother's older sister cautiously enter the kitchen. She had a somewhat startled appearance on her face. My mom and I looked at each other, both of us wondering *what now?*

"Hello, Carol Jean." She spoke softly with the gravelly voice I had come to know. Though she had grown weaker over the last year, she was determined to celebrate Christmas with us.

She put her hand on the counter, steadying her frail body. With her head slightly cocked like a pigeon, she added, "That old bird smells good." I masked a smile.

"By the way, Carol..." she continued. "I love that adorable kitty ornament."

Closing my eyes, I shook my head. "Say what?" Immediately I regretted asking the question. But my dear aged aunt simply repeated her statement about some nonexistent cat ornament. She looked at me with clouded eyes, turned and slowly exited the kitchen.

My mom asked, "I wonder what that was all about?"

"Don't know and don't want to know." I finished basting and covered the roasting pan.

"Great Grandma!" The cafe doors slammed open as the twin tornadoes announced their presence. They grabbed my mother and hugged her hard, almost knocking her over.

"Okay, everyone out!" I waved the baster as a scepter and playfully shooed the trio from the kitchen.

The doors mercifully blocked most of the cacophony from the living room. Yet from the occasional cheer or groan coming from those watching the football game, I surmised that Those Idiots were playing against A Bunch of Losers. As I returned the roaster to the oven, a wet black nose poked under my armpit.

"Get out of here, Bear!" My big black lab retreated and trotted out to the friendlier territory of the living room. Closing the oven door, I took a quick appraisal of the kitchen: Potatoes boiling, two pies cooling on the counter, dough rising for the rolls. Exhaling with a contented smile, I wiped my hands on the large flour-sack dish cloth tied around my waist and left the kitchen.

Entering the living room, I came upon an incredulous sight. In one corner stood our splendidly decorated Christmas tree, under which piles of brightly wrapped gifts were stacked. My brother Bill and my eldest son sat sprawled on the couch; an assortment of children lay on the carpet with the dog; and my mother, aunt, sister-in-law Barb and daughter-in-law sat around a card table near the tree working on a jigsaw puzzle. Though my aunt held a few puzzle pieces, she seemed more interested in the ornaments on the tree. Whatever makes her happy, I thought. Though the scene was fairly idyllic, my father's absence was sorely apparent.

My extremely pregnant daughter-in-law reported she was having mild contractions.

"Wouldn't it be fun if I went into labor today?" she asked.

"NO!" came the resounding answer. Kay just smiled. The twins got up and ran out of the room, followed by the dog.

"I need someone to set tables, both the grown-ups table and the kids' table." I announced. "Whoever's volunteering has to wash their hands!"

"I will, Mom." Of course – my son John. It was so good to have him and Kay to the house for Christmas. My youngest son Matt was in the military and couldn't be home this year. Though I'd rather have both sons present, I was thankful John and his family made it. He gave me a quick kiss on my cheek as he walked past me. But before he could get much further, he was assaulted by his twins who were brimming with news.

"Daddy! Bear ate one of the pies!"

Groans arose from everybody at the loss of one of Kay's homemade pies.

My mother was the first to ask. "Which pie did that dog eat?"

With grimacing faces, the twins looked at each other and exclaimed, "Mincemeat!"

Cheers rippled through the room. Exasperated, I threw up my hands knowing the dog would soon perform a similar action. "John, put Bear out please..."

My aunt softly touched my hand and smiled, nodding toward the tree. I followed her gaze to the beautifully decorated Fraser Fir and taking a step for a better view, peered between the lush green branches. In amongst the other ornaments and twinkling lights sat our gray cat.

As John returned to the living room, I cried, "Look at Wolfie in the tree!" Interest in the game was lost as everyone's attention was redirected to the tree. Choruses of laughter erupted from adults and children. As I gazed about the room, I thought of how much my father would have enjoyed this moment. Though he was not with us physically, I knew he shared our laughter in spirit. I was thankful for all the wonderful memories of my dad and looking at the close-knit family gathered in my home, smiled at the thought of memories yet to come.

I looked again at the cat in the tree and joined in the laughter. This was going to be a good Christmas after all.

I AM HERE FOR YOU

ALAN MEYROWITZ

Emma had been the social one, planning lunch and dinner dates, theater outings and backyard gatherings with other couples. John was never comfortable with any of that.

Friends and neighbors sensed it. After her passing, invitations to him as widower werefew.

For several months, he delved into the backlog of Dean Koontz and Stephen King novels that had been accumulating in his den. But he lost patience with those and an overwhelming loneliness enveloped him, the slowly growing fog of it denying him focus on anything else.

It was then that the thing in his stomach exerted its first gentle pressure.

John placed his hands, fingers linked, over his abdomen and gently pushed back.

Perhaps it was not too odd that he allowed the notion of companion to intrude as loneliness retreated, or that he could not be sure if he was speaker or listener when *I am here for you* resounded, and repeated, in his mind.

During the days that followed there would be no hint of anything unusual, until he again pressed a hand over his stomach. He had to smile as the pressure was returned, reassuring. Nights were different, as the thing inside him took the initiative to let him know it was there. John welcomed that. In the quiet and dark, he would otherwise only be thrashing about in despair for Emma.

After a few weeks, there was an intermittent nausea. So, he began to eat smaller meals, and more of them through the day.

That helped, as did the thought that what he was eating provided nutrition for two.

He slept less and less at night, but found solace in lying on his back and rubbing his palms gently over his tender abdomen. The words *I am here for you* became his mantra, repeated by him in a whisper through the night even as the dull cramping became a sharper stab.

When the pain became too bad, one thought overtook all others: get out of bed and call for help.

Too late, though. A worm thrust up his esophagus and then down his throat, inspiring a vicious cough. Its entry into his windpipe shut down his breathing and ended him. His last thoughts were not of Emma when, just before all went dark, he managed a barely articulate *I loved you.*

THE HATCHLING
EDDIE D. MOORE

Jarin watched as the dragon hatchling playfully snapped at a passing butterfly. The tree from which he watched the mountainside den gently swayed in the wind, and he nervously glanced at the ground below. When he turned his attention back to the den, the hatchling's red scales sparkled like gems in the sunlight, and the corners of hia mouth turned up slightly. The hatchling stretched his neck up into the air, and he froze with his tail outstretched behind him. Clearly, something had caught the creature's attention, and Jarin feared that little dragon might dash back inside.

A limb shook as a squirrel leapt from one tree to another, and the hatchling followed it intensely with his eyes. Jarin relaxed and nodded his head as he considered the dragon's interest in the squirrel. Lord Tybalt would pay handsomely for a live dragon hatchling to add to his personal collection of exotic animals; besides, a red dragon was the centerpiece in his family crest. Catching a squirrel to bait the trap would be easy, but finding a way to keep the hatchling from drawing the attention of his mother was another problem.

Jarin soon lost himself in thought while he considered the different methods of quietly capturing the hatchling. Designing a trap to release ether when the door closed would be tricky, but he already had a good idea of how to build it. The hard part would be making sure that the creature received the proper dose and ensuring that the dragon continued to breathe while he made his getaway. Fear shot through his chest as the thrashing of nearby leaves caught his attention.

Fearful of drawing unwanted attention, Jarin slowly turned his head toward the sound. He heard small pieces of shell fall to the ground and saw the flick of a tail inside a clump of leaves. He glanced back toward the dragon's lair and released a long slow breath when he saw that the hatchling was no longer tracking the squirrel.

The squirrel scurried down the limb and froze when it spotted Jarin. Long seconds passed as Jarin and the squirrel stared at each other. Suddenly, the squirrel screeched and jumped to another limb. A moment later, the squirrel began to bounce up and down, shaking the thin limbs it clung to while it barked at Jarin.

"Quiet, you stupid tree rat." Jarin said in hushed tones while his eyes darted back to the dragon's den. The hatchling's head swiveled to face Jarin's tree, and a moment later, he dashed closer a few steps. The little dragon froze when it made eye contact with Jarin.

Hoping that the squirrel would jump to another tree and draw the dragon's attention, Jarin held perfectly still while the hatchling stared at him. When he couldn't take the burning in his eyes any longer, Jarin allowed himself to blink, and the hatchling bellowed a high-pitched roar that seemed way too loud for such a small creature. A low rumbling growl answered the hatchling's roar.

Jarin burst into motion and dropped from limb to limb as fast as he could. The hatchling scratched at the ground and roared at Jarin as he descended the tree, but it didn't come any closer. As his feet landed on the ground, he heard loose rocks clatter against each other, and a long deep roar reverberated in the air. Fear almost paralyzed him, but he forced himself to run.

He heard a whoosh and the sound of popping wood as something burst into flames, and he felt a hot wind pass by him as he ran away from the dragon's den. He leapt over rotted logs and scurried under half fallen trees, hoping that the squirrel didn't escape the dragon's flames. A sense of relief washed over him as he heard the running water of a nearby mountain stream, but the thumping sound of large wings renewed his flight of panic.

He jumped when he reached the ledge that dropped to the stream while hoping that the water would be deep enough to keep him from breaking anything. The cold water stung his skin as it swallowed him, and he let it hold him for a moment before he began to fight his way to the surface. He sucked in a fresh breath as he surfaced and looked up to see the tail of the dragon as it passed overhead.

Jarin allowed the current to take him downstream, and he kept a careful eye on the sky, searching for any sign of pursuit. He didn't believe that the mother dragon would travel far from her hatchling, and he sighed with relief when he heard a distant roar that came from the direction of the dragon's den.

When he pulled himself out of the stream, he rolled over onto his back and watched the trees above him sway in the breeze. He winced and leaned forward as something stung his back. His fingers fell on blistered skin, and when he looked over his shoulder, he sucked in a deep breath at the sight of the burn. Jarin gently prodded a large blister on his shoulder and said to himself, "I wonder if Lord Tybalt would be interested in a kitten."

APRIL

ALEX MORGAN

"Remember tonight...for it is the beginning of always."

-Dante Alighieri

It seems like I've watched her slip away from me a thousand times already. How many times has it been? Four?

Five?

I think four.

Even if it was more, I don't want to fathom the thought.

April...my center of the universe, is laying in her hospital bed, again. Only a husk of her beauty remains. April, you used to fill my world with joy, happiness, and peace, and now the only thing keeping you alive is a fucking machine; IVs, tubes, and other miserable things, are attached to her mangled body. Assimilated in this perpetual contraption of anguish—both hers...and mine. Modern medicine...both her salvation and prison.

Fucking bullshit...

I can't take this anymore. I'm losing my fucking mind in Purgatory! Is this God punishing me for being a shitty Christian? For not going to church every Sunday? For using his name in vain? No, that can't be the reason...April was a saint, and look at her.

What kind of "God" would punish someone so...good?

What kind of "God" would make someone like her suffer through so many deaths?

Maybe something completely different? Maybe I'm just in some fucked up coma—maybe *I'm* the one laying in that bed. No, no…I don't think I'd be capable of having a nightmare this bad.

Jeff bursts through the door, disrupting my thoughts. "Jesus! Chris, I came here as fast as I could.

I got caught up in fucking traffic and…"

Jeff pauses, probably due to the shock of seeing April in this condition. I didn't get a chance to tell him how bad she was.

"Christ, April…how—what are they saying?" This time's no different, Jeff still has genuine concern in his voice. I try to muster together a definitive answer, but how can I? I've been in this—well, not exactly "this" situation…but others. Some not as horrifically traumatizing, others though…

Well, I still have nightmares about the others.

I notice Jeff set his jacket down on the chair next to me as he sits down. "Chris, I'm—look, there was nothing you could do, man. It's not your fault, so don't sit there and blame yourself for it." I'm not even sure what to fucking believe anymore. I'm not even sure why I'm even sad. I know this will all happen again soon. Sure, everything else will be different: The mornings I spend with her, the days at work, the sex…the way she dies; but one thing will always be the same every time…the fact that she'll die. No matter how hard I try, no matter what I fucking do, I can't stop it from happening again. I'm starting to wonder if I should just embrace what little time we have together, how long is it usually? About a week or so? I know it's always before the wedding.

200

My concentration is disrupted again, but this time by the doctor. "Mr. Harris? When you have a moment, I'd like to speak to you..." He glances over at Jeff, who's anticipating receiving a dose of information. "In private, if you will."

I briefly bury my face into my hands, stand up, and then follow the doctor out of the room. The man closes the door behind him, ensuring no third-party hears.

"Mr. Harris, Ms. Cochrane's—" I interrupt him, for what seems like the hundredth time I've had to say this.

"April. Just...April, call her *April*." The doctor clears his throat and continues, heeding my last statement.

"*April's* condition is...severe. We need to continue with the surgical procedures we discussed earlier, or else—"

"Let her." The doctor gives me kind of a disgusted look. I can't say I blame him. "Is there any way to make sure she dies painlessly?"

I can feel the tears coming again, but also feel a little relieved, at least this time she has a chance to go without all the suffering I've seen her go through before. The doctor looks completely surprised, and slightly disturbed.

"Mr. Harris, there could still possibly be a—"

"No, *look* at her! Christ, just look at her...if you told her what you told me, she wouldn't want to live through his either. What would be the point?" I lie. There would be a point, I'd give everything to see her live through this, I don't care if I have to take care of her for the rest of our lives...but I know in a few days, I'll just wake up to her smile and watch all of this happen again.

"At least do her—us a favor and end her suffering."

Damnit, I'm about to lose it again.

"Mr. Harris, you do realize that this is a decision to be made by her family, specifically her next of kin. Do you understand?"

I collect my composure as I explain to him her mother overdosed on painkillers when she was ten, and her father passed away from cancer when she was twenty.

"I am the closest thing to family—no, the only family she has left." I tell him.

The doctor then explains the legal procedures required to proceed. I nod, and keep nodding in acknowledgement until the doctor finally returns to his office. As I re-enter the room, Jeff almost jumps from his chair.

"Chris, for fuck's sake, what did the doctor say?!" I stare at Jeff for a moment and force a smile. I can't remember the last time I was actually able to smile naturally.

"He said everything will be fine. They're going through with the surgery ASAP, Jeff. They're going to do everything they can." Jeff looks relieved. Good.

"Thank God. How long did he say? I can go grab us something to eat while we—"

"Go home, Jeff."

"What? No fucking way! You both are—"

"Go. Home."

"O-okay. Chris, man, please fucking promise me you'll let me know what's going on? Fucking promise me that one thing, will ya?"

I stare at him, and reassure him with another empty promise. He reluctantly leaves the room and disappears down the hallway. Don't worry, Jeffy…you won't remember any of this soon enough.

I lean over and embrace April's soon-to-be corpse. Holding her tightly, I whisper to her.

"I pray I won't see you again. Not in this world, life, or whatever the *fuck* this is."

"I'm…sorry, I just can't do this anymore. Please, don't come back. Not again. Just…wait for me. Can you do that? Just please wait for me."

The only response and closure I receive is just the artificial, computed sounds from her vital-sign monitoring equipment. It provides little solace…

But it's still better than the other goodbyes.

FOREIGN FAMILIARITY
ZACHARY MULCAHY

"…Of course, she looks the same to me, just as beautiful. There isn't a single, possible, way for her to be anything but more beautiful than everyone else. At least, that's what I thought. She deserves anything positive that life was generous enough to grace her with. Which is exactly why she doesn't deserve me. Or even you. The only thing equivalent to her, is herself. So, who gets to be the lucky one? Who gets to set the standard for all to see that that man, the one unwillingly sucked into her aura of energy, gets such a granted treat. Who would deny an invitation to her estate? An opportunity of embracing the joy of her retreat she offers from the ugly face that the world rears oh so effortlessly. Portraying her strength as she stifles its process just as easily. Woman are all created and born with this substance that man nor woman cannot claim name for. They say, 'If you look hard enough, it is surely there and easily identifiable!' For every heartened trait and inspiring piece of existence they share, lies a wretched, determined, beast. People eat up the duality of man, but there is no vitality more damning, more daunting, and more peaceful than a woman who claims relation to you. For she is both your mother's grasp, and your mother's scold.' I couldn't find who wrote that. But I remember when I was studying at University I came across the excerpt in some BS writing class and thought there was no better collection of words to describe Pamela."

Peter smacks his papers together on the podium where he had just delivered his farewell speech to the deceased woman whom he thought he would spend the rest of his life with. He blows a kiss to the casket, decorated in eccentric flowers and maroon cloth. Applause rain over riddled with positively afflicting mumbles – mostly from the older crowd. There had to be close to two hundred people squished into this tiny community center. If only the woman had been as loved as she was missed by all 199 figures in the room, except Peter. He begins to walk off and allow for Pamela's mother to speak, but he returns to the podium.

"If anything were to come out of this passing that wasn't tears, I would say love more than you already do. Because there's always an opportunity to love more than you do."

The applause did not roar this time, but rode across a somber wave of confusion and dismay through the open room. The mother hugs him and takes the podium.

Instead of returning to his seat positioned near the front of the ceremony, Peter walks through the aisle on the side holding a fake smile assuming those who had listened would try to comfort him as he passed by. The air got colder as he neared the side exit door.

The air hits him like the wave of shock that came two weeks prior to the death of Pamela. Wondering to himself, how could this be reality? How could, what is feared most manifest itself and become real so easily? The tears begin to fall, flushing his system. He holds himself as he weeps. Peter slowly crouches. The weight of the life he knows causes him to fold inwards. Still sobbing, basking in the release of pain. The worst hurt he's ever felt. What a rush for the poor soul.

Peter pulls his jacket over his face. All senses of his sorrow are in full throttle. With streaming tears, he stops and looks around. No witnesses of his fully exposed display of weakness. Peter gets up, still whimpering. His car becomes the destination. The world cannot see him like this. Or, at least he insists it doesn't.

He enters the car, closes the door and immediately senses the ringing silence. An easy catalyst for a dejected blubbering session. Tears don't even fall this time. Just the flexing tenseness of his body. Jolting from the withdrawal of the woman he thought he could no longer crave.

He reaches for his phone. His rhythm and habit takes course. Within a matter of seconds, he is checking the news and finds himself buried in a breaking news article. After becoming self aware of scrolling, he comes to.

"Fucking idiot" Peter mutters, no worry of spit falling onto his dress clothes or leather interior. "That easy to lose it all, huh? FUCKING, STUPID, IDIOT! Do you even care!?" He stops and yet again, begins to cry.

"NO. Quit fucking crying, you PUSSY!" Peter bangs on the center console of his SUV. Causing it to rattle and shake. This time he battles with himself silently in his head.

"Do you miss her now? Oh, someone you found so mundane and inconvenient, inconveniently leaves your life and now you're sad? But you're free now right? It's what you wanted the whole time. How's it working for you?"

Peter batters himself internally. He looks down at his phone again. This time opening his messages. He scrolls to "Brooke" in his contacts.

"Are you working?" is written and sent. Seconds pass before a response is received.

"No, come over."

That was enough for Peter to put his car in drive and bolt. Just as he is pulling out, Peter sees small crowds that are beginning to make their way to the parking lot.

"Just in time" he thinks to himself.

The streets are empty and easy to navigate. Peter resonates with the silence again, but it does not harm him as it had before. It cues him to turn on the radio. He instantly regrets his decision, as the radio and empty passenger seat reside as a symbol for previous times that are now gone forever. He switches it to a talk station. Two men argue on the radio about injury reports for football as Peter focuses on maintaining his speed limit and switching lanes.

"I'm here, come out" is sent as Peter pulls into the guest parking in the Maple Woods apartment complex.

"You've been here enough times to know where I live, dummy" is playfully rebutted by Brooke. Peter waits patiently. Suddenly, through the street lights and the glow of the lively windows emerges a curvaceous womanly figure. Peter gets a dopamine spike. He tucks his phone into his pocket and locks his car as he approaches Brooke.

"You coming from work this late, or were you out with another woman?" Brooke questions sarcastically.

Peter fails to realize there needs to be an explanation for his dressy attire at such an odd and late time. He is taken back by the shrill questionnaire of "another woman," reminding him of what has taken so much effort to repress.

"No, no" Peter musters up. "It was some dude's birthday at work. It would have been weird if I hadn't gone."

The couple enters the building up the stairs and merges to the left for her apartment. They find the TV already on with the smell of a hot dinner from the previous hours that lingers throughout the confined space. A vibe of home and uncertainty settles in with Peter. But, it seems familiar. A foreign familiarity if you will.

FOR ALL ETERNITY
TED MYERS

When Sarah died, we had been married for fifty years.

At twenty-three, she was a dazzling beauty. Many men were vying for her attention. There was one in particular, Roland, a tall, dashing Frenchman, and I knew she was attracted to him. He was rich, handsome, and erudite. He proposed to her. He wanted them to live together in Paris, but she had strong family ties in New York, and so I won the contest. When she agreed to marry me, it was the happiest day of my life. And every day after that was just as happy. Even after the heat and passion of youth cooled, she was everything to me, my center. Then the stroke hit. It left her paralyzed. She always made me promise not to let her die in a hospital, and so I ministered to her as best I could for that last week. Finally, mercifully, she slipped away. Even before they took her lifeless body from our bed, I made the decision.

"I'm coming with you, my darling," I whispered.

Then I lay down beside her and took a dozen of her strongest pain pills. It was a very pleasant way to go. I highly recommend it.

When I awoke, I was standing on a dock, squeezed in on all sides by strangers. The crowd was enormous. There was a big, white cruise ship. It looked like a giant, ship-shaped layer cake. People were boarding, ascending a long gangplank, one-by-one. I couldn't see what was making the process so slow, but it was clear everyone wanted to get on board that ship. I doubted there would be room for everyone on the dock. I scanned the crowd, frantically searching for Sarah. I saw someone who looked like her from the back.

"Sarah, Sarah!" I cried. But it was not her.

I couldn't be too far behind her; she had only been dead an hour when I followed. Looking around, I noticed that no one in the crowd looked old. Everyone seemed to be in the prime of life. I looked at my hands, and they were young. Eventually I got close enough to see that people in uniforms were making everyone form a line. We entered a terminal, walking single file between two ropes.

Inside, each aspiring passenger had to pass through a scanner, like the ones they use at airports to detect bombs or guns. But this scanner was scanning for something else. I believe it was scanning character. As each person passed through, he or she was either allowed to ascend the gangplank, or moved aside. The crowd of those who had been rejected was very large, and they looked unhappy and worried. I wondered what would happen to them. I wondered with dread if I would be one of them. I was sure Sarah was on that ship, and I didn't want her to sail without me. Then, in that sea of distraught faces—those who had been moved aside—I saw her. It was the young, beautiful Sarah, the one I had married fifty years ago. I ducked under the rope and ran toward the crowd of rejects.

"Sarah!" She saw me, and fought her way through the mob to the rope that held them in. "Sarah, why are you here? Why didn't they let you on the ship?"

"Because I was unfaithful to you, my darling," she said, and broke down crying.

I couldn't believe my ears. "No. That's impossible. We were so happy. All those years…" Then I saw Roland making his way through the crowd of rejects. He stood beside her.

"I'm sorry, Sam," he said to me. "Sorry you had to find out this way."

Then a uniformed guard gently guided me back to my place in the line. I was crying. It was my turn to enter the scanner. Inside, it was not like the ones at the airport. I found myself staring into a mirror, at the young me, the me of fifty years ago.

"Your character has been as close to blameless as anyone I've seen," It said to me. "Except for the suicide. Suicide is a big sin… However, since your motivation was not borne of cowardice, but of love, this sin will be forgiven. You may board."

"I don't want to board," I said through my tears. "I want to go where Sarah goes."

"That's not possible," said my image in the mirror. "You must board."

And so it was that I became the first person in anyone's memory to board the ship to paradise with a heavy heart. As I ascended the gangplank, I looked back at the crowd of rejects. Sarah and Roland were at the front, and they waved a sad goodbye. When I told her I would love her for all eternity I didn't lie.

MY UNCLE'S MAGIC HANDS
CLARKE O'GARA

My uncle used to live in a cottage. Visits to his cottage are among the most vivid memories I have. Everything in his cottage was made with his hands. I remember moments. The log fire spitting. The earthy smell of the kiln. The bright acrylic paint on his hands. The nudge against my leg of the latest 'stray' he'd rescued.

"What's this one?"

"It's a cat."

"It doesn't look like a cat."

"I haven't done the body work yet, but look at its eyes, look at the way it moves." Its eyes were yellow with black, narrow pupils. It rubbed its exposed circuitry against my jeans and raised its tail in that ulterior, feline way.

When I was younger, I thought my uncle's hands were magic.

My uncle had his own children, then divorced from his wife, lost custody of his children, lost his cottage that he built with his magic hands, and moved to a barge moored in a basin. He would spend a lot of time walking and taking photographs. His hands got older. They still made things. Just a lot less often.

On one of his walks he found another 'stray' laying under an old railway bridge. A dog; deactivated. One eye missing. A leg twisted. The tail broken. The skin was torn at points across its little body. It revealed the wiring and aluminum frame. What fur it had left was mottled and matted from the rain. It was supposed to be a little black and brown dachshund.

My uncle picked it up and carried it home in his camera bag as if it were a cradle. He handled the dog as if it were wounded and alive. He could see the life in everything. He could see past what things were, to what they should be.

When he returned to the basin it was almost dark. But even in the twilight he could recognize everyone's barge. Each profile home was unique. He turned on the power and climbed into the barge.

His barge overflowed with stuff, but it never appeared untidy. All over the barge there were plastic boxes full of things. He had to sell the cottage to pay for the divorce. But he refused to sell his stuff. He simply crammed it into his new life.

He laid the 'stray' down on his bed, then he rummaged through the plastic boxes. He found vertebra for the spine. The tools to untwist its legs. An eye that didn't match. He removed the fur from the body and used the last of his hot water to wash it in Swarfega. Gently kneading the oils out, like he was washing a baby's hair. He used some leftover conditioner to soften it. A light-brown pelage was slowly reborn in his hands.

By the morning he had a healthy, operating, android dachshund. The personality ROM was still intact. It was a chipper but needy dog. He lifted it up and looked into its mismatched eyes. "Bowie," he called it.

My uncle had two children, Jack and Saul. 17 and 13 years old. At 3:10 he walked down to the school. Work was slow at the moment so he was enjoying his free time. His low expenses combined with the money from selling his little creations meant he always found enough money to make ends meet. Sometimes money was good, sometimes money was tight.

The little dog bounced, yapped and circled his ankles. Its buoyant, attention-seeking personality revealed that it was designed to thrive with hyperactive children. Soon Jack and Saul would be able to shower it with attention, and maybe put down their Holo-Pads for once. When Bowie made his next pass, my uncle picked him up and turned him off.

He saw the back of his ex-wife's Range-Rover as he approached the school. So, he left to wait in a small memorial park adjacent to the school. After half-an-hour Saul and Jack came to the park. My uncle watched them from a bench at the park's perimeter. His children played with their Holo-Pads.

The Holo-Pads projected holograms onto the cropped lawn. The light figures battled, controlled by Jack and Saul. My uncle simply waited patiently. His sons knew he was there, but they had to wait and be sure their Mum didn't follow them. After school, she always went to a boutique cafe near the park to gossip with the other divorced mothers. Jack and Saul would annoy their mother until she let them go to the park. This was my uncle's limited, unofficial and illegal time with his kids.

My uncle picked up Bowie and turned him on. He jumped and chased his newly fixed tail. Saul and Jack saw him straight away. Immediately they turned off their hologram fighters and sprinted over to their dad.

"What's that?" asked Saul.

"It's a dog," said my uncle.

"Is it a real dog?" asked Saul.

"Real dogs are way too expensive," said Jack. "Where did you get it from, Dad?"

"I found it under the railway bridges past Headrow Farm. Someone had thrown it away."

"It's so cool," said Saul. "Are you going to keep it or sell it?"

"It's for you two - if you can look after it."

"No way," said Saul. "Dad, you are the sickest." Saul hugged his father for the first time in months. My uncle nearly cried as he embraced the smell and weight of his son.

"How will you hide it from your Mum?"

"We'll just say aunt Caroline got it for us," said Jack.

"You better go," said my uncle. As he said it he broke his own heart. In his only act of cruelty to his children, he hoped it broke their heart as well. Jack hugged him and left with his brother. Bowie didn't follow the brothers immediately. My uncle pointed and said, "New owner, follow," in a flat voice. Then Bowie bounded after his departing children. My uncle felt comforted that at least one of his creations would be able to walk his sons home.

My uncle couldn't meet his children too often. While the custody battle was ongoing he wasn't supposed to see them at all. But he took his chances when he could.

During rush hour, it was possible to get close enough to the school to see Jack and Saul without being spotted. Everyone just assumed that he was a parent of one of the children. Which he was.

The familiar black Range Rover was outside the school again. He kept his distance. But he had noticed that their mother never left the car until Jack and Saul came out of the gate.

The children started to spill out of the school entrance and into the playground. Jack and Saul came into view after a few minutes. Leaving the building last with the laggards. They had a group of friends with them. They looked excited. Jack made them form a circle, removed his backpack and gently lifted out Bowie. He placed Bowie in the middle of the circle his friends had formed. Saul turned him on. The children laughed as Bowie woke up, looked at his surroundings, then began gently jumping up at their knees and running around their legs. "He's so real," my uncle heard one of them shout. Although he doubted any of them had seen a real dog. Soon they were the only children left in the playground.

My uncle felt warm and useful watching his gift bring so much value to their lives. Then she stepped out of the Ranger Rover, with a face like a botched abortion.

"I told you to get rid of that stupid dog," she shouted. "If you want a dog, I'll get you a dog. You're not keeping that scruffy second-hand reject."

"Mum. Don't. It's Bowie. Someone made that for me," shouted Jack as she picked up Bowie and slammed him onto the floor. It took three attempts until Bowie stopped moving. Then she picked him up and threw him over the school fence into an overgrown patch of wasteland.

Once everyone had gone home, my uncle must have searched the wasteland next to the school, found Bowie in the long grass, taken him home and stayed up all night repairing him.

We know he repaired him because the police found Bowie next to where my uncle died. He was barking in distress and jumping against the wooden gate that led to the railway foot-crossing where my uncle had laid down.

After two weeks, the police let me have Bowie. When I ran a diagnostic on him I noticed my uncle had turned off his emotional inhibitors. The only reason I could imagine for this was that my uncle wanted to be sure that something was hurt by his death.

The damage to Bowie was permanent. He wouldn't stop barking and lashed out wildly. I couldn't bring myself to wipe his memory. So, I dumped him under the railway bridge by Headrow Farm.

HER FELLA

CARL PALMER

She rubs my head, runs her fingers across my face, and she cries. She holds me tight, her head next to mine, and she cries. I tell her that nothing has changed. I try to explain, but she doesn't understand. She hasn't understood anything I've said for the past five years.

We've been together since she was a little girl. We understood each other then. She'd talk with me for hours, look into my eyes, and tell me all her secrets. Evenings on the porch swing or in the yard, laughing and playing, or in her room, lying on her bed watching her every move.

I learned so much from her. She taught me what she liked, what she didn't like. She'd ruffle my hair, give me a hug and a kiss, speak to me in her special way. She called me her Fella. She'd say, "Come here, Fella" and I'd be right there by her side, ready for anything she wanted to do. That was then.

As she grew older, became a teenager, became busy, became popular, she had less time for our long walks together. Our talks were what I missed the most. I was still her Fella, still there for her, but she was outgrowing me. Soon she didn't talk with me at all. Sometimes at me, but never a conversation, and sometime during that time, she stopped hearing my words altogether.

Now, barely out of her teenage years, time seems to have gone by so quickly, our fifteen years together. Her, so full of life, so vibrant, so youthful, but me, I feel so old, as if I have aged seven years for each one of hers. Some days I feel at least a hundred years old.

And now she treats me like that, too. Lately she's spending more time with me. I love she's doing that. It's just the crying. I wish she wasn't so sad. She holds me close, rocks me, and she cries. She carries me everywhere and won't let me do a thing. She does everything for me, and she cries. We get into her car. I love to watch her drive. She used to look my way and smile. Today she stops several times, takes me in her arms and cries and cries and cries.

We enter the cold, bright room, yet I feel peace. I feel her tremble as the doctor shaves my wrist just above my paw. The needle is withdrawn. I feel warmth and am happy. We romp and play in the yard, her and I. Laughing and shouting in words we both understand. Just like before, before she began to cry.

ANXIETY

J.M. PAUL

Relapse always lies just around the corner. It sits, it waits, it watches, springs when you least expect it. It doesn't care what you've been through, all you've done to escape it. It's always going to be lurking there, just biding its time as it waits for you to weaken.

Before— before you pushed it back, repressed it, and beat it into the ground— it ran your life. It dictated your every action. It took things you loved and made you dread them. It took things you knew and made them foreign. It took the easiest things and made them terrifying. Your daily habits became laced with paranoia. The unknown became paralyzing. It ran your world, and filled it with imminent menace.

Even now that you've beaten it, it still lurks at the very edges of your vision, reminding you that it's been there and that it can come again. It will never truly be gone. You know this, and you hate it. No matter what you do to stave it off, it will always be there. All you can do is hope you're strong enough when it strikes again.

It is ominous. It is disturbing. It is hateful. It is pathetic. And it loathes you.

You will never be cured, but that doesn't stop you from trying.

You shake the bottle, listen to its contents rattle softly. Is this sanctuary?

"Just enough for a trial," your therapist said. "See if it helps any."

One pill a day. Even out your serotonin levels, and your problem will be solved. Winning without fighting. Perhaps it sounds dubious, but it can't hurt to try.

It's a toss up: staying medicated for the rest of your life, or struggling on until you find a therapist that thinks you're worth really treating. Who will take their time, work out the root of your issues, and help you banish them forever.

What if you lose before you find them? What if the constant terror drives you out of your mind, or drives a bullet through your skull? Is true sanctuary worth the risk?

You twist off the cap. You swallow the pill dry.

Sometimes you just have to take what you can get. It's hard not to dream of an easy life, however. Of a life without fears and hardship, or overwhelming emotions and daily defeat. You've never known a life like that, but the fantasy won't leave you. How beautiful must it be to stride through life with confidence and good humor. How freeing it must be to face life with courage instead of crippling fear.

This is your fondest dream. How sad is that? Others dream of unimaginable riches, or of love, or of adventure. That's what they strive for: a life of *adventure* and *love* and *luxury*. You? You can only hope to someday shake away everything that holds you back, and live like everyone else. That's it. That's what awaits you at the farthest ends. It's the light at the end of the tunnel; the triumph from the struggle.

You dream of freedom from yourself. You imagine a world without terror. You yearn for simplicity. This fantasy is different, but it's yours, and it'll do. All you need is a motive, after all; no one said it had to be a fancy one.

So you live on, pursuing this odd dream of yours, but that's just it:

You live.

HILARIA IN WINNIPEG
DAVID PERLMUTTER

From *The Winnipeg Free Press,* February 6, 20--:

 WINNIPEG (CP)- Those used to the typical tedium of Winnipeg City Hall meetings were treated to an unexpected spectacle this morning that will surely eliminate what little respect remains in the city for that particular institution. It all has to do with a particularly bacchanalian event from the distant past, which most of us modern people have totally forgotten about until it was brought to our attention then.

 Rather than the usual political exchanges between Mayor and Council, those in attendance at the session were unexpectedly presented with a Mayor and Council they had *not* elected. Granted, that tends to happen with a lot of people in any sort of election. But this morning's session was exactly and literally such a case.

 This group, more racially, culturally, sexually etc. diverse than the actual Mayor and Council, pretended to act in their stead, and did so for the better part of an hour before the fraudulent nature of the proceedings was discovered and the police finally called to remove the miscreants. What tipped them off was the fact that the final order of "business" was to throw water balloons at themselves, and then, unexpectedly, at the audience, who offered no defense to this, despite being rather surprised and shocked at the whole thing.

 Intrigued by the display, I caught up with the group after they were imprisoned, and was allowed to speak with the mock Mayor, a woman studded with tattoos and other body art known only as Norma Rae.

 She explained that their activity was an attempt to revive a custom I had never heard of before: the festival of Hilaria.

"So, it's a comedy-related thing," I said. "Assuming that "hilarious" is one way to describe good comedy…"

"Not exactly," she responded. "Hilaria was invented by the Romans, and was something of a masquerade type thing where anybody could imitate anybody else, regardless of what position they held."

"Which explains…"

"Yeah. They don't always get that they're not nearly as important as they believe, so we decided that this would be as good a way as any to let them know that. Unfortunately, we got stopped before we could go ahead with the next part of Hilaria."

"And that is?"

"Death, and resurrection. So that this world can become purified."

"So…. you were going to….?"

"Yeah. As many of them that needs to go that can go that way. Only way to get change in the system."

She paused as soon as she saw my nervous look.

"What's *wrong* with that?" she said, angrily. "You got a PROBLEM with that?"

"No," I said, nervously. "Good luck with that."

And then I came back here to warn you. To be careful to notice whether or not the people conducting government business are actually around to revive the weird and deadly custom of Hilaria.

Of course, a lot of the time around here, it's hard to tell the difference.

HOLIDAYS
MELISSA QUIGLEY

It was the summer of '75 when everything changed. My cousin Edwina and I had finished our first year of high school and were on holidays at our grandparent's house in Amphitheatre. They lived in a tin shed on top of a hill overlooking the valley. Our uncle Bomber arrived mid-morning with rabbits slung over his shoulder and a shotgun wedged between his armpit.

'What are you lookin' at?' he said.

He grabbed a rabbit and swung it in my face. Its rigid body hit my cheek and I blinked and recoiled. The pungent smell of gunpowder, earth and blood made me sneeze. He threw his head back laughing.

'Leave her alone,' said Nan.

'I can't help it if she's ugly,' said Bomber.

She spat on a handkerchief and wiped my face.

'Go hang two in the cool room,' she said to Bomber.

'You can skin the other four and I'll make a stew for lunch.'

Nan folded the blood splotched floral material back into her apron pocket.

'Don't listen to him,' said Nan.

'We're going for a walk,' said Edwina to her mum.

Bomber stood at the makeshift table outside and slit one of the tiny bodies down the middle. He frowned and waved his knife in the air at a myriad of flies and lunged it at us.

'Look out or I'll dissect the two of you.'

We squealed and ran across the unmade road.

'Wait up,' said Edwina's mum.

A piece of paper flapped back and forth in her hand like a winning lottery ticket.

'What the fuck does she want?' said Edwina. 'WHAT?'

'Come here young lady and don't use that tone with me.'

We walked over to her.

'Be good girls and get these things for Nan at the general store.'

She handed Edwina a list and five dollars.

'I'm not eatin' that shit,' said Edwina.

'You'll do as you're told. Now get going.'

'I'd rather die than eat rabbit,' I said.

'They're pets – not for eating!' said Edwina.

Aunt Evelyn ignored us and headed back towards the house.

On the other side of the road we lifted the barbed wire and stepped through the gap in the fence. Cows grazed around us. We laughed and raced each other down the valley to the creek galloping over dung. The sun was warm on my back and I took my cardigan off and tied it around my waist. A kookaburra in a nearby gumtree watched us step on rocks across the creek.

The water was shallow, the earth moist around it. I slipped and my runners squelched with water cooling my feet.

Edwina pulled out a packet of cigarettes and a box of matches hidden in her socks beneath her jeans. She lit two cigarettes and handed me one. We walked through unkempt bushes and turned onto the main road. We stubbed our cigarettes out when we heard tyres crunching on gravel. A car pulled up beside us. The engine revved and the muffler rattled competing with music inside the cabin. A man, with an earring in his ear leaned his tattooed arm out of the window and tapped his fingers on the door. I could see our reflection in his sunglasses.

'Ladies, how are we this fine morning?'

We ignored him and kept walking. A bald man dressed in jeans and a t-shirt stood mashing a can, in front of the pub. He had a long beard and his moustache curled on the ends. The same car pulled up near the entrance and the man got in beside him.

'Where are you ladies goin'?' I can give you a lift,' said the driver smiling.

'Nowhere,' said Edwina.

'Come on, you must be going somewhere. What's your name? What's your friend's name, if you won't tell me yours.'

'Who are you?' said Edwina.

'I'm Brett and this here's me mate, Dave.'

'Come on, let's get the fuck out of here,' said Dave.

'You'd better wear a belt otherwise you'll get your pussy milked,' said Brett.

They laughed and we ran towards the general store. The bells jingled above the door to announce our arrival, and the shopkeeper greeted us. She was full of mirth telling us who we were before we could open our mouths and marvelled at how much we looked like our mums.

'Silly old duck,' said Edwina when we were outside. 'We don't look anything like them.'

I walked back towards the creek.

'No, let's go this way,' said Edwina.

'But it's longer.'

'Who cares?'

Edwina lit a cigarette and handed it to me and lit another one. Music blared and a haze of dust enveloped us. The car we'd seen earlier drew closer and this time Dave was opposite.

'Where are you off to?' he said.

'None of your business,' said Edwina. She drew back on her cigarette and blew smoke in his face.

'Bitch,' he said. The door clicked open and Dave got out of the car. He grabbed Edwina around her waist and she tried to butt her cigarette out on his hand.

'Let go of her,' I said.

I kicked him and my heart pounded.

'Run, Liz, run,' she said.

My cigarette fell out of my fingers and my feet faltered. Brett ran after me and twisted my arm in a vice grip. I kicked him and he held me tighter and pulled me towards the car.

'Help,' I yelled, but it was useless. Our only witnesses were sheep in an adjacent paddock.

Edwina sat in the back of the car beside Dave. Brett shoved me in the front passenger seat and locked the door.

Dave's hand clenched my shoulder while Brett ran around the other side and sat beside me. The car smelt of stale beer from empty cans that littered the floor. I bit my bottom lip and the scenery blurred.

'If you played nicely this wouldn't have to happen; your friend has no respect,' said Brett peering at Edwina through the rear vision mirror.

'She needs to be taught a lesson,' said Dave.

'I've done nothing wrong,' said Edwina.

'Leave her alone,' I said.

'I'd shut up if I was you,' said Brett.

He drove towards our grandparent's house. The kelpies chained to the metal drums barked to let Nan and Pop know there was a car approaching. I wished Dad and my uncle were outside. Apart from smoke coming out of the chimney and our parents' cars out the front it looked like no one was home. We stopped in front of a disused mineshaft several kilometres down the road.

'If you're nice you won't get hurt,' said Brett. 'Ain't that right, Dave?'

'Yeah.'

'Okay, who's gonna go first?' said Brett.

I could see the smirk on his face out the corner of my eye.

'Come on, don't all speak at once. If you don't answer me, I'll have to pick.'

I thought I heard a car pulling up behind us and glanced at the side mirror but the glass was smashed. I didn't dare turn around.

'Who the fuck is that?' said Dave.

'Don't know,' said Brett. 'Keep your mouths shut or I'll shoot you.'

I licked my lips and tasted blood. Urine trickled onto the seat beneath me and my head throbbed.

'What's up, mate?' said Brett.

'That's where you are. I wondered why you'd forgotten these.'

I stared at Bomber in disbelief. He was holding up the bag I'd dropped.

'It's not mine, buddy. You've got the wrong person.'

'Not you, yah drongo,' said Bomber. 'Me nieces. Best you let 'em go otherwise I'll have to introduce yah to me friend.'

He raised his shotgun just above the door.

'Your nieces?' said Brett. 'Well I'll be… We were just showing 'em around the area weren't we Dave? No harm done.'

'Come on girls. I'll take you home,' said Bomber.

He glanced at Brett and Dave.

'I'll deal with you two knuckleheads later.'

We sat in the backseat of his car and I viewed the dry barren landscape while listening to Edwina tell him what had happened, grateful he'd found us.

'You girls deserve much better than them larrikins. I'll kill the bastards. No one treats my nieces like that.'

I'd always disliked Bomber but now I wanted to hug him and thank him but I didn't know how. It was nice to know that beneath his gruff exterior he respected us and strangely I felt closer to him than I'd ever felt before.

GRANDMOTHER'S TYPEWRITER

SALLY RAMSEY

Sephora gazed at the old machine in the corner of her home office. It was useless. Ribbons were no longer made for it. Even if they had been, the keys stuck so much with age, typing on it would be impossible. For years she had crafted her tales on a laptop, but she would never get rid of the relic, as one well-meaning visitor had suggested. It would be like tearing away a part of her life. She stared at the beat-up metal, and a lifetime of images swirled in her brain.

Young Sephora had always been dependent on her grandmother. Even before her mother and father were divorced, her mother had very little time for her. Her older sister, Jan, was the one always in trouble, so she got all the attention. She also got the new clothes, while Sephora wore her hand-me-downs. Sephora received a few things for birthdays and Hanukkah, but it always seemed that Jan got what she wanted and Sephora got what her mother could spare from whatever time and meager funds were left over.

Grandma Lena's heart was weak. She always had a bottle full of tiny pills in her pocket. Every so often, when her breathing came hard, she'd put one under her tongue. Despite her illness, she'd always seemed to have time for Sephora. She taught her how to make brownies and how to shell peas from the garden. At Lena's instructions, Sephora turned scraps of cloth into doll clothes. But the best thing Grandma Lena ever did for Sephora was to give her a little black notebook.

Sephora first started writing in it when she was six. She could only print, and a few lines would fill one of the small pages. Still, there was enough room. Sephora's thoughts flowed from the tip of her pencil in simple poems. Words came easily to her, even in rhyme. When the first notebook was full, Grandma Lena gave Sephora another. As Sephora grew, little stories joined the childish verses. Sephora didn't share them, even with her grandmother. The words were hers, something precious, something her sister didn't have.

When Sephora was in fifth grade, Grandpa Jossi, Grandma Lena's husband of forty-five years, died. Grandma Lena was sicker than ever, and the family decided that she couldn't live alone. She would move in with Sephora's Uncle Hershel and her Aunt Margo, three states away in Massachusetts. Instead of a house, Lena would have a small room on the first floor of Hershel and Margo's home. The bedrooms upstairs were larger, but Lena couldn't handle stairs. The many things Lena had no room to take with her were given away.

Lena had an old Remington typewriter. Sephora had never seen her use it. It was heavy and would have been difficult for Lena to lift. It wasn't light for Sephora either, but it was gifted to her as a writer. Sephora was fascinated with it. The ribbon had two colors, black and red. The keys were not the easiest to press, but she managed. She wrote stories. At first, they were not much longer than the ones she'd written in the black notebooks. But the typed words seemed to take on a life of their own, popping from the page. While Sephora hid the pages at first, she finally got up the courage to share a story with her one and only friend, Ellen.

Ellen was everything Sephora was not. While Sephora was short, Ellen was tall. Sephora's hand-me-down outfits were behind the fashion. Ellen was the daughter of two furriers. Her clothes were bought new every year, sometimes more often, because she grew so fast. She was always in style. Ellen's hair was short, curly, and perfectly trimmed, Sephora's was long and unkempt, so much so that Ellen sometimes used her own hairbrush to banish Sephora's tangles. Ellen excelled at math, Sephora's worst subject. But Sephora had the ideas. She thought up new games. She developed complicated scenarios for dolls, and came up with the plans for school projects. Writing was a talent Sephora had that Ellen didn't share, or even understand.

But Ellen believed wholeheartedly in her friend. She wanted Sephora to bring a story to school, so their teacher and the other kids would know that Sephora had something worth their admiration.

Sephora resisted, afraid that the ridicule that was often heaped on her clothes and her hair would be aimed at her words as well. If it was, she wasn't sure she could live with the shame. But Ellen kept on her, threatening that if Sephora didn't share her writing with the world, she'd find a way to share it for her. Sephora still resisted.

"Look," Ellen argued, "Your grandma was always trying to help you. She wouldn't have given you the typewriter if she didn't want you to do something with it. I wish I could do what you do, and if you show everyone, I'll be really proud of you as my friend. You can write to your Grandma Lena and tell her what you did, and she'll be proud too."

Pride was something Sephora had very little of herself, but she desperately wanted to enable her friend and her grandmother to feel it. She took her story to school and hesitantly gave it to Mrs. Singer, who asked for permission to read it to the class. Sephora was terrified, but Ellen kept nodding at her. Sephora echoed Ellen's nod to Mrs. Singer. The class was strangely quiet. Not one spitball, and only one wadded note, flew from the desks. When Mrs. Singer finished reading, Sephora was amazed but relieved. Her work was met not with disdain, but with applause.

Across the distance, Grandma Lena was still guiding her granddaughter. Across the years, her spirit in the heavy metal antiquity always would.

.

THE GO-AWAY BIRD
ANNA REICHERT

Grief sat upon her wing.

She stared at it tiredly and sighed.

Why did grief have to be the color of a lima bean? Perhaps if it had been the color of something, well, *more*, it wouldn't cling to a feather so?

Grief had no purpose. It didn't fiddle or flutter. It didn't even yattle or prat. Grief simply sat and clung.

Half-heartedly—*again*—she twitched the tip of her wing—*again*.

The lima bean of gloom remained... And, now, wasn't that the most featherbrained of thoughts? A snicker almost made it out her beak.

"Did you just—laugh?" She felt the terrible need to roll her eyes, but since birds did not do such things, she did not. Neither did she reply. Let the Ruddy Shelduck think what it will.

"You just surprised me, is all. I didn't think you—could." The duck hemmed, right before it hawed, "Laugh you know."

Such foolishness for a fowl. It should really know better. She looked again to her wing, wiggling the grief about ever so carelessly.

"Why do you do that, miss?" The orange Ruddy bent low to the ground and bobbed its head about trying to catch her eye. "Flap your hand around like—that."

The duck had a stutter. It really shouldn't honk so. Somebody might put it away like...

"Do you want me to call a—nurse or someone, miss?" The Shelduck pecked a rag out of a tuft of its feathers and dabbed it toward her eyes.

What was the fowl doing? Sharply, she clacked her bill shut and startled the intruder back.

He stretched out his wings and puttered them nervously about. "It's ok, miss. I can get—somebody here— right quick. I just don't want—you to cry."

Was she crying?

She nuzzled her face with her wing.

Perhaps, she was. She wondered why.

The Shelduck squawked again, "Don't you worry—now. Help's coming."

"Ah, Miss Phoebe. What's got you so upset?" It was the Hottentot Buttonquail, of course. Dumpy and noisy, the little bird always skittered about in dark corners, leaping out when you'd just managed to forget the fussy old thing. "Something scare you, honey? You remember Franklin. He's the janitor, been here way longer than even you. Say "Hi," Franklin."

"Hi," the Ruddy Shelduck chirped.

Would the inanity ever end?

Jumping up—legs straightening, toes unclenching from their perch— she prepared to...

"No Miss Phoebe, you just sit right back down. You've got another 15 minutes in the meditation garden before you can go back to your room." The male Buttonquail clucked, "Oh, and don't give me that look, Miss Phoebe. Your doctors want you out socializing with others at least two hours a day. No pouting.

You know it's good for you. Now, how about you smile for me?"

How absurd! Go-away birds didn't smile. Surely even a Hottentot Buttonquail would know such a thing?

"Miss Phoebe" had been born a go-away bird thirty-five years ago. She'd pretended to be more for twenty-seven of them. An ornithologist. A professor of it, even. But then the wind shifted, and Miss Phoebe simply molted away.

"There you go, Miss Phoebe. That's a beautiful smile."

There was no smile. There would never be a smile. Ask the lima bean on her wing. She flapped it around so the silly bird could see.

The Buttonquail stilled the flailing feathers, patting the wing with a deep call of 'there-there.' "Alright, I'll let you get back to your thinking, Miss Phoebe. You let me know if you need anything else, ok? I'll be right over there."

"G'wa-ay! G'wa-ay!" she called with all her might.

"You're right, Miss Phoebe," the Hottentot Buttonquail trilled. "Today is a good day."

And, thus, grief sat upon her wing.

MY BROTHER'S KEEPER
ELLENA RESTRICK

You were everything to me. My shelter. My playfellow. My constant companion. You were my everything. Do you remember the Monmoths' estate in the autumn? We used to play in the orchards, collecting vermilion and burnt orange leaves. For hours, we would hide in the alcove and fashion crowns for each other, dizzy with the scent of petrichor and white gardenias. There was never any point in going back. Lady Monmoth would have a coronary occlusion when we returned with our clothes muddied and dishevelled. Even then, you were always willing to take the blame for me, weren't you mon petit agneau? No matter how many times she threatened you with the cane, you never let her harm me. You never let her leave welts on my back or cuts on the back of my legs that never seemed to heal and wept pus. I don't think you know how grateful I was to you; how it broke my heart to hear your screams from behind a locked door and how I sobbed when they separated us. You were my every thought. You were my everything.

It doesn't change what you did, I know that. I didn't want to believe…I didn't want to believe that I had not really known you. That you could be capable of doing such a thing. Yet here I sit with the evidence right in front of me, forwarded to me from an unknown sender. The words seem to claw at my eyes, ripping apart the images of you that had become the god of my idolatry. I have a solitary candle to illuminate this page; it would be so easy to burn it. I could exonerate you mon agneau. If these are the last things I say to you, know that the thought crossed my mind. Know that, just once, I was willing to save you. I wanted to, I really did…but I can't and I won't. You scare me. That poor family…they were innocent. What you did was completely deplorable and heinous and brutal…but I still love you. You are still the blood of my blood, the bone of my bone. When my heart ached for your dulcet tones, I often ran my finger across the scar on my forearm and thought of the vow we made. You extracted my soul with your father's combat issue blade and bound it with your own. You are more myself than I am. But I can't change who I am, what I am. You always used to say I am my father's daughter.

You have to protect yourself and to do that, you have to kill me. I understand. I have come to terms with what must be. I love my murderer and I always will. I forgive you but I can't forget. I am the final piece in a grand design that extends beyond us. When Baptiste finds out what I know, you will hang. The thought of seeing your face distorted, your eyes bloodshot, your hands gripping the rope haunts my worst nightmares. Even now I want to throw that file into the fireplace to save you from that fate but I can't. You hurt them so badly, mon agneau. I'm sorry.

I felt this place was as fitting as any. This is where we began so isn't it fitting that our story should end here. I'm going to leave a message that only you will understand:

'When the east wind dies and the sun doth rise, the lone wolf dies but the pack survives.'

I set down two crystal glasses on the window sill and pour whiskey from the antique decanter. The frigid wind screams like the tortured ghosts that occupy my every waking moment. I raise the glass to my lips and swallow a mouthful; I have to stop myself from gagging on the pungent contents. The aroma burns hairs on the inside of my nostrils. I can hear your footsteps on the gravel, the turning of a key in the door. It seems so puerile but the thought of seeing your face, embracing you one last time, gives me the courage to face what may lie beyond this mortal coil. I can feel your eyes bearing into me. You still wear the cologne I bought you from Paris; Pour Un Homme de Caron.

"Mon agneau, long time no see," I say as I turn to face you. Time has not withered you at all. Your olive, green eyes, the scar above your lips, your mousy brown hair. I have yearned to see you for so long. "Please sit, have a drink. We have a lot to discuss, do we not?"

"I would rather get this over and done with, if it is all the same to you Lady Amelia."

"Oh, I'm Lady Amelia to you, now am I? I really have fallen from grace."

"You are Lady Amelia Del'Accort; I am only addressing you by your title m'lady," you say, adjusting your watch strap. You always used to do that; you really haven't changed at all. It's only now that I look down that I notice your fingers curled around a blade, glittering in the candle light, your knuckles white with tension. It's a shame you would choose such a beautiful night to commit this ungodly act. You would smear a canvas of stars with my life blood. Your hands are shaking. I want to hold them still, to reassure you that everything is fine, that I understand but I can feel the animosity radiating from you, forming a barrier between us.

"A knife? Not the way I thought you'd do it. So blasé and messy. I imagined you'd steal daddy's gun and make quick work of me," I say, taking another sip from my glass. Your eyes dart around the room. Even now you can't bear to look me in the eye. "I have but one question. If you do this, how are you any better than him?" You lurch forward. It takes a few seconds before I even notice the knife embedded in my chest. The pain is searing, burning. You draw me into you as my legs buckle.

"I'm sorry ma moitie," you say, stroking my hair. Your voice is brittle and tremulous. I grasp onto your jacket, focussing on your scent.

"I forgive you, always." This was always the way my life was supposed to end; falling into oblivion in your arms. I will be with you always, my love. Remember our message, our secret code, the vow we made. I know I will not. There are worse pains than this.

'When the east wind dies and the sun doth rise, the lone wolf dies but the pack survives.'

RUN

JON ROBINSON

To date, I've run two thousand, four hundred, and six miles. 5K's, half-marathons, triathlons, anything. It's cathartic for me. Trails put my mind at peace. Endorphins, spirituality, healing, chakra, I don't even know. It's just that when I'm running, filled with the deep inhale and exhale of every mile, I'm transported. Like a ghost, an out of body experience. Yet, still completely grounded - present. Running is a paradox for me, and I'm wild for it.

My mom never saw me as a runner. "Lamar," she'd say, "you're just runnin' from your problems. You need to just sit still. Give it a second." God bless her, I've never stopped. I can't sit still like that. I'm too good at running. Races - individual, relay, short, long - they're all my strong suit. I get to chisel away at a personal best, pass whoever's ahead of me, bust the tape at the finish line. No shackles - nothing - just sweet freedom. Deep breaths and endorphin highs.

When mom passed she was sixty-two. I didn't really expect it, but I didn't *not* expect it either. We all knew the cancer could, I don't know, come back and everything. But, we didn't believe it.

Not for mom. But it did, and later that year I ran my first Iron Man. I got first place and dedicated the medal. Not that anyone really remembers or even cared, but I dedicated it anyways. That's actually the race where I met Miranda. Her blonde hair was pulled back, sunglasses resting on top of her hair, no use to her eyes, and she was speed walking something fierce. It was funny to see, a speed-walker at an Iron Man. I mean, at first, it was actually kind of insulting. But, later, I found out she was dedicating a medal too.

We got married last year, she and I. We're pregnant now, too. Well, she's pregnant, I just helped. I hate when guys say "we're pregnant," like, no you're not. But Mom would faint if she knew. Who am I kidding, she probably does know. I'm thirty-six, though, and Miranda is thirty-four. We don't really want to have kids much later than this. We definitely want them, but you know. I mean, it's just, yeah, we don't want them much later than this.

Miranda started running after that Iron Man. The medal had been for her dad. He'd always wanted to be an "Ironman" but never was. Never got the chance. She crossed the finish line, though. Crushed it, in her own way. I think her old man is with mom, laughing at us, putting in a good word for their grandkid. My mom is probably the one speed walking, and he's running the streets of gold. God's just laughing with them probably. I like to think so, at least.

That's actually why I'm here today on the trails. When we found out we were pregnant - Miranda was pregnant - I told her I needed to sign up for a race. I wanted to give myself something to run towards. She understood, laughing, jealous she couldn't join, saying she'd barely be able to walk another race by the time the baby was here. But she found a race online for me. It's a half that goes through a series of nature trails off the coast in northern Delaware. It's only about forty minutes from where we live south of Dover. So, this weekend is the long run. It's the last one before the race. Which is next week actually. Oh goodness, it's next week. But, from there, we're only about - she's only about - fourteen weeks from delivery.

I love this trail. The whole course is fifteen miles, perfect for training. It starts in a black gravely, parking lot and has a few wooden benches to sit and tie your shoes. The trail itself winds like none other, though, up and down, left then right. It's uneven, full of rocks and roots, even narrowing to the width of a bike wheel at certain spots. It grabs for your ankles, desperately trying to sprain them, but it's made me tougher, and added another layer to my endurance runs.

It's hard, yes, but it ain't ugly. This race is in the summer, so the trees are in full bloom, green and tall, with grass and dirt mixed across everything that's not literal trail. There's this certain spot, too, that opens into a field, and, my goodness, it's beautiful. It takes your mind someplace else, someplace broad and open, someplace lovely.

It's scary having a kid this late. Things can happen. They can happen to the kid or even Miranda. The doctors have said it's all good, but there's always this chance, this sneaking suspicion that something - anything - could go disastrously, irreparably wrong. I don't want to dwell in that kind of headspace but I just do. I go there constantly, except for when I run. Well, okay, excluding right now. It's like this illogical belief, though, that the worst can and will happen. It's this grosser, prenatal version of Murphy's law. I hate it. I hated when my mom died.

By the time I'm done, today should mark, roughly, my two-thousandth, four hundred, and twenty-first mile. But who's counting, right? They start to run together after awhile, the miles, but they still feel unique and special. Like, this run is every bit as thrilling as my first half-marathon. That might sound crazy, I know, but it's true. That's just the way it is for me.

We chose not to know the gender, just the results of various tests. We didn't know how long that could last, depending on what the doctors said was happening developmentally. But, honestly, it's going smoothly, all as it should. They keep saying everything is alright, and the next step is a safe delivery. That there's nothing to worry about, it will all be great. I just don't know, though. How can anyone be sure of something that hasn't happened? How can anyone tell me that the unknown is certain - like they're some sort of medical prophet?

This field is so gorgeous. Purple and white flowers sprayed across the trail and openness. I just get to run through it. Nothing stopping me. I love this part of the course. Best for last I guess. It's the final quarter mile before the trail starts coming full circle, back to the trailhead. Sometimes I wish the entire trail was like this, or, at least, that this part was longer. That's not how it is, though. It just isn't. Maybe that makes it sweeter. I wonder if our kid will like running. Maybe Miranda and I can push her in a stroller, do family trails or something. That would be pretty cool. We could even do this trail sometime, just start backwards at first, walking to a picnic in the field. That would be great. It would be totally fine if she didn't grow to like running, though. Or if *he* didn't. Man, I just wonder what it's gonna be like. "It." So weird to call him or her an "it." I can't wait to find out what we're having. Just a few more weeks.

Made it. There's those benches. They're just so convenient. And, woah, Miranda's already here.

"Hey babe," she said, sitting on a wooden bench next to our parked car.

"Right on time," I said, slowing at the trailhead in front of me, the parking lot coming hot.

"You killed that run," she said, smiling, "lot on your mind?"

I smiled back at her. She already knew. We've talked about it all.

"Babe. We're gonna be fine," she said, "Seriously, Lamar. Kiddo's gonna be fine. I'm gonna be fine. We're all gonna be fine. Believe me?"

"I believe you," I said.

She's right. She really is.

"Now let's eat," she said, "I'm starving."

"Same," I said.

241

"Maybe one day we can do a picnic around here," she said, "with the kiddo."

"I'd love that," I said, "the field would be perfect."

"Cool," she said, smiling again.

"Cool," I said, smiling too.

ROCKSTARS AND BROKEN DREAMS:

AN EX-SUPERHERO MOM MAKES PEACE WITH HER NEW LIFE

NAOMI BRETT ROURKE

I am a superhero. Really. I am. Or was. Until I became pregnant, had a kid, and settled down to wipe snotty noses and look under the bed for nonexistent monsters. Not that I don't love my kid. I do. Really. I guess. It's just…hard. Gimme a Rockstar.

When I was Fantasticgirl, I made a difference. No criminal could best me. No crime syndicate could stop me. I put hundreds of bad guys in jail without even powdering a second time. Now, my nose is oily, my hair is lank, and my eyes are bloodshot. No make-up for me – sometimes I go to the grocery store and don't even realize I've got dried oatmeal in my hair until I catch my reflection in the silver trim around the frozen foods section. Sometimes, when my little darling is going strong, I don't even make it to the shower. The gym? Forget it. Last time I was there I was so out of shape that I couldn't even press 600, and don't even get me started about the childcare. You would think that they never even had a child of a superhero before.

"Mrs. Fantastic, your child threw a toy today. It's not that we're complaining, but the wall does need to be replaced. Can we assume your insurance is going to cover it?" I mean, really. Do they want me for a customer or not?

When Dennis was a baby, he was so sweet, crawling out of bed at three months, holding up the car at six. His cries broke glass but the neighbors got used to it and we replaced everything. Oh, there was that one old fart who moved away, but I really don't think that was due to us. Probably lowering property values or something. Denny didn't mean to blow down his chimney. After all, he was just doing what the wolf did in that kiddie story. Alright, it was a little bit of a mess. And the old fart was in the hospital for a while, but we did pay for it, and he was so ungrateful when he got home. Good riddance, I say.
You can't stifle a boy's creativity. Gimme another Rockstar.

Mmmm, that's good. You know, I wasn't always this sloppy. My alter ego, Chris Wickens, was a very put-together junior editor for the newspaper. Shoot, my heels matched my hat and who wears hats anymore? It caused a little hiccup when I changed into my superhero costume – I'll be honest – I forgot it was on my head several times. Went out – whoop – superhero on the bottom and junior editor on top. People looked at me strangely but I made it work. That's what you gotta do, you know. Make it work. That's how Wonderman got hooked. I wasn't trying to hook him, but he saw me flying through the air, titian hair a-flying, svelte spandex costume hugging the curves, just the right amount of superhero make-up. You know, not too slutty, not too virginal. Just right. It was superhero love at first sight.

We were married in front of everyone. I mean, everyone! Where? At the Blue Star Ballroom. That's right. The one that burned down; just between us, Flameman can't hold his liquor. That was a *great* party, let me tell you. That was when I had my first Rockstar. Hey, gimme another, would you? It was so good. I had to have another. And another. You want to know the truth? I wasn't even awake for the first night of my honeymoon. It was all those Rockstars, believe it or not. I was gone. Blotto. I know they're not alcoholic, but alcohol never worked on me. Just made me jittery, you know? When all the high school boys tried to get me drunk to have their ways with me, hoo boy, did they have a surprise in store. I dislocated more arms that way. I didn't mean to. And when the parents, the principal, and the football coach all blamed me, all I had to say was the "r" word. What? No, not "rape." "Rum!"

    I love my husband. Really, I do. He's a sweet guy. Even when I beat him at arm wrestling and break the dining room table doing it. And Denny! You'd think the sun rose and set on that boy. Actually, these days, he wants to spend more and more time at work. He says because there's only one superhero in town, there's more crime. I don't know about that. Seems like the crime rate is going down, not up. He's away a lot. At night, too. Probably doesn't find me attractive anymore. Probably thinks I'm dumpy. The dumpy little wife. The homebody cow who has oatmeal in her hair and hasn't had a bath for three days because her little monster won't let her! I had dreams too! All broken. All because of a rubber that couldn't stand up to a little superhero nookie. I'm still attractive, aren't I? Aren't I? Look at me! Answer me!

    Oh, sorry, man, I didn't mean it. Look, I'll pay for it. Yes, and your hand too. Look, I didn't mean it, ok? I'm just a little stressed right now, is all. Ok? Hey, let me write you a check and while I'm doing that, gimme another Rockstar. What? Cut off? You can't cut me off. What do you mean I can't come back? It was just an accident. Oh, I see. People like me aren't good enough for you, huh? People -- superhero people -- aren't good enough to sit in your bar, huh? We're good enough to catch the bad guy who robs you but not good enough to . . . I toldja that was an accident!

    Ok, fine. Here's your freakin' check. I'm going. Keep your shirt on. Next time you get robbed, ask Superman or Batman or something. Oh, that's right. THEY'RE NOT REAL!! Sucker. Hey, uh, how about one more Rockstar for the road?

LAST PAGE FIRST
VALERIE J. RUNYAN

"I know you're in there. I saw you get your mail."

"I didn't know stalking was a part of your job description."

"Well, it's a new skill I can add to my resume."

"What do you want?"

"What do you think I want?"

"Oh, I don't know for it to rain Benjamins every time you snap your fingers just like everybody else."

"Funny, maybe you should weave a book out of that idea."

"I forgot what a bitch you are in person."

"Well, that would stand to reason since I was a bitch to you on your voicemail several times mind you. I also was a bitch to you in your emails and text messages yet again several times with no acknowledgement whatsoever; so here I am!"

"See that door over there don't let it hit your ass on your way out."

"I don't have time for this shit! You're behaving like a child and you know how I feel about children. I'm ready to throw your ass over my shoulder and shove you into my trunk and drive you to my office and slap you silly until you write something!"

"Damn, for a mother you sure are violent."

"Children make you violent."

"No, that's just you."

"Whatever."

"If I go willingly the trunk is off the table, right?

"Get the hell in the car."

***

"I changed my mind, I'm getting out!"

"What is wrong with you?"

"Well for starters I didn't get to finish my perfectly prepared Whiskey Sour and I was right in the middle of watching one of the good episodes of Star Trek also…"

"I swear to God I will bitch slap you into next week if you don't give me a straight answer!"

"By the way will you please open this damn door!"

"Alright you want out? Fine get the fuck out! But know this, I am the only thing standing between you and prison, where, ironically, you don't have to write anything there either!"

"What?"

"Oh, now I have your attention… what did it for you? Prison or not having to write anything?"

"Prison. I couldn't give a shit about writing anymore. Why would I potentially be going to prison?"

"Plagiarism is a felony nowadays, fortunately for your ungrateful ass I went to the mat for you and now I could lose everything, thank you very much!"

"Honestly, I did know it was that big of a deal, it was just using the last page first. I need a drink."

248

"Oh no you don't, you're going to process all this shit sober!"

***

"Who the hell is in my office? Excuse me, can I help you?"

"Back up ma'am, FBI."

"Fuck this, I'm getting a drink."

"You listen to me, if you are not where I think you will be when I'm done here you will be a homicide victim. Do I make myself clear?"

"Perfectly."

***

"Hey. Scotch, two rocks and a lime."

"Coming right up."

How the hell did I get here? All I wanted was to just someday be like Ernest Hemingway write and publish some stories, travel and drink with other famous Expats! Why did I believe all that shit about being the next whoever and Nobel and Pulitzer prizes? Hemingway got both of those and then nothing until after he died! Well, at least he remembered writing most of his stuff, I don't even remember writing that damn book!

"Another?"

"Until I say when."

"All those fucking reporters asking me, 'What's your writing process?' They want to know what my writing process is? Whiskey and Autocorrect! Well, it's funny to me."

"And only you, now pay up and let's go."

"Hey, I'll order the appetizer plate. Sit, let's eat."

"No! You are the worst behaved client I have; God I wish I knew what is wrong with you!"

"I'm in love with a woman I can probably never really have."

"You know what, I've been in love but I have never resorted to an act of criminality!"

"She is literally out of this world."

"Be that as it may, this is the world you and I live in and this publishing world will kick your ass ten ways to Sunday and not give a shit about you come Monday!"

"You know, on one of those writer personality quizzes I scored Hemingway! Did you know that?"

"No! Just like I don't know why you plagiarized not one but two manuscripts!"

"I'm sorry."

"I don't give a shit if you're sorry! You can be sorry til the fucking cows come home! I want to know why? Why are you ruining not only your life but mine as well?"

"I was scared, alright! I was afraid people would think I was a fraud, especially since I have no memory whatsoever of writing the damn thing and all those accolades about how great a writer I am even comparing me to my literary idol Ernest Hemingway! I didn't want that bubble to burst, so I cheated and now I feel so ashamed that I don't deserve the comparison, I'm afraid that I might not be that great ever again."

"Honestly you probably won't, but I am not going to let you fall into that rabbit hole that so many great writers have which led some to their self destruction and others to their self exile until their death. Now get your shit together and write the damn book! I want the first draft in three weeks and it better be something I've never read before!"

"I'll sell my condo to pay back the advance."

"Don't bother. I took care of it. But if you don't deliver, you'll be lucky to be able to write your name on a parking ticket in this town! Do I make myself clear?"

"Perfectly."

CURIOUS

JO-ANNE RUSSELL

"Someday your curiosity will kill you," Rick said to me. "You're lucky you didn't fall off the edge."

"I couldn't help it. If people are going to do that, in a canoe, and make such a ruckus I think anyone would look."

He kissed my cheek. "I'll call you tonight, okay?"

I just smiled at him and started my long walk home. Kill me, I thought, some people just have no sense of adventure. Night was quickly overtaking the day, and with it came a deep chill. I shivered as I walked down the dirt path through the woods to my cottage. Somewhere in the distance, an owl screeched and around me the chill grew colder. I walked faster trying to beat the darkness. The evening shadow quickly overcame my strides and soon I found myself staggering along the path. Branches reached out scratching my face stinging me in the cold October air.

Something ran by me brushing against my leg as it went. My breath caught in my chest. I ran faster veering from the path into the thick woods. Blindly, I went with my hands searching in front of me for the invisible branches. Again, I heard a screech but this time it was somehow different. The sound was almost human.

Before I could decipher it, a small faint light shone in the distance. I sighed with relief and slowed my pace. Walking closer I could see it was a light in the window of a small stone cottage. Strange, I thought, I don't remember this place. I approached quietly to peer inside before disturbing the occupants. Perhaps they could turn me in the right direction of my cottage.

Inside a small girl of about six sat on the floor. Her knees were pulled up to her chest and her head was cocked to the side. She was staring intensely at a poorly lit fireplace. I suddenly heard a rattling followed by a thump. It sounded like it came from the side of the cottage. Slowly, I made my way through the darkness and stopped near the back. I could feel a cold hard wet surface. I felt around a bit more and grabbed onto a metal object. The lock was connected to another metal piece on the surface.

How odd, cellar doors on a cottage? Just then, the doors bumped up and rattled, as if someone were inside trying to push their way out. I heard a loud thump, then silence. I jumped back. My hands shook with fear and cold. Quietly I waited for more movement. The brush around me clawed and scratched at my legs as if it were alive.

I drew in a deep breath and leaned close to the doors. "Hello? Is anybody there? Do you need help?"

Rattle, rattle, thump!

I fell back, and then scrambled to my feet. The sound came again but louder. I took a step closer to the doors and suddenly felt a burning in my right arm. A branch had snagged me. The warm blood trickled down to my hand and I winced in pain.

The thing in the cellar rattled and thumped some more. I swallowed hard and put my face closer to the door.

"Can you speak to me?" I asked, but no voice replied.

"Ahhh!" The bloodcurdling scream of a child rang out like a siren.

I scrambled to the front of the house as fast as I could, falling twice over things I could only imagine were twigs or roots. The scream came again with seemingly more terror. I didn't even glance into the window as I passed it I simply burst through the front door.

I tripped. My face slammed to the wooden floor, my nose shattered. Hot blood spewed forth pooling on the floor in front of me. The soft glowing embers flickered laughingly in the fireplace. I gently squeezed the bridge of my nose and tried to stand when I felt the sudden slam into my shins.

I screamed out and fell in the bloody puddle. Too dark to see and too sore to stand, I dragged myself across the floor toward the cellar door. I heard soft scuffling sounds coming up beside me.

My heart slammed harder and harder inside my chest trying to escape, with or without me.

Something blocked out the light for a second then rattle, thump!

The sound came just as a sharp object pierced my back. I bit down hard on my tongue. The blood from it gagged me, making me heave.

"Stop!" I screamed, but the attack continued. The weapon in my back pulled out and slammed back in.

I screamed again.

The thing behind the door rattled and thumped. "Stop," I choked out but felt a searing sudden pain to my head, and a quiet blackness overcame me.

When I came to, my eyes blurred with the brightness that crept through the cellar doors from outside. Thick blood was crusted to the rags tied over my mouth. My hands and feet were bound and chained to a metal link in the floor. Across the room another victim sat in his bloodstained prison. "Warn you," was written beside his mutilated corpse.

Too hoarse to scream I sobbed through my gag. The door at the top of the stairs slowly opened, and the child walked down. I watched as she stared intently at the body and then at me.

"Help me, please!" I begged.

She walked over to the corpse and forced her hand through a wound in his side. She pushed and jerked until her arm submerged to her elbow, then pulled back out. I wanted to turn away, but my fear forced me to follow her every move.

She stepped toward me and revealed her bloody prize. In her small hands, she held his dripping organ. She raised her face to the ceiling and opened her mouth. Her ear-piercing screech echoed through the cottage and beyond, sending a shrill pain through my tormented body. A series of howls and clicks followed. Her pink smooth skin now shimmering yellow crawled on her skeleton. Her smile revealed long curled misshapen teeth with chunks of flesh dangling from them.

She devoured the organ and leaned into my face. Her breath smelled of feces and rotten flesh.

Behind her, more creatures tore away at him, piece by piece.

I found my voice and screamed. My muffled half-squeal didn't faze them. They feasted and screeched their calls of victory.

"Someday your curiosity will kill you!" Rick's words wrung out like alarm bells. As she reached for my eye, I could only hope she would kill me quickly.

GOOD SAMARITAN
MATT SCOTT

It all comes down to choices. Nate smile as he wishes he had thought of that first. The alley smells of urine and garbage. It's a shooting gallery. The lingering scent of ammonia burns his nostrils as tears mix with blood. They trail down his cheek and find their way to the gash above his lip. It is split open from mouth to nostril. Blood flows freely from his wounds and he sits on the wet asphalt, among the shattered beer bottles, needles and rotten restaurant trash, his broken right arm hanging limp in his lap.

Nate is leaned up against the dirty brick wall of the Chinese restaurant. There is a service door to his left, metal and solid. The security light is gives off an incompetent glow above Nate's head. The electric hum echoing its amusement through the alley, welcoming the coming of the dawn. It all comes down to choices.

When Nate left the precinct after his tour, he walked down Greenway Avenue and turned left on 8th Avenue. A veteran law enforcement officer of twenty-one years, Nate was also a transplant to the city. He was from a town in the Mid-west where it was better to be from then to actually still live in. He walked this route every morning enjoying the city before the filth woke up and crawled out from their dens to hustle and harass the people of this city. He never had any trouble before. People usually don't mess with a beat cop this early in the morning this close to the precinct. People don't usually do a lot of things. He had to help her when he saw the bastards attacking her in the alley. She looked so scared, so lost, so completely out of place. He'll never know why she was there. Never know what her name was, never no where she was from or where she was headed. He will never speak to her again after this morning.

His legs are stretched out before him, but Nate can't feel them. He is getting drowsy, not sure how much longer he can stay awake and only hoping that they are gone and she is ok. He's lost a lot of blood. Too much. It pools around you and mixes with the run off from the downspouts. A dirty crimson stream swirls into the storm drain a few feet down the alley, and he can hear the blood, water, and urine swirling into the drain as it descends into the sewers. What was he thinking? He's not a young man anymore. Age and the beat has taken their toll on him. Diminished his reflexes just enough. In what world could this have possibly have had a happy ending? What did he think would happen?

The woman is frantic now, standing before him. Her cell phone clutched tightly in her hand as if the devil himself were intent on stealing it. She is screaming and pleading for them to hurry. She keeps saying that they are gone but that 'he' is really bad. What did that mean? How bad?

She begins to whisper into the phone as the sounds of the burgeoning city filter down into the alley. Though her movements are animated, even frantic, he can barely hear what she is saying. He thinks that he can hear the sirens approaching from the south, or maybe they're just birds. Maybe coyotes. Coyotes? Now why would he think that? There are no coyotes in the city. Wolves' maybe, in sheep's clothing. He thinks he smiles.

The wolves are gone now. They had skulked away like the cowards that they are when he stepped off of the sidewalk and ran down the alley. One lying dead across the pavement from him. She was screaming. They had knives and were trying to hurt her. To take the innocence he knew she might still possess. She is still young, still beautiful. Wolves destroy beauty. They devour it with serrated teeth and wicked tongues. With sharp needles and bags full of poison. This city is a cesspool. She would not have recovered. You don't ever really survive something like that. She may have endured it, learned to live with it. Buried it away someplace deep within herself, only to let it slowly burn, and fester. It would grow claws and dig its way

257

out someday, shattering her sanity. No, he wasn't about to let that happen. Not on his watch. No one deserves that. Not even him.

    He sits there now, staring up at this woman, still whispering into her phone, her small hands waving frantically toward flashing lights that have just entered the alley. A four-inch blade is buried in his spine. Blood soaks his uniform shirt around his right kidney. He is pale. A bluish white, like snow falling beneath a streetlight, his color draining into the sewers. So, this is it. This is how it ends. Sitting on his butt in an alley surrounded by the smell of rotten garbage, urine and… copper. Copper? Oh, yeah. Blood tastes like old pennies and motor oil. He tries to smile again, not sure if he really is. The gash above his mouth is almost visible to him if he looks down in just the right way, though he doesn't have to move his head to see it. In fact, he can't move your head. He can't move anything. The sirens are growing dimmer and the woman's innocence has been saved, for now at least, and that is all that he can hope for. He did his part, saved the day. Now he is too tired to think about what comes next. All Nate can do is briefly understand what he has done. He saved the young girl from the wolves. The city didn't get her. It didn't strangle the light and life from her like it wanted to do, like it tried to do. That doesn't happen on his watch. No sir. It's all about choices. And he would do it again, no questions asked. A man is never off duty

REIGN OF THE FOREST
PAMELA A. SCOTT

A soft breeze rustled dead leaves near his feet, a reminder of the crisp autumn morning. The dusk was so cool yet silent. Justin reached his destination and climbed up the ladder into his deer stand. What other fool would stand out in the middle of a dark forest alone waiting for some white-tailed deer to nibble and feast while he set his scope on the targeted spot?

Instead the blow of its warning nearly made him fall from his stand. They say the deer sounds like the loud whisper of a ghost and that is when the message is sent to the rest of the clan to warn of danger.

Justin's heartbeat was strong and fast until he realized what it was, and then he relaxed, zeroing in with his scope. By then it was too late. Too far. In the view of his scope he saw the magnificent buck, with tall and full spread antlers. He had to be at least twelve years of age.

It was rut time and in the background, he heard the fighting, the hooves pounding against rock, and round, antlers clashing against each other. May the strongest survive and win his mate.

It was a busy day in the forest already.

Justin relaxed again in his stand, the deer turned and walked deep into the forest.

Daybreak was on the horizon, and he'd almost fallen asleep. Sun glistened through the trees making a photographer's nightmare of image, black shade against sun streaks of rays, blinding rays.

And then he thought of his brother David, his twin. The total opposite of him.

Justin loved to hunt, for the thrill of it, and for the survival of it.

There was absolutely nothing wrong with deer hunting. It was encouraged to keep the populations down, and for their own survival too, if that made any sense. Without food, they would not mate, and without mates their population would eventually cease, but the deer have been around for centuries, since ancient civilization and ruled the forest. They were considered the magic of the forest, their quiet nature and camouflaged fur that could turn to gray from reddish brown to melt into the hues of the forest during autumn and winter.

He heard more rustling of leaves and the sound was coming closer.

A hungry coyote. They say for every coyote a man sees, there are eleven in hiding just waiting to feast. He swallowed hard and tried to keep his calm. At any minute, he could be attacked.

Justin raised his gun and unlatched the safety.

It's just you and me, Coyote. He aimed and shot once, then once again.

It was happening. The thrill of the hunt filled his nostrils with the scents of the forest and his eyes took in the tantalizing sights of it, bold orange and crimson leaves glistened against the hues of the rising sun.

One coyote down. But it didn't make him feel any better.

No life taken could replace his brother David.

David didn't hunt. He admired the love of wild animals and the rain of the forest. He was a tree hugger and vegetarian.

And then he was gone, Justin thought to himself as he shed a tear and tried to hide his emotions. If it weren't for that deer, my brother would be alive. There were times when life and death didn't make sense.

Despite their differences, they were brothers through thick and thin.

He aimed his shotgun one more time, thinking another coyote was near but then took a double take of his view. Through the scope, he saw the unexpected, a buck staring right back at him.

The adrenaline rose, and he slowly released the safety zeroing in on his target.

Slowly, his finger rested against the trigger and just as he was about to shoot,

the buck vanished into a mist. Instead a dark figure appeared, his twin.

"David" Justin shouted. He couldn't believe his eyes and looked through the scope again.

"Go home, Justin." David said.

"I will be okay. You must let go Justin. There was nothing I could do when I rounded that corner that night when the buck jumped in front of my car. Nothing you can do, David, but to help take care of Mom and Dad. This is hard on them, I know."

"David." Justin whispered now, tears streaming down his face, his voice weak and broken.

He shook his head and laid down his gun.

David's shadow became larger and closer, and Justin climbed down from his stand and started walking closer towards him.

"David, wait. You are alive."

He held out his arms to hug his brother. Beams of sunlight through the forest blocked his view.

"I am alive spiritually, Justin. I am fine. Now go home and take care of Mom and Dad and stay out of these woods. You know how I feel about killing deer."

"I know, I know." Justin shook his head back and forth then lowered it humbly.

When he reached out to touch his brother, the mist was cool to his hand, then it vanished with a fading voice. "Go home now, Justin."

The shadow was replaced by antlers, and Justin was face to face with the buck.

He'd left his gun up on the stand and slowly reached for his hunter's knife. The deer was snorting and grunting. It bent his head forward and bucked. His two front feet jumped forward against David's torso, knocking him to the ground.

Strike one, and his chest felt like he was hit with a hammer, unable to breath.

Is this how David felt when he hit the deer with his car? When the deer jolted straight on in the middle of road and leaped into his vehicle, causing the fatal crash? I'd given anything to bring David back, even if he was a tree hugging type of guy. We were blood. We were brothers.

The buck then ran off into the forest looking for his mate, and the coyote howled.

Dizzy, he managed to stand up. He retrieved his gun and headed home satisfied.

He knew his brother was at peace. No one would ever believe him.

Justin followed the sunlit path. Much different from his brother's yet he felt at peace and was ready to take care of his mother and father. They would have never believed him if he told them what happened that day in the forest. He made himself a cup of hot coffee and sat out on the back deck with his guitar and played a new song he wrote.

In the distance, he saw a tall buck standing proud and, in a sprint, the deer dashed off into the forest. Justin smiled. It was the same deer he had seen every morning for the past week. He knew he was not alone and vowed to carry out his brother's wish. And what better way to carry out his wish, but on their birthday.

Rain fell silent upon his shoulders as he played his music like he never played before.

MY SOULMATE
DENNIS SINAR

My given name is Elizabeth, Lizzie to my friends. I'll tell you a story that gives me the most fear, because it will be by undoing at judgment day. It's said that God will forgive any sin, but forgiveness requires repentance, and I cannot repent. No matter how I squirm or twist, the slimy fingers of the sin are around my throat, pulling me back into the memory of what I've done. If calling down a curse is not a capital sin, it should be, because the results are as devastating. I've had time to reflect, to enjoy the havoc I caused, and yet to wish for more. If I could rewind these thirty years to the beginning, would I choose differently?

Within a week after I met James, he insisted on calling me Elizabeth. He felt that formality engendered respect, and respect was the quality I most treasured as the relationship evolved. James was the first man who called me his soul mate and the only man I've believed. He was handsome, but not catch-your-breath gorgeous, and his flyaway mud-colored hair and limpid blue eyes stirred me like no other man. Within a few months, we moved in together and started planning for marriage, good jobs in Charlotte, and children.

James and I met Kerri at the annual garden party after we'd been together for a few years. Mother was with us and after a disconnected conversation and a spilled drink, she judged Kerri to be little more than a dressed up drunken slut. Maybe it was a harsh judgment, but mother was an opinionated woman. However, at the garden party the following spring, James joked that Kerri was just one drink away from proving my mother right. Looking back, I should have recognized their attraction.

Was it his curiosity or her availability? Probably both - a slow play with Kerri's easy sexuality pulling him closer each day. It started with his unexplained absences and hushed phone calls, then moved to a weekend away on business. I sensed his growing distance and our sniping turned to hurtful confrontations. I was devastated when he left. It was so sudden, without emotion. He went to work, left a typed letter on the bed and never came back. A few days after he moved out, I discovered that he'd emptied our bank account. After the tears and the anger, I chose seclusion to puzzle through why he'd chosen her, stolen my money and left town. His leaving crushed my soul and my spirit. I was sick for weeks. It was an ugly sickness that resisted sleep, medication, food, or tears. Each day and night pain and anger squeezed my soul. I stumbled in a dark place for months before realizing that seclusion gave me no comfort and so I turned to God for solace.

The church offered peace for my soul and recovery from my pain. I suckled at the breast of mother church and became the model of involvement in bake sales, in cleaning the church, and in prayer circles. In the choir, I sang a good hymn, forcefully, an enthusiastic voice to lead the congregation. I created a new identity. If not for the succor of the church, I would have become a drunk on a street corner in Marsden.

The church taught me that God constantly passes his loving eye over the world, taking in every thought and every action, now and forever. He cares deeply for every being and provides the strength to overcome life's difficulties. I heard God's message, but did not believe. The God of mercy and healing could not assuage my anger. In desperation, I turned to the devil and to his magic. Magic filled a void in me that God could not abide.

My friend Elise doubted the power of magic. When we had coffee, she looked over her glasses and asked, "Isn't magic siding with the devil, aren't you using his power to get revenge? I know you still hate James, but I hope all this devil talk isn't part of your plan for revenge. I love you, but that's crazy."

"Of course, it's about revenge. When I was at my lowest point of despair, I came to believe that the devil's magic lives in each of us. He knows our deepest thoughts, the evil ones, and knows our weaknesses."

"Now you're talking like one of those witches we've laughed about, the ones who live in the coven in Varnamtown. People say they worship the devil."

"Don't get me wrong. I don't want to go all the way to living in a coven and wearing black clothes and funny hats. I just want to learn a few tricks from a clever witch. I believe that stupid people believe in luck. Maybe luck exists but I've never seen it. Good or bad happens when God randomly lifts his right hand or his left. There is no randomness in magic, the devil knows it will work, every time.

After more wine than usual, Elise smiled and asked if magic included the ability to create a curse. I smiled a smile more evil and whispered that we all have the power of a curse deep within us, but we only lack the means to awaken it. I looked into Elise's eyes and smiled again ... "a curse is the only sure vehicle for the wronged to avenge themselves."

The next day, I sought out a witch outside of Varnamtown, learned a powerful curse, and paid her well for her knowledge. She cautioned me that such a powerful curse could be used only once, reserved for someone who deserved it most. James was the prime candidate.

The next night my room was dark except for three candles burning around the circumference of a circle as I invoked the dark spirits with the words and actions the witch had taught me. A cutting of James's mud-colored hair lay in a locket in the center as the channel, and a stick of balsam fir incense, his favorite, burned beside it. Summer breezes floated through the room and the candles flickered. When the time was right, I whispered my wishes for ill will to him and his family from that day forward: pain, sickness, bad dreams, mental instability, paranoia, loneliness, financial loss…and severe gum disease. After my wish was spoken, the candles flickered and went out. All was dark again with the lingering smell of balsam. I knew the curse had taken hold, and I smiled.

Moving back into a normal life took considerable time, but the transition was smoother, eased by the belief that the curse was at work. I looked beyond a foggy and uncertain future and considered how I could get back to mental health. The days stretched ahead, one lonely tedious dawn and dusk after another. Gradually I passed through the cloud and met Lester, a good man, but not a soul mate. We married and found a kind of happiness and, eventually, financial independence. No children came, but we enjoyed each other's company. Years passed and Lester died after a long illness. I was alone—too late in life to start again. To combat the loneliness, I returned to the church with a healthier perspective, reestablished my place in the choir, and spent time volunteering in the ministry with friends. I missed the close companionship and simple shared talk of marriage, but my friends were enough. Occasionally, I thought about James.

As if he appeared out of my thoughts, I saw my James in the grocery store early this fall. We nodded as people do who have not seen each other in thirty years, wondering what happened in the interval. I stopped to talk, anxious to hear what misfortunes had happened to my soul mate. He'd married Kerri and she'd died in an auto accident, in a dark wet field, alone, drunk. There were three grown children, two in prison and one nearly there, all on drugs. James' sculpted hands were deformed by arthritis. He told his story with no emotion, only with resignation. In his blue eyes, I saw a glimpse of my soul mate, but I didn't feel love. He asked, and I told him my story, of Lester, of growing old in Marsden, and of my life in the church.

As we parted, I relished that he had suffered mightily, but not as much as I had suffered. By then I knew the curse was a sin, but the pure joy of revenge outweighed any guilt, and I needed more. Drawn on, some moral principle gnawed at the back of my mind guiding me to ask for forgiveness, but I pushed it away. As if by magic, last night in a dream, the devil showed me a way to make him feel even more pain. With the devil's guidance, James would suffer more—sleeplessness, constant pain, financial ruin, and the gum disease would take his teeth.

THE DIVINE WOW WOW
FIONA SKEPPER

You know the saying, nothing comes from nothing? Maybe it's everything comes from nothing? No, but I think you understand the sentiment. Look at religion. They've dug up statues of fat goddesses with multiple breasts that are over ten thousand years old, and many people, even though they don't do the whole established religion thing, still say they believe in God or at least aren't willing to say they don't. You could make an allowance for quietness on the subject because of fear, especially in countries where atheism makes some people cranky, but a lot of society says they believe in God, simply because they do. I believe there is something out there, greater than ourselves. And this leads me to what I want to discuss: my Maltese Shih Tzu, Wow Wow.

Wow Wow, you should try calling it at the dog park. I didn't choose that name. I called him Sam. The name changes happened when I first brought him to a family gathering. My four-year-old niece immediately began to torment the dog in very 'cute ways', including whacking him with her doll and pulling his tail, which he objected to and gave a few loud barks in response. Sally and her evil twin spawn, my nephew Sam, thought this outburst was hysterical, and they both began imitating the barking by yelling 'Wow Wow', pointing at my poor harried pet. He has been called that ever since.

I want to make it clear that I never thought my dog was particularly special when I got him, but it's been a year now, and I can no longer deny it. I think, well, basically my dog can see dead people.

Hear me out before you judge me.

Wow Wow is a pretty timid dog. When I try to get him to interact with other dogs who bound up to him, tongues a-salivating, he usually retires to near where I'm sitting. He likes to lean against me when he sleeps, to make sure I'm there. He is basically miserable by himself, trying to squeeze past me out the door when I leave, or whimpering until I give in and take him with me. Until recently, I didn't realise there was a deeper reason behind all this.

It started about six months ago, not long after I'd moved into my new flat. Wow Wow was lying comfortably on the couch next to me, showing no interest in *Judge Judy* but making no comment. The next moment I felt a vibration. Wow Wow stood up and his whole body trembled, minutely but violently, as though he'd been plugged in. He then started making strange, gruff, little hiccup wow wows, before he eventually broke into a tirade, barking, as though the hounds of hell were nearby. He was staring with great concentration at the living room window. There was nothing out there. The view was mostly blocked by the thick branches of trees full of twittering birds.

That was only the beginning. Sometimes when he followed me to my mail box, he would break away and run out to the front nature strip and bark furiously at something unseen in the air. He was so fierce that sparrows scattered.

Another time when the door of my bedroom had been left open, I heard him howling, and I rushed in, only to find him transfixed with terror, and barking at the mirrored wardrobe, although the only thing I could see was his reflection.

The vet declared that Wow Wow was 'perfectly healthy', and added the very unhelpful comment that 'dogs sometimes bark.'

It was clear that no one else was seriously considering the world of the spirit. I have always been open to the possibility that our world sometimes collides with the next. When I was a child, the spirit of my grandmother tried to reach me. I was contacted by a grey cat, with eyes exactly like my grandmother's. She came to my back door several times, eating the salmon I provided (Grandma's favourite). No one had believed it then either, saying that Grandma hadn't even died but had run off to Rio with her Latin dance teacher, but I knew the truth.

    I confronted my landlord, asking if any strange occurrences or tragic events had transpired in or around the apartment block. He feigned perfect ignorance, mumbling something about the structure only being built in '86'. I reminded him of how in the *Poltergeist*, they'd built the house on a Native American burial ground. He looked at me in even greater wonder. I think I gave him something to think about.

    I then did what I should have done earlier. I Googled. This was how I was blessed by finding Great Master Simeon. His website was called *Creature Links to the Other World: I'm willing to believe you!* It explained how animals, as simpler forms of creation, were closer to the natural state of existence and as such could contact the realm of the spirits that was barred to humans. It was however, only specially chosen humans (like him) who could recognise the messages.

    I tentatively emailed him, explaining my situation. He responded almost immediately. He didn't dismiss my ideas; he embraced them, confirming what I had come to suspect in my heart, that I had been chosen to possess something truly special. Amazingly, he was willing to come to me, all the way from his ashram in the suburbs of Moscow. He didn't mind as long as I sent him the plane ticket. He turned up at my door only a few days later, dusty and hungry from his travels, but with what seemed to be a light emanating from his soul.

    'I have come.' He put out his flat palm, as though stopping traffic, to indicate I shouldn't say anything more. He then mentioned the cab driver, and I placed some cash in his hand.

    You have to believe me, I mean Wow Wow went right up to him even though he was normally wary of strangers. He put his little paws up on the sage's leg, his big eyes looked at him, his tiny tongue moved quickly, and he kept trying to reach up to him and give him some welcoming licks. He then whimpered.

'He is attempting to communicate with me. Oh really Wow Wow?' The Master patted Wow Wow on the head and gave him some pieces of meat that were in his pants pocket.

'He and I need to meld tougher.' He picked up Wow Wow. 'Where is the bedroom?' I pointed and they disappeared. An hour later he stuck his head out the door. 'I need to replenish. Bread is fine, maybe in a toasted ham and cheese sandwich?'

I moved towards the fridge. His voice soft and melodic came again from down the hall.

"And drink, the fruits of the earth are the best, I think a bottle of Bordeaux.' I ran to the bottle shop.

When he emerged a hours later, he announced proudly that I had an extraordinary creature that was 'in touch with the other side.' He needed to have several days of conferences with Wow Wow. No one interrupted him except when some of the Master's priestesses arrived (I was lucky enough to get a group rate with Qantas). Chanting and other noises associated with transcendence emanated from the chamber, including a lot of yells of 'Yes Master.'

The Master took Wow Wow on his special spiritual investigations. 'We owe it to future generations,' he said, 'to try and make contact with the other side and counteract any malevolent influences.' They visited several people that were in need of guidance.

The servants of Evil found another way to disrupt our mission, however. One day there was a loud knock on the door. 'Immigration.' What a fuss they made! They charged into the bedroom/temple, but he had disappeared. For a second I thought he had transformed into pure spirit. However, he was found two blocks away, limping from a fall, and my drainpipe was bent at a ninety-degree angle.

They way those enforcers went on about visas. Yes, he accepted payment but all for the good of *Creature Links,* and his interest rates were far more reasonable than a bank. It was a vocation, not work. I visited him at the detention centre just before he was put on the plane.

Right now, Wow Wow sits beside me, mediating, and grooming himself a little. The Master has passed the torch to me, and although I am not in touch with the fellowship of the universe like him, I try my best. I forward all gifts from grateful contributors to a bank account in Geneva as the Master directed. I am Wow Wow's protector. I wait anxiously for a tremble to indicate contact is occurring again. The questions I had been asking all my life have been answered. I am blessed.

BETTER THAN DREAD
ALLISON SPECTOR

I was born in a shivering-white nest under the sliver of a pale-faced moon. My mother was the Blue Fairy, my father a night-mare. Each evening, she'd ride him through fallow-field and weep salt tears into the earth so that only what pleased her grew there. Their bridal bower was a tangle of brambles. Their nights, long. Their love, relentless. My mother shrieked and clawed, and my night-mare father spewed flame from his nostrils and bucked against leather whip and spurred heels until at last a child emerged in a tangle of flesh and feathers.

But it's not my story you're concerned with, is it? You came here for him—for the babe you loved so dearly. Shielded so carefully. You weren't expecting him to look so different now, were you? Ten tender years under my tutelage have made him a perfect being, purged of all distraction—all sensation. He is a perfect vessel now to carry on the work to which you bound him.

What? You don't like him this way?

Does the hollowness of his eyes unnerve you? Are you concerned by the twitch of his mouth and the blankness of his expression?

Oh, I assure you. This is still the child you held to your breast, who nuzzled you and stared at you with wide-eyed wonderment. Oh, how that tiny hand grasped at your finger! How those tiny lips smacked hungry and helpless! And he breathed your name, "mama, mama," over and over again even as you abandoned him to me.

Entrusted him to me.

You refused to allow the typical Guardians and Godmothers anywhere near your blessed babe. You decided to travel deep into the harsh reality of dreams to seek the Old Companions; the ones half-buried in slanderous lore and blurred recollection.

Good mother. Wise mother. Sweet, protective mother. You were so astute in choosing me over the Fear-Feasters, the Hate-Drinkers, the Siphons of Malice.

Those twisted creatures are not suited for children.

No. Of course you would never be so foolish as to entrust an ugly thing with an ugly name to guard and guide your beautiful boy. So, when you read the tea-leaves, and heard the rustle of the trees, saw me in your dreams and in the winking constellations, you knew that it was only sensible to choose the Harvester of Hope over the Devourers of Dread.

And hope is such a lovely thing, so light and delicate like the laugh of a newborn child at the promise of its mother's arms.

Surely your charity and wisdom were not a mistake! Surely your choice was deliberate. Did you not set out blood-tinged milk on the full moon next to your child's cradle and sing sweet words beneath the open window?

Aye, you did.

And I traveled on the wisp of a moonbeam's shadow to heed your gentle, generous call. I crept upon your windowsill and lulled you quiet and docile as I drank of the child's blood and the life-force of your bosom.

It had been so many moons since anyone had remembered my needful skills and special appetites. But you, my dear remembered! You knew the power that I could grant the babe.

And I did care for him as you asked. I did all I promised—all that my name suggests. I gave him gentle spring breezes and garlands of wildflowers. I gave him the deep, well-hidden incantations. We gathered seeds of light in the darkness and planted them in the soil with the hope of spring. I whispered sweet promises in his ear, even as one-by-one they remained unfulfilled.

And then came the dungeon and the great gray walls as I slowly removed the toys, the friends, the dreams he held so dear. But then I'd kiss his forehead and promise better days. And his sweet bright eyes would shimmer at me and his tiny, uncertain hand would squeeze my finger and dream of you, his dear sweet mother. His hope was as sweet as the milk he supped from your bosom. It filled me. Sustained me. And I, in exchange gave him my guidance and protection—taught him the secrets of my trade.

Oh—the boy did not like the silent suffering and despair of his hosts that followed his feasting, but how readily does starvation make an apt pupil! So quickly, your child learned to cherish the flowing colors swirling around the heroes at the beginning of their journeys when hope is rich and sweet and overflowing. He learned to dangle promises just out of reach—to offer much and give just enough that the anticipation of light, and good and rest and comfort drew out the sweet nectar of hope from which we deeply drink.

Dear mother, sweet mother! Why do tears well in your eyes as your son stands before you? Why do you choke, and tremble, and accuse?

The gift of your precious offspring means more to me than you can imagine. So gentle, so fragile—like a butterfly's wing begging to be ripped from its tiny, trembling shoulder.

But fear not, sweet mother, for his condition is merely a temporary state. He is young and healthy and returned to you, and his power shall be the envy of all others.

Yes, my dear. Please rest assured that there is hope for your boy. So much hope, sweet and delicious, flowing like honey, waiting to sustain his hunger.

COWS OF NETHER ALDERLEY
PATRICIA LESLEY STAMMERS

I was aboard the bus hurtling towards a town in the Peak District when through the window I glimpsed a mill and Mill Cottage. The fact that it was a damp, cold, January afternoon could not check the impulse, so I leapt up, grabbed my backpack, and made my way to the front of the bus.

The driver was not too distracted by my panting in his ear,

"Next stop, please."

He brought the bus that was screeching "new brake pads please" to a halt. I disembarked in Nether Alderley.

The rustic architectural group that had caught my eye was now hidden by a series of bends and mature chestnut trees, so I swung my backpack aloft, and hiked until the ancient buildings seen from the bus reappeared.

There was a broad, tiled roof that sloped dramatically from a height of about six to within one metre of the grass. The roof belonged to a mill that reminded me of the Malt House in Far From The Madding Crowd; mossy, crumbling and camouflaged with age. On the opposite side of the road, the diamond paned windows in a black and white, timber framed structure winked. The burbling of the nearby mill stream sent my sentimental soul skyward as I awaited a response to my knock on the plank door.

The latch lifted, and the door opened with a creak.

"Hello!" I said. "Please, may I have a bed for the night."

"Come in please," said the proprietor.

The room into which I edged from the doorstep was dusky and cluttered with objects. Paintings, prints and wall lights hung between declining wooden beams. I had not seen such a collection since childhood visits to our ancient neighbours. Flowers, pottery, books, and carvings perched on the crowding furniture like a flock of roosting birds. A carved stone fireplace filled with logs presided over all. Brass and copper fire irons hung, glinting within the fender.

The ceiling was so low that I could have touched the rough wooden beams with my fingertips. A thick carpet covered what little there was to see of the floor. No trilby or overcoat hung on the coat hook. No shotgun hung on the wall. If men shared the house, they had left no evidence of themselves.

I stared around, almost oblivious of the hostess but managed to murmur,

"What a beautiful room." My pleasantry did not amuse her. She seemed suspicious of me and wanted to know what I was up to in Cheshire. I told her Macclesfield was my mother's home town and that I was on a pilgrimage of sorts. She was reasonably satisfied with that and offered tea.

Later she drove me into town so I could go to the bank because she wanted cash payment. On returning to the cottage, she showed me a room upstairs. Compared with the stark midland hotel where I had passed the previous three nights, the room seemed like a warm hug.

Low wooden beams glowed in the lamplight. The floor scattered with mossy coloured rugs was more like that of a woodland than a bedroom and creaked in time to our footsteps. I eyed with longing the huge bed that crouched beneath a patchwork quilt. Television, a novelty for me, and a deep upholstered armchair together seemed to promise an interesting and comfortable stay.

The colours of the soft furnishings were warm; brick red curtains and a duvet of brown patchwork. Finally, the height of luxury, an adjoining bathroom. Two long windows less than a metre deep, one behind the bed and one beside, opened on the Manchester road beside which grew a row of chestnut trees. Behind their trunks and scooping, bare branches rolled a country estate that reminded me of Mansfield Park? Yes, I thought I would be comfortable at the Mill House, for a few days.

"Go walking," said the hostess, "and at the back of this cottage, you'll find a church." That's what *most* visitors did, she implied.

"Okay. I'll probably go out later", I said, "when I have unpacked and had a rest."

The going was wet but a cold, grey cloud promised more rain. Dusk was imminent so I kept to the path but was nonetheless surprised by two shaggy cows that grazed the flanking pasture. They had long curving horns and reminded me of highland cattle that I'd seen in old oil paintings. At the end of the lane, there was a rectory that seemed to be melting like a giant portion of ice- cream amid a shrubbery.

"Ring the bell." The landlady of Mill Cottage had advised me. "Ask to see inside the church."

I pulled the bell and a responding sound echoed like the rumbling of a mighty stomach throughout the building. A dog barked, but no one came to the door. I didn't care and crunched away along the gravel drive.

By the path there stood a fancy facade of a much smaller building. I knew it wasn't a big, stone dolls' house, but that comparison was inescapable. I peered through the gothic hooded window and realised that the floor of the small room was below ground level. The furniture, a miniature sink, cupboards and desks stood on the beautiful fitted wood plank floor.

"That's the old school house." said the landlady when I returned and mentioned the quaint little stone building.

The evening passed happily. I read, wrote, made plans for the following day, crept into bed early and slept like a dormant bug beneath a drift of autumn coloured bedclothes.

The following morning, I went out at dawn.

"You've been out already?" She sounded surprised when still clad in my overcoat I entered the dining room and found landlady serving breakfast.

"Erm ... yes."

"Where've you been," she asked when I was seated at the table.

"I walked along the footpath," I said. While helping myself to orange juice, I noticed that my hand shook. "Beyond the church there's a stile."

"Oh yes I know. I go that way sometimes with the dog." I nodded and tried to smile appreciation for the plateful of hot food that she put before me. I had often craved for the old days when my family were farmers. I would go wandering 'deep in the meadows', with insects and birds for company. In our hayfield on the edge, there was a hollow tree lying like a decaying dinosaur that I used for a seat.

One day whilst I was there something emerged from the dense cover of haystalks. A soundless patch of russet with eye like a bubble of burnt umber, paused in mid stride. Quivering black nostrils sniffed the air from my direction. I was too surprised and excited to move. His shoulder stood more than a metre high and his head was impressively antlered. Slender legged, he moved across the path and vanished into a ditch that was overhung with sloe and hawthorn bushes. Those childhood days were gone but fascination engendered by that stag and our domestic animals remained.

"Did you go to the Harebarrow?"

"The what? I don't know," I said. There weren't too many signposts. "A peculiar thing happened though." The landlady seemed more companionably inclined now as she settled into a chair by the carved stone fireplace.

"Oh? And what was that?"

"There were two cows grazing in a field." She reached across to pour me some tea. I raised my chin and breathed in to steady my nerves. "One of them spoke to me." She blinked at me, dropped the pot, stood up and backed off a step or two.

"Please don't worry. I was probably only daydreaming."

"You're joking of course."

"No, I'm not. I hoped that you'd be able to offer an explanation."

"Um, excuse me" she said and backed into the kitchen.

I had to laugh when a few moments later the door opened a fraction and her eyes peeped, warily, at me.

"What happened next?"

"They asked me if I could look into the future." Her eyes narrowed.

"Oh yeah." She was probably planning how she could have me safely incarcerated, but I had to go on with the story.

"When I said no, they told me to go into the wood and pick a bunch of flowers. They said if I put the flowers at the foot of the elm tree and waited, I would discover who my husband would be." The hostess, obviously thinking I was crazy, reached for the wall phone.

"You didn't do as the cows said?" Her voice rose to a squeak.

"I would've, but I couldn't find any flowers. Anyway, as I approached the Elm tree there was an ear-splitting crack. I stopped just in time to avoid a great branch of the tree as it crashed to the ground before me.

"Ah!" The landlady letting go of latch, and phone covered her mouth.

"I thought that someone was playing a trick on me and then I heard a voice from somewhere say, 'Sebastian is the name of the man you will marry'."

"Perhaps you went out a bit too early in the morning," suggested the landlady obviously trying to seem serene, as she replaced the phone, and opened the door wider. "You might have been a bit light headed."

The next, day feeling relieved that nothing else weird occurred, I returned home. There was a letter from a publisher. He loved the manuscript I had sent to him and wanted to know if we could meet. The letter was signed Sebastian Jervis. My hand shook as I picked up the telephone to contact him.

TURNING POINT

M.E. SYLER

The sidewalk is a speedway. To avoid a collision, I stood at the curb. Too many people with a phone stuck to their ear, others with their heads down thumbing the screen and mixed in the mob are clueless teens and tweens.

Chinatown is always busy, and usually, I avoid downtown at lunchtime. But there is the exception. One that I tried to escape, but Phillip wouldn't let me off the hook, and as always, I'm on time, and he is late. That forces me to wait outside of Chengs Chinese Carry-out where we agreed to have lunch.

It doesn't bother Phillip in the least to keep me waiting. Lost in one of his stories again, no doubt, an author, laughable. Two publications, one in an obscure digital magazine, and the other a self-published eBook. In my opinion, it's a waste of valuable time. He needs a real job. Despite my opinions, we are friends. We grew up together. Phillip always had his head in the clouds, and me, grounded, practical, and ambitious. I tried to guide him, but impulsive Phillip never took my advice. He married Helen, the only girl he had dated in High School. She ended up shouldering their financial load, and, to her credit, she never complained. How their marriage survived these twenty years, I don't know. *A woman's love does not share my life*. We are opposites, but Phillip and I have a common interest in history. Occasionally, when Helen's at work, we tour the historic areas of the city.

I passed the time watching patrons file in an out of Chengs with containers filled with the best food in the city. Each time the door opened a whiff of rice and soy made my stomach growl and tempted me to eat lunch without Phillip. I disciplined my urge to wait him out.

Then I saw the man, a wall-hugger, dressed in soiled clothing, sporting a long thick coat, even though the temperature is in the eighties. A dirt-crusted bum with shoulder-length hair matted and tangled with his beard knotted by leaves, twigs, and other debris. No doubt he's infested with lice.

The man is disgusting, but I can't turn my eyes away, his grimy hand gripped a shopping cart filled with rags and cardboard. Possibly used to build a shelter and a mat to sleep on. He stopped and leaned against the building near the door at Chengs.

I observed everyone passing by and those going in and out of Chengs, they all ignored the man, as though he were invisible. I could not help myself. For some odd reason, I was compelled to stare at this vagrant.

For several minutes, I kept my eyes on him, my hunger was forgotten, people walked up and down the sidewalk passing between us. The man patiently leaned against the structure, oblivious to my gazing.

Then a woman exited Chengs with two containers, in passing she handed one to the bum. She didn't stop to speak or to look at him; it appeared, to me, she went out of her way not to acknowledge him, as she quickly exited down the sidewalk.

The bum opened the container, and with grimy fingers, he scooped the white rice into his mouth. Then a thought came to me, *can I see Jesus in the face of this wretched man*? An unusual thought that I can't explain. I am not religious like Phillip and his wife who practically live at the church. At that precise moment, with his rice-filled hand near his mouth, the man lifted his eyes to mine. My heart leaped. A broad smile of decayed teeth crossed his face as though he knew my thought, my heart thumped against my chest, and then I knew the answer, yes. I can see.

For a few seconds, we held our gaze. Then the man lowered his eyes and continued to eat half of the rice in the container. I looked down the sidewalk to locate the woman who had given him the food, but she was out of sight. Strangers walked up and down the sidewalk unaware of my encounter. To me, it seemed loud and clear. After a few moments, the homeless man placed the container in his shopping cart and pushed it down the walk.

My opinion of the vagrant changed. The words in Deacon Bill's homily, this past Sunday, prompted the thought. The one time I gave in to Phillip when he prodded me to join him and Helen at Mass. Deacon had told the story about two disciples on the road to Emmaus. They had followed Jesus, and after his crucifixion, they were disillusioned. Their expectations of him died. The destitute I watched did not meet any expectations I would hold true. Then if I'm being truthful, and admit, I'm selfish, autocratic, and arrogant. Then why do I believe Jesus would show Himself to me?

"Daniel," Phillip startled me out of my thoughts. "You look like you've seen a ghost."

"Not a ghost," I said. My voice filled with disbelief.

"What are you talking about?" Phillip said.

"The Road to Emmaus, I saw Jesus today in the face of a homeless beggar."

"Where is he?" Phillip looked down the street, in the direction I pointed, but the man was gone. Phillip gave me a look, and I knew he didn't believe me. We purchased lunch at Cheng's and walked in silence until we reached the steps of the Museum of American History. We sat down to eat.

After a while, I said, "Phillip, you're the religious one, why did you doubt what I said?"

"Daniel, I've known you all my life, and until last Sunday you never stepped inside a church. I'm your best friend, and you're the most non-religious, unbelieving, man I know. How could you see Jesus?"

"It's hard to explain. When our eyes met, a voice inside of my head, posed the question: can you see Jesus in the face of this wretched man? When the man's eyes met mine, my heart skipped, and that affirmed the question."

"Okay, as your best friend I believe you. But, if I were you, I wouldn't tell anyone else," Phillip said.

"Why? If I have come to believe, why not tell others. Is this supposed to be my secret? I had equated it with the road to Emmaus story."

"From Saint Luke's Gospel. You've never opened a Bible in your life. How would you know about those events?" Phillip asked, and then stuffed fried rice into his mouth.

"Then how did I recognize Jesus?" Phillip swallowed. Then he said,

"That's in the Bible too. When you feed the hungry, shelter the homeless, and visit the sick and the imprisoned; that's where you see Jesus."

That must be it, "When I witnessed the woman feed the man. Words from Deacon Bill's homily prompted me to ask, can I see Jesus in the face of this man."

"Really, you remembered what Deacon said in his homily?"

"Don't you?"

"Some, but he gets long winded and my mind wanders," Phillip replied. We laughed.

After we had eaten, we stood. I heard Phillip say something, but my thoughts went to a woman's scream. A child, he looked to be about four years old, ran trying to catch a dog. His mother attempted to grab him at the same time she clung to a baby stroller. The little guy was fast, but he would not catch his dog. His path crossed near us, without hesitation, I ran to apprehend the child. *I have the angle, and I should be able to intercept him before he gets into the street.*

The boy ran with his head down, and his hand tried to grab the dog's leash. I'm within his reach when we passed the curb. Tires squealed, horns blared, my eyes fixed on the boy, I lunged forward with my left arm stretched out, my fingers grabbed his shirt collar, and I yanked him backward into my hands. I spun around and threw the boy, like a forward pass on the basketball court; and Phillip caught him. My heart pounded. I felt joy. Then the impact.

A woman sobbed, a jumble of incoherent voices and sirens blared. Phillip spoke in my ear, "Hang in there, buddy."

Then my heart burned when I saw him again, the face of the vagrant Jesus standing above me. His arm outstretched, I clasp His hand, and He pulled me up.

GRYPH

PAT SIMMONS

It rained on Saturday. Soccer was cancelled. Dad told me to stop complaining about the weather and do some jobs instead. Thanks Dad. But it was OK because he asked me to clean out the shed.

I love the smells in the shed. They're a mixture of earthy things, chemical things and old things. There are tools that Dad never uses, old tins and boxes, toys I've grown out of, toys my sister Rosie's grown out of (must get those wheels off her bike, they could be useful), things Dad said he'd fix (Mum's still waiting) and a bird cage. I always felt sorry for that budgie. What's the point of having wings if you don't have room to fly?

I'm glad no-one else goes in the shed. Mum sometimes stands outside the shed and tells Dad, "It would make a lovely craft room if only someone would get rid of the rubbish." So, he stays away from the shed. So does Rosie. She's scared of spiders.

Anyway, I filled a couple of garbage bags with rubbish to show Dad I was making an effort. Then I found it, underneath some sacks. An egg. Definitely not a chicken egg, heaps bigger, and a sort of greenish black colour. It felt hard like a rock. But it was warm. I know Dad stores some strange things in the shed, but an egg?

A bird wouldn't just lay an egg and leave it, so I waited. It would come back and sit on it. Maybe something bad happened to the parent. I was a bit relieved when nothing appeared, because whatever laid that egg must be big, very big. Why would a bird lay an egg in our shed? Maybe it wasn't a bird. Platypuses lay eggs and they're not birds, but they live in water. Some snakes and lizards lay eggs too.

Was it an emu egg? As if there'd be an emu in Newtown. Well, there might be. I've seen a guy walking his pet pig. So, you never know. On google, emu eggs looked like my egg. Maybe the emu was caught and taken back to the zoo.

I didn't want whatever was in the egg to die. I knew I had to keep the egg warm. We had a chicken hatching incubator at school once. When those cute little chickens hatched out everyone made a fuss of them and cuddled them. Then they got bigger and uglier, and after a week, no-one liked them. Pretty slack. I reckon. No-one that is, except for me and Robbie. Robbie's my best mate. We've been friends since pre-school. Robbie begged his Mum and Dad and they let him take two chickens home. He still has them. Their names are Taylor and Miley.

I told Robbie about the egg and he came around to my place after school to have a look. We hung out in my bedroom and played computer games. Then we went out to the shed. I explained to Mum that we were doing a project on spiders. Rosie heard us and screamed. At least we knew she wouldn't bother us. Mum looked a bit worried, told us to be careful and not to touch anything with eight legs.

I lifted up the sacks and showed Robbie the egg. He was gobsmacked.

'Can I touch it, Joe?' Robbie asked.

'Go ahead,' I said.

'It's warm and kind of like a rock,' he murmured.

I know,' I said. 'What do you think it is?'

'Haven't a clue,' he said, looking around the shed. 'We need something to put it in so when it hatches it'll feel safe.'

We found an old tin box.

'Perfect,' Robbie said.

We lined the box with some scraps of material.

I held the box and Robbie gently put one hand on each side of the egg. He looked at me wide eyed. His face was going red.

'What's up?' I asked.

'It's heavy,' he gasped. 'Really heavy.'

Puffing and panting, Robbie lowered the egg into the box. His eyes looked like they were going to pop out of his head.

'Look,' he said, 'Look.'

The egg was glowing.

'Are you boys still in there?' Mum called.

We looked at each other in horror. We thought she might actually come inside the shed. I ran to the back door where she was standing.

'We've nearly finished Mum. Just writing up our notes.'

'Well, don't be too much longer,' she said, frowning. 'Are you all right? You look a bit flustered.'

'I'm fine. Didn't realise there were so many different spiders in the shed.'

I heard another loud scream. Rosie must've been listening.

I ran back in the shed.

'It's hatching,' Robbie said.

We crouched over the egg, hardly daring to breathe. It was cracking, splintering. We touched the crumbling shell. It was still glowing, but wasn't hot. Then suddenly, there was just a pile of dust with something sitting in the middle of it. We had no idea what it was. We could see damp feathers, a beak and these big eyes staring up at us. As the feathers dried we saw they were a golden colour.

'What do we do now?' I asked.

Robbie couldn't take his eyes off the creature.

'I dunno,' he replied. 'It's awesome.'

I gently picked it up. It sat in my cupped hands, looking up at me.

'It's got feathers on its head and chest and fur on its back half,' I said.

'And a tail,' whispered Robbie. 'It's got a tail.'

Sure enough it had a tail with a tuft of hair at the end of it, swishing from side to side.

'Hurry up in there, boys,' called Mum.

'Let's take it up to my room,' I said.

We wrapped it in Robbie's jacket. It gave a little squawk then closed its eyes and fell asleep, which was a relief really. We went inside.

'Just finishing our notes,' I called.

Robbie switched on my computer and started typing like a maniac.

After a few minutes he said, 'I think I know what it is.'

'What?'

'Yep, here it is,' he grinned triumphantly. 'It's a gryphon.'

'Are you crazy?' I whispered, keeping an eye on the bedroom door.

He showed me some images.

'Gryphons love gold and they like to hoard it. They can find other treasure too, emeralds and stuff. They hate horses. They live for around one hundred and fifty years.' Robbie gabbled excitedly.

'But, but they're just a myth.' I spluttered.

'Well this one isn't. Look at it. Just look at it,' Robbie said.

I opened Robbie's jacket and studied the little creature.

'Yep,' I agreed. 'Feathers, wings, big hooked beak, four legs, front legs like a bird, back legs furry. A tail. I can't believe this. OK what do they eat? And more important, what do we do with it?'

Robbie's fingers were flashing over the keyboard. 'They're omnivores. They eat berries and meat. Baby gryphons stay with their parents for two years.'

'So where are its parents?' I asked, not expecting a reply.

'Don't know. But we need to put it back in the shed in case they come back. And we can't tell anyone. Agreed?'

'Agreed,' I said. 'Adults will take it away and do experiments on it, for sure.'

We went downstairs.

'Just seeing Robbie out.'

'OK love,' Mum said.

She and Dad were watching a wildlife documentary on television. If they only knew!

I took some blueberries from the fridge and we settled the creature in the old budgie cage. It seemed to like the berries. As soon as it saw them in my hand it opened its beak and squawked.

'Here you go,' I said as I popped them one at a time into its wide pink mouth. It swallowed each one whole and squawked for more.

'Let's give it a name.' Robbie said.

'We don't know if it's a boy or a girl,' I said. 'What about Gryph?'

'Yep, I like that,' Robbie said. 'Goodnight Gryph.'

We closed the cage door.

That night there was a huge thunder storm. I listened to the thunder and watched the lightning out of my bedroom window. I saw an enormous flash that lit up the sky and I'm sure I saw something on the shed roof.

When I went into the shed the next morning the cage was empty. Gryph had gone. Lying on the floor was a huge golden feather.

Robbie's checked. Gryphon feathers have magical powers.

We wish we could've said goodbye to Gryph. We've never told anyone about what happened. Who'd believe us anyway? But maybe one day Gryph will come back to where it was born. We take turns hiding the golden feather under our pillows and we keep wishing.

FLASHES

CARL SMITH

I don't want to die.

They say when faced with death your life flashes before your eyes. I disagreed. I believed your brain was trying to recall similar scenarios you'd survived.

I was wrong.

I saw her. I saw her crooked smile lifting up on one side of her mouth – that's her genuine smile; both sides go up when she's forcing it.

But my recollections of her can't save me.

She didn't want me in her life anymore, so I acted. I couldn't imagine life without her, but I'm sure she wouldn't want this.

I regret stepping off the ledge.

THE EARTH CRACKED IN TWO

LAUREN SUCHENSKI

The earth cracked in two and showed its slightly-tinged blue center - the little place where all thoughts meet, where they glow under our feet, and where they tap and twist and tingle through all the mingling of the clouds. The deep spinal tissue of the roots of the world showed themselves to just be words - and inside of those words: deep twisting twirls of curls of ghosts of thoughts never formed. The tongue of time whistled inside of itself and rained through the rainbow reflections slicing and reverberating through the air. We were all there, and we were all careless and cobwebbed and careening like flocks of frozen fragments. We knew our names, our times and our tastes. We knew the names within our names and the voices within our vibrating songboxes. wW all gave each other just enough soul to breathe, and we planted our dreams in huge wells of wind that we dug into the sides of the earth. We all created our food out of deep nourishment - our leftover words, our lingering pleasures, the slightly sweet sadness dripping out of the sides of our mouths. Time began at the beginning, played backwards through a radio and two old speakers - projecting all across the projection of space, but we could all hear it, whether near or far from the source of the singing radio river. And thus, time beat to the rhythm of the music the trees were singing, to the violin strings and bows and arrows of desperate attempts to be free from the trapped tinkling souls of tied up trees - twisted and bony and brown.

Tiny and shoe-laced and turnip tongued - the days passed like soft sounds of cerebral sunsets. Huge museums of mountains mumbled up great patterns of poetry and prose. Cathedrals of art and science trembled in suspension and light - architecture of archaic accolades of all our accomplishments, yet we cared not for city walls and halls of sentience - we dangled and dabbled for brief moments in the shining sour apple sweetness of our glory, just to soak up a big fistful of inspiration before we tip toed back to the broken open wounds of the womb of the earth, to care, to tend, to listen, to mend, to remember, to remind ourselves to resound, to reverberate, and to rebirth ourselves. We spent the long trumpet hours of the afternoon staring at reflections of pools of deep purple water- the water from ages and ages of tears of travesties, tragedies and truths - honoring and belittling our sacred sorrows. We swallowed whole the great salt flats that had persisted even after the tears had evaporated in the sullen swaths of the sun and let our tongues get tortured by the tingle of the chemistry and charisma of taste. We jingled and jangled and let our weaving entanglements of deep rhythms escape us. We tumbled and turned and burned at the edges, folded up at the spleen, and one day evolved. Or devolved - I can't quite remember which.

A GALAXY FUR, FUR AWAY

JOHN TALONI

T'Furr was a very angry kitty.

Mrrowl had been chasing him all day. Now he was creeping towards T'Furr's spot on the couch. Inch by inch, he moved into T'Furr's comfort zone.

"Mrrowl, I have had enough!" said T'Furr. "We were not sent here to play these kitty games!" Mrrowl continued to inch forward. He reached a paw slowly towards T'Furr, then extended a claw. T'Furr felt the fur rise on his neck despite his training. "Put that down, or I will be forced to respond in kind meow Meow Meow!" The kitty brain overwhelmed his training, and he jumped to his feet, back arching.

"Mraaaarrrrrrr!" he exclaimed, almost completely overwhelmed. With the last vestige of self-control gone, he leapt off the couch and rushed past Mrrowl, hissing full force, into the bedroom.

T'Furr lay on the bed, tail twitching. Mrrowl padded in and sat down a safe distance away. "You act like we need to be working all the time," he said in their native language. It sounded strange coming out of the small mouths of the Earth cats.

"And you forget our mission," said T'Furr. "We must discover the language and culture of our brethren. They have so far escaped us – not just us, but every team on this forsaken planet."

"Bddddddddt!" One of the other cats came into the room, tail high. For some unknown reason, he allowed himself to be called by the undignified name of Bobo. "See, here is a perfect situation," said T'Furr. "Bobo, we call this a 'bed.' What do you call it?" But Bobo's only response was "Miaow?" And he sat on the bed licking his paws.

"Rrrrright," said Mrrowl. "I see our subject is ready for his language lesson. Look, maybe these cats just aren't like us. They seem to have these humans trained to take care of them, and they look like us, but what other evidence of civilization do we have?" asked Mrrowl. "Perhaps they're so advanced that they prop up the entire human civilization. Or maybe they're just, well, not all that smart."

But T'Furr wasn't convinced. "We just need to discover the key to their culture," he replied.

"Come on, I want to play a little," said Mrrowl. "These small cat bodies can move remarkably swiftly." Mrrowl, T'Furr, and the other felinopologists had transferred their consciousness to bioengineered bodies created from the genetic material of the local cats. Their much larger bodies lay in stasis light years away.

Mrrowl jumped on the bed, stalking T'Furr. "No," said T'Furr, "I'm not interested right n- "T'Furr cut off mid-sentence as Mrrowl leapt at him. "Leave me alone mrowr!"

The human rushed into the bedroom. "No fighting!" she said in the strange, throaty language her kind used. "Break it up!" T'Furr ran off into the other bedroom. Apparently, the human thought T'Furr had caused the fight, and she chased him. "Bad kitty!" She carried a broom and made sweeping motions toward T'Furr. "Get away from him! Bad cat!"

T'Furr scurried around the bed, barely escaping the broom, and ran under the other bed. With a twist of his neck, he engaged the Safety Portal. Jumping through, he landed in a small fold in spacetime outside normal reality. Distantly, he heard the human ask "Now where did that cat go? He seems to disappear every time." He heard her get on hands and knees and look under the bed. "I'll never understand where that cat gets to," she said.

Still angry at the exchange, T'Furr paced around in the Safety Portal. It was only a few feet wide, and had no particular texture. The floor felt like dull metal, but was actually more like a dense force field. T'Furr remained in the Portal for almost an hour. While useful, the Portals were not stable, and he chose to leave before being dumped unceremoniously on the ground. A short time later, he heard the sound of a can opening – and he realized that he had become quite hungry.

Trotting to the kitchen, T'Furr saw several bowls of food. He went to one and began to eat. Bobo hissed at him, trying to take the food for himself. T'Furr's kitty brain impulses overloaded his emotions. He hissed back, raising a paw and batting it at Bobo. The human came in right then and saw only T'Furr's retaliation.

"Oh! Mean kitty!" she exclaimed. "You eat over here." She picked up his dish and moved it a few feet away. T'Furr walked to the food, his tail twitching. No one would order around an adult feline in such an insulting manner on his homeworld – at least not without risking a fight. Mrrowl ate a few feet away, showing his amusement at T'Furr's situation with several twitches of his whiskers.

After the meal, T'Furr went back to the couch and began cleaning himself. Tongue on paw, then stroke the head. Lick back and sides as much as possible, clean the rest with the paws. While he much preferred the warm mist bath of his homeworld, the local custom was at least efficient. He hardly noticed when the human sat beside him.

"Do you want to be a good kitty? Yes, you do!" she said, stroking his fur. T'Furr reacted with a start. No cat allowed himself to be touched so casually on his homeworld.

"Who's a happy kitty? Who's a happy kitty!" she said, scratching behind his ear. Involuntarily, he moved his head toward her hand. His kitty emotions began to overwhelm his consciousness.

Next, the human began to stroke him under the chin. Inch by reluctant inch he moved closer to her. His life's training told him to run, to flee, not to let anyone touch him so easily.

But it was too late. The emotions of his small kitty body overwhelmed him. With a cross look on his face, he started to purr.

Oh, the indignity.

WHAT IS THIS THING CALLED LIKE?

CAROLINE TAYLOR

It was the night before Ginny's annual mammogram, and she was having trouble hooking up with the sandman. Thoughts of "what if" kept him at bay, long past the hour at which she could say she'd had a good night's sleep.

Counting sheep didn't work. She tried summoning pleasant memories but kept wondering what would happen if they diagnosed stage four cancer, not that she had found any lumps or anything, but still …

She tried thinking about her trip to Aspen next month, but looking forward to a pleasant event even in the near future seemed a bit too much like tempting fate.

For reasons known only to her subconscious, Ginny asked herself an odd question: Of all the people she'd known in her life, how many of them had really liked her? She'd long since realized that she was the kind of person who had lots of friends she didn't particularly like, so it probably wouldn't be a huge surprise if the opposite were also true.

As for the term itself, Ginny decided that like has nothing to do with love or lust or respect or admiration. Like means feeling an affection for someone that tolerates and perhaps even embraces that person's shortcomings and that persists, regardless of distance, over time. How did that definition apply to various categories of people she knew?

Family. Ginny's mother and father and older brother—even her two daughters—might have loved her in the way that is unique to families, but did they really like her? There was too much evidence to the contrary. Her brother Tom, for example, had started out not liking Ginny because she was a girl. Then he didn't like her because she hogged the bathroom. Now, he didn't care for her because, unlike Tom, Ginny had managed to find a career she loved and had retired on a comfortable pension.

Nona, her eldest, hardly ever kept in touch. Her busy career and all-consuming passion for running marathons were typical excuses for not calling on anything but Ginny's birthday or holidays. If Nona actually liked her mother, Ginny figured her daughter would call or text whenever she felt the need. Jessie, her youngest, had been a rebel as a teenager and seemed stuck in that persona at age twenty. Four years ago, she'd run away with a lowlife roadie for a going-nowhere rock band. Ginny knew she was still alive only because Nona said so. Jessie's last words to her mother, as she'd thrown her clothes into a black plastic garbage bag, were, "Leave me the fuck alone! I hate you!"

So. Scratch the two daughters. Maybe they'd make an appearance if Ginny ended up in the hospital or on a slab at the mortuary, but duty is not like.

Schoolmates. Considering Ginny's father was an army officer, she and Tom had spent much of their childhood traveling from one place to another. That made it hard to think of any schoolyard friendships that had survived the family's inevitable reassignment to a new post. If any schoolmates remembered her, it would only be a matter of curiosity, as in, "I wonder what happened to that shy girl with the orange hair and freckles?"

Boyfriends. Many of Ginny's so-called boyfriends might have been attracted to her physically (after the orange hair turned dark and the freckles got covered up with makeup), but did they actually like her? After much thought, she could recall only two who fit her definition, neither of whom was a factor in the love-leads-to-commitment, let alone marriage, department. Some of them might have been in love with her, but love is not like.

Like Daniel, for example. They'd been madly in love, until Ginny realized that the man of her dreams didn't seem to like her. He never laughed at her jokes, which was not a good sign. Things between them had progressed to the stage where Daniel had gotten down on one knee and pulled a jeweler's box out of his pocket, but it was all she could do not to crack up laughing at the relief he couldn't hide when she'd said "no." Most other males she'd encountered after that sorry episode could safely be consigned to the category of sexual attraction period.

Girlfriends. As with schoolmates, Ginny blamed the impermanence of her peripatetic youth for having very few. Most of her girlfriends were acquired in college and afterwards in the workplace. The college girlfriends, though, were like her schoolmates. There wasn't enough *like* in the relationships she'd had with them to make those friendships last. Well, except for one. Sandra Olson had remained in touch with Ginny for fifty-seven years. But did Sandra like her? Ginny had no idea. Their lives had diverged, and they now had little in common; yet, they remained in touch. For all Ginny knew, this was mostly because neither of them wanted to be the one who severed the connection.

There is—or was—only one other woman Ginny considered a girlfriend. In retrospect, however, she might have been wrong. She'd imagined they were close until Maria had cut off contact and later moved over to the dark side of the political spectrum, leaving Ginny wondering if she'd ever really known Maria at all.

Coworkers. That was tricky. Many of the coworkers who might have actually liked Ginny had also worked for her, so a case could be made for their affections not being based on anything more than staying in the boss's good graces. Some of those people had kept in touch, but was it because they liked her? Maybe respect would be a more accurate term. Even those coworkers who did not actually despise or hate Ginny most likely considered her to be tough, exacting, not a team player. Definitely not.

Neighbors. Until recently, Ginny had never really had neighbors, in the neighborly sense, that is. Before, as they got transferred from post to post, she would be in the neighborhood too briefly to be noticed. Later on, the neighborhoods she'd lived in had tended to be lifestyle enclaves where privacy held sway and neighborliness was sneered at, if not outright discouraged. Even now, Ginny had no idea what the neighbors thought of her, but like was probably going a bit too far.

Husband. It was getting on to four o'clock by then, the sky just beginning to lighten. Too late now for sleep. Ginny was pretty sure Cal had liked her, quirks and all. Like Cal, Ginny was selfish, lazy, and antisocial. Unlike her husband, she also tended to be judgmental, vain, and a control freak. Cal had probably even loved her as she had him, God rest his soul. Still, she couldn't help feeling that their marriage had been long and happy because of the shared sense of humor and a common background.

Four-thirty now and time to throw in the towel. Ginny sat up, wondering why she'd wasted the night constructing such a strange inventory. What purpose did it serve? It certainly led back to the obvious question: Was Ginny herself likable? She thought not. It didn't bother her, either. She couldn't recall ever wanting people—especially strangers—to like her. Sure, she'd wanted various men at various times to love her, but love is not like.

Ginny did not wish to be disliked. Considering her innate selfish, lazy, vain, stubborn, judgmental, and antisocial proclivities, she did what she could not to make enemies. But making friends? Even if there were an answer as to whom she might befriend, there would remain the question of why. Of course, she knew the general consensus was that people need friends. But Ginny did not feel needy. She did not feel lonely, nor was she any kind of misanthrope.

She was, however, willing to consider whether she might be missing something wonderful because of her rootless childhood. But what good would that do, considering she seemed to lack the necessary skills? It seemed an awful lot like telling a dolphin how wonderful it is to climb a mountain.

Short of Twitter, which she refused to use, there ought to be a way to circulate her definition of *like* to a wider audience, before the term became totally meaningless, thanks to Facebook. Probably way too late.

But it might not be too late to indulge in one last bit of mischief. She'd send some e-mails to the few remaining acquaintances she could claim, asking them just one thing: "Have you ever wondered, what is this thing called like?"

MEMORIES OF NOT GREECE
TRUDI YOUNG TAYLOR

     Hospital chairs are cold, especially in waiting rooms of the emergency department on a late night. Or was it now early morning? A Friday night? Saturday morning? The cold air of February buffeted her being every time someone walked or ran or pushed a gurney through the doors leading to the covered parking area where ambulances and cars parked with the injured or dying or just frightened stop to unload their people, the most important people in the world, to them. She pulled her knees into her chest making herself as small as possible. The chairs were weird, hard plastic in washed-out shades of green and orange stuck together with poles against the puke pallid walls. Like anyone would seriously think about stealing from here, or maybe they would create a scene throwing a chair through a window or door or block the paths of the gurneys and the EMS team wheeling people in.

     He had held her hair back as she vomited into the toilet, as exploding blueberries and raspberries covered in cream, careened out of her nostrils and mouth. Her eyes felt so swollen like they could bulge right out of their sockets and plunk like overripe fruits into the sea of puke, but he had her head too in his hands, elongated fingers that suited his large frame. She wasn't frightened just uncomfortable and wishing it was over and that she hadn't had so much to drink on their Valentine's celebration in her special dress. The one she had saved for this occasion, crushed red velvet with the tie-up bodice and long swirls of skirt; a little like the dresses Anne Boleyn wore for Henry the Eighth, before the animosity and beheading. She always whoopsied when she was excited, always. And her hair was red and curly not in any way like Anne Boleyn's thick brown strands before her husband lopped off her head. She looked up at him with only love, love, love silencing the tummy ache of crab cakes and chocolate éclairs and one too many glasses of champagne.

• • •

She had been an ill bride, just out of the hospital, still under a doctor's care, when they said, fuck it. And got on a plane with thirty-two dollars and a new visa to fly to her homeland where the food was bad, and the scenery was lush even in October with the birds of prey circling close overhead and never landing. Her family kept them for a few days; the In-Tourist Centers set them up with bed and breakfasts for the other nights. Somehow, she managed to drive a stick shift on the wrong side of the road because he was too large to fit behind the wheel of the small car they rented. But even if he did fit, he couldn't drive a stick, so she was stuck. Even when she told him, I think I've made an awful mistake. He poured some more tea, added milk and sugar, pushed the heart decorated mug towards her, before saying, we're here now, let's make the best of it, shall we? They did, walking old railroad tracks through one town, washing their undies in one city, downing port in the pubs in another, sprinting through brisk mornings for a newspaper. Two days before their departure, they took a detour. Look up the sign said, and they did seeing a blue sky, air frigid but clear floating above the dilapidated runway doubling as a road. They found castle ruins sitting on a mossy hill, beaten by the harsh winds of the North Sea. The foam sprayed them from deep below as he pulled her back from the edge, wrapped her in his elegant arms, to drive to a tea shop in the nearest town, where life seemed okay, and marriage was not so scary or smothering or settling down. She woke him up that night to listen to the couple next door having wall-pounding sex. Giggling from their secret snooping, they tried for a syncopated rhythm but couldn't stop laughing, and fell asleep to sounds of a headboard crashing like the waves from earlier. No time for showers the next morning but she led him to the sink, tipped his head forward and washed his hair, letting the blue-black strands iced with silver, thick as her wrist, slide forward into the basin. Never cut your hair she said, and he replied as long as you wash it for me. The shampoo was slippery making his head silk-shrouded, sleek as a seal, heavy with hair and head and gray matter to become heavier again as she poured jug after jug of warm water to rinse. She smiled thinking of the times they would have together, traveling around Greece on rented motorcycles, renovating their little house, caring for their dogs and cats instead of the children that she couldn't have. Jug after jug, she rinsed out the suds and promised herself to wash his hair, always.

    They had been playing Trivial Pursuit, a game she was lousy at except when playing on a team but they were playing alone that night, drinking tequila and dark beer in the only circle of light of a dark woody bar. She felt giddy with the completion of the semester, contemplating another round. That night was before the crackdown of DUIs and MothersAgainstDrunkDriving and their maturation, so another round was possible and even probable when he asked her something else. She had been caught unaware, concentrating on the sunny yellow wedge of pie missing in her wheel, when he posed the question of marriage or Greece. Without hesitation she said Greece, been married before don't want to do it again. He pushed the long hair away from his face and held her gaze with those long-lashed green eyes, moo-moo mouth pursed, white skin so soft that it showed the bruise of her words. Tears ran down her face knowing her time was up and this was it, and he would leave her if she chose Greece but still she tried. Can't we do both, no, why, not enough money, I want to go to Greece, I want to get married? Full stop.

    After two days of him feeling not quite well, she worked late that Friday until checking on him she saw he looked worse than that morning. Color grim, and she called his doctor, but he was not worried, flu season, and she said to do something please for my husband. Pharmaceuticals didn't help, and her beloved looked at her as he said, I'm so scared. She didn't know what to do so she asked him. Stay at home. They knew they knew. Blue, the skin around his mouth and eyes turned blue, and they knew as the seizures came that his brain wasn't getting enough oxygen. She asked again. Stay at home. Massaging him as muscles died, rocking him when he shook, whispering little love memories into his ear until he smiled. Then the smiles became fewer, frozen in pain. She dialed 911. Paramedics jumped through the door, attaching lines and tubes, speaking to him in progressively louder voices as the gurney wheeled in. She watched from the hallway, out of their way, shaking.

She twisted the heavy gold ring on her finger; first one way, then slipped it to the middle joint, then back down and twirled it the other way. The hard edge of the plastic chair cut into her thighs. Her sweater was not warm enough against the aseptic cold air rushing through the room and down her spine. She shivered and fidgeted as a way to keep warm, keep away the thoughts of the other room, what they were doing. The slip-sliding sound of the doors announced a visitor even before she saw his green-clad booties, stained scrubs, red-raw fingers wringing together. I will not look up. Nothing good will be said.

She knocked her head against the patched wall of the waiting room. Straight back. Bouncing her scalp against the plasterboard, feeling trickles of blood plaster hair against her neck, many feet scurrying towards her, hearts-blood from her scalp, the give of the wall, trying to knock out all the little love memories of Not Greece.

THE CHESS GAME
ROZKO ILIEV TZOLOV

I have never smoked, and have always led a healthy life, lung-wise, breathing as much fresh air as I could. Considering that we also never had lung cancer in my family, my diagnosis came as a surprise to me.

For some time, I had been coughing, was short of breath, and felt a vague malaise, but I thought that it was just my age. I was seventy-five years old and in good health—or so I thought. At last, I decided to address my symptoms, and went to my family physician, Doctor York, for a checkup. After he listened to my lungs, and tapped me here and there, he said that he needed to take a CAT scan. When I returned for the results, the doctor said, with what I imagined was a cold, distant face, although he assumed a mask of compassion, that I had terminal lung cancer. To prove it, he brandished an X-Ray image in front of me and showed me some lighter patches on it, saying that was it.

"How long have I left, Doc," I asked him straight.

"Not too long, Mike. Maybe two months. At this stage, I don't think there's any point in having chemo," he said, and scratched his head with his pen. "I would say that it would be best to prepare yourself. Make a will, say your farewells to your family...you know."

"Actually, I don't have any close family," I said. "I've never been married, and the only relatives I have are some distant cousins who have enough of their own problems without burdening them with me dying. And I don't really own very much to be worth it to write a will either."

The doctor thought again: "Well, then spend your last days as happily as you can. Go on a vacation," he said, and shrugged his shoulders.

"All right Doc. Thank you for your advice," I muttered, and left his office.

In the beginning, I didn't think so much about my impending demise. I thought of taking Doctor York's advice and taking a vacation, but there really wasn't anywhere I cared to go, and I didn't have much money—my pension was meager. At first, I lived day-by-day the way I had before I learned that I was dying. In a week, though, it hit me: even at my age, it's hard for one to know that he is dying. However, what can one do about it? Even if you don't want to watch the hands of the clock keep rotating, time passes by, the cancer grows, and death approaches. After a month and a half, I started feeling ill, with shortness of breath that prevented me from climbing the stairs, and my entire body started aching a lot as well. In the end, I was admitted to the hospital. I think that I had an unspoken gentleman's agreement with the hospital administration that I would die within a couple of weeks, as I couldn't pay for my maintenance therapy and was a burden to the staff. Well, two weeks passed and I was still alive. I didn't get better, so they couldn't release me, but I didn't seem to be in a hurry to kick the bucket either. It seemed to me that the physicians began to give me mean looks when they were doing their rounds and found me still kicking.

At first, the time spent in the hospital was lonely, mostly because nobody wanted to befriend a geezer on his deathbed—it makes people sad—and why would they want to get upset? My roommate was some fellow who was breathing through a big machine with a fan inside. I wasn't even sure if he was awake. I spent my time slouching up and down the hallway looking at the closed door at the end of it, leading to the big beautiful world, knowing that I would go through it only when I was dead. I know—I was being dramatic. I could have asked to be wheeled out in the hospital yard, but I didn't want to just peek at the world, knowing that I was stranded where I was.

Luckily, during the second week of my stay, I met and befriended Joe, a patient in the next room. He was my age, and like me, he had no close family. He had been married, but never had children, and his wife had died several years ago. He was in the hospital because he had a heart attack and was waiting for a transplant, but how would he get a transplant at that age? He was simply waiting to die as I was.

Eventually, I became bedridden and couldn't move around anymore, so Joe walked slowly from his room to mine, pushing his glucose bottle on a stand next to him. He would sit in the chair next to me, and we would talk for hours. What were we talking about, you ask? About everything: our lives, our youth, past loves—all kinds of memories we needed to get out of our systems. I discovered that he played chess, as I did, and after we had a nice talk, we would lay out the chessboard on my bed, and play a few games. He was a tad better than I was, but I still managed to win a game sometimes.

The weeks passed by in that way, and still I was not getting out of the hospital either way, upright or feet first.

One night, the ward was quiet. Joe slouched into my room again and spread the chessboard before me. We started a game. It was a contested match. For some unknown reason, I wanted to win more than I usually did. Joe also was absorbed in the game; clearly, he wanted to win as well. At one point, I took my eyes off the chessboard. Joe's face was serious and sullen. Outside in the corridor, someone had turned off the lights, and the room was dark and cold. Shadows ran up the walls, the man-machine on the bed next to me was making his beeping sounds, breathing in and out regularly; in the corner behind him, there seemed to be a human figure. Joe followed my eyes and stiffened, and then looked back at the chessboard immediately. We continued our game. I had never played better in my life. I thought that if I lost, it would be the end of me. It seemed that Joe thought the same, because he also was giving his best, but he still couldn't win either, no matter how hard he tried. In the end, after a long exchange, we were left with just a few figures. Besides the king, I had a queen, and Joe a queen and a rook. It looked like he would win. Sweating, I saw out of the corner of my eye that the shadowy figure in the corner had stood up. I looked back at the board. Meanwhile, Joe had made a mistake and moved his queen behind his king. If I checked him in my next move, I could take the queen. Suddenly I felt bad. How could I beat him at that particular game? He was my friend, after all. Rather than checking him, I moved my queen to threaten his rook. He moved his queen next to mine checking me, I took it, he took mine with his rook, and I his rook with my king. We remained with just a king each. It was a stalemate. I looked at him. He was staring at me and smiling.

"Stalemate," he said.

"That's how I see it," I said, and we shook hands. It occurred to me that maybe Joe had moved his queen deliberately so that I could take it. I looked at the corner, but the figure had disappeared.

It had become dazzling in the ward. The light from the lamps above me was blinding. I felt a flow of vitality. My body, bedridden under its weight for so long, felt light. I rose in the bed, and Joe helped me stand. We went out in the hallway, limping. There wasn't a living soul there, but at the end of the hall, I saw that the door was open and the light was streaming through it. Joe and I exchanged glances and started for it, unstable on our feet, leaning on each other. Shoulder to shoulder, we limped by the other patients' rooms. The door could have been a mile from us; we passed what seemed like a thousand rooms, but together, supporting each other, we kept inching forward. At last, we reached the door. Joe looked at me and asked, "Are you ready to go?"

"Let's do it!"

"You understand, there's no going back?"

I looked back at the ward with its sterile white walls and floors and just shrugged my shoulders.

RADAR LOVE
ROBERT M ULLRICH

My human is hugging me on his lap. I'm wrapped up in a big old comfy towel. He is sad. I don't know why he's sad because I am real happy.

I have never been to this place. There are lots of smells. There are dogs and cats and other animals, too. I don't like cats much. My human has one. I only met her once. That was three days ago when he brought me home. It has a fence and grass to run around in. The big building where I used to stay didn't have any of that.

The nice lady human came with us. She lives at the nice house, too. I like her. She loved on me the first time he brought me home. She seems sad, too. I'm going to lick her hand for awhile. That made her smile, but she still looks sad. I don't understand, but there is a LOT of stuff about humans I don't get, so I'm just going to snuggle.

***

I didn't used to have a home. The human I had before put me out of a car and left. I didn't know where I was. I don't see so good because of the thingies in my eyes. They make everything fuzzy. I couldn't find my way home, and it got bad. I couldn't find no food and only mud water to drink. Then I smelled meat! There were humans eating by a big building. One of them tossed me a bone to chew on. He went and got another human who gave me meat and rubbed my head.

I had bitey things on me. He got some stuff and sprayed it on me. All the bitey things died just like that! I couldn't believe it. Then he carried me where it was cool in the big building. (I had a boo-boo on my leg and couldn't walk so good.)

The boo-boo hurt a lot. It was all red and icky. He put smelly stuff on it every day until it got all better.

He made a bed for me by his feet and got me food and water and a nice blanket. Then he put a little door in the big door so I could go in and out by myself. The building was huge so I had lots of room to run around chasing mice and possums and bothering the other humans.

One of the nice humans started calling me Radar. I'm not sure why. I'm pretty small. He calls me a Chi-hyena. He says I look like my mommy was a Chihuahua and like my daddy must have been a Hyena. It's funny.

My human took me to the nice house once before. That's when I met the nice lady. I think I could have stayed but a dog that lived there bit me. I got too close to her human, and she got mad. He said it wasn't safe for me there, so he took me back to the big building.

I stayed at the big building for almost two years. My human would take me for a walk every day. Lots of times we would go down by the water. I got to walk around and sniff everything. Sometimes we would just walk around the block, but he always took time just for me. It made me happy. I never knew a human could love me so much.

Then I started to not feel too good a lot. I started making messes when I was sleeping. He never yelled at me. He told me "Good girl!" even when I peed and pooped in my bed. He would clean me up and never made me feel bad. I couldn't walk too good anymore either. He would carry me when I got tired. I would put my head on his shoulder and love him bunches. Sometimes, he would stay with me when I was sick. He made a bed on the floor and slept right by me. It starting to get really hard to breathe sometimes and I kept throwing up my food. I was getting sad because I couldn't see his face too good anymore. The thingies in my eyes were making the pictures go away.

***

Three days ago, he packed up all my stuff. He put everything in the car. I don't know why, but then he gave all his stuff to this man, and we drove away. I didn't care. As long as I was with him, I was happy. I couldn't believe it when we got to the home where he took me before! I was really nervous because of the other dogs, but he kept them away. He never left me alone and even slept beside me for three nights in a row. The first two nights was outside, and it was really neat. Every time I woke up he was right there. I love him a lot. He makes me feel better even though I am sick.

The last two days were the bestest I ever had! We went to a place where dogs run around without leashes. There were lots of smells and other dogs, but I wasn't afraid. I runned away from two big pitbulls when they came into my building! He took me for lots of walks and carried me a lot of the time. My one leg doesn't work so good. Maybe it's because of the boo-boo I had a long time ago. We went to lots of places and I got treats; LOTS of treats. I even got ice cream for the first time. It was amazing! I still made messes in my sleep, but all he did was tell me "Good girl!" and loved on me.

***

This morning I felt terrible. I threw up all my food again, too. He looked sad, so I licked his leg until he smiled and picked me up. Then we went for a ride. The nice lady came with us to this place with all the dog and cat smells. Then another lady came in. She seemed nice, but she tried to take me away from my human. He said "no" and wouldn't let me go. I don't know where they wanted to take me. He keeps hugging me and telling me he loves me. He is smiling at me, but I know he's sad. I don't want him to be sad, so I licked his face. That made him smile and then he licked me on the nose. I love him so much!

The other lady came back and sat down. She said something to my human. He made a big sigh and wrapped me tight and kissed me on the head.

The lady just stuck me with something! It stinged a lot, and now I am getting really sleepy. Everything is slowing down. He has his nose on my nose. It's weird, but I can understand human words now. He is crying. Then he said; "I love you, Radar. You breathe out, and I will breathe in; capturing your last breath. Now you will live forever in my heart." That was the last thing I remember before I went to sleep.

***

When I opened my eyes, I was a little scared. I couldn't see him, but I feel him all around me so I'm not scared anymore. I see a bridge that looks like a rainbow. There are dogs and cats and humans and all kinds of animals on the other side. A big horsey is telling me to come over. It's weird to understand horsey talk. All the animals and peoples look happy, so I walked over the bridge. I feel like a puppy again! The horsey told me to wait and play by the water because someday my human will come over the rainbow bridge, and we can be together forever.

Radar got her name from her oversized ears. She was a source of comfort in a stressful time. I had health issues and was working 60 to 100 hours a week. On the bright side, I was able to spend more time with her. She never left my side when I was at work. She was in poor health when she found me, and I was able to give her two more years of a better life. I carried her to the rainbow bridge on September 21, 2015. I held her in my arms as she drew her last breath, which I captured as she slowly released it.

I've heard it said many times that Dog is God spelled backwards. It's the other way around.

HOT TRACKS
JUDY WANG

Cameron wipes the sweat off his brow. He hates New York in the summer, the way the heat boils away the city's layers and peels back its reeking core. You can smell everyone's business, and it mostly smells like hot piss.

He takes his phone out of his pocket and turns it over in his hand. He clicks it on and off, watching the picture of him and his girlfriend flash across the smudged screen. Lindsey is wearing a form-fitting white sundress. She looks pretty, but also kind of stiff. She is posing with one hand on her hip and the other wound tightly around Cameron's arm. Cameron grimaces at Lindsey's perfect smile, and then at his own stupid, bemused grin before putting the phone back in his pocket. *You fucking idiot*, he thinks.

Cameron slumps back on the wooden bench. The Canal Street subway station is empty save for a few others lurking along the tiled wall. A middle-aged man in a Mets cap is leaning against the wall nearby and whistling Glory Days with his head bowed. An old woman on the far end of the platform fans herself with a magazine. Strands of bone-white hair fall out of her bun.

It's not too late, says a voice in Cameron's head. *It's not too late to bail.*

He looks down at his backpack, filled with a fresh set of clothes and swim trunks. He's been thinking all week that this is a bad idea. Instead of breaking up with her for the fourth time like he'd planned, here he is, waiting for a train that will take him to Penn Station, where he will wait for another train that will take him to Great Neck, where Lindsey's whole family was congregating for their annual Fourth of July barbecue.

On the other end of the platform, a man with skin like weathered teak walks in. He wears large, dark sunglasses and whips a thin white cane in front of him. It darts lightly through the air, back and forth, back and forth.

Cameron is furious with himself. The thought of Lindsey's family standing on their deck with their Moscow mules, madras shorts, and yapping dachshunds made him want to reel. *It's not too late.*

The man with the cane draws nearer. His shirt is unbuttoned at the top, exposing a small patch of silver hair on a bony chest. His jeans are thin and worn around the bottoms. He is walking down the platform at an angle, a slight one. It's only when he is less than one foot away from the edge that the others realize he is going to walk into the pit.

"Whoa!" someone yells. The shout echoes around the chamber, scattering Cameron's thoughts. But the man continues walking. He either hasn't heard, or he is used to blocking out the city's cries.

Everyone else hears. They see what's about to happen, but no one moves. The blind man will fall into the pit and drown in its noxious effluvia. If he's not instantaneously electrocuted by the third rail, a train will run him over and squeeze the life juice out of him.

Cameron wants to look away. He doesn't want to see it. The blind man lifts one foot, and Cameron sees the cracked leather loafer move through the thick air as if it's in slow motion. It dangles over the edge.

A microsecond balloons in front of Cameron. An alternate universe rises inside it. He sees himself doing the unthinkable. Before he knows it, Cameron is racing toward the man. He grabs him around his thin waist, fingers interlacing fragile ribs, and jerks him sideways.

As he loses his center of gravity, the blind man's mouth opens in surprise. He doesn't realize at first that someone has grabbed him. He stumbles and drops his cane, but he swings out his arms and catches himself. Then his senses return. He can see Cameron without seeing him. The blind man draws back and punches Cameron hard and square on his mouth.

Cameron feels sharp knuckles slicing through his lips and then he is falling backward. He hits the ground on his butt. Blood crowds the back of his mouth. He looks up to see the blind man crouching down and reaching out his hand, searching. He finds his cane on the floor and stands up.

"Asshole," the blind man says in a raspy voice. Then he turns and walks away slowly. Cameron can see the worn undersides of the blind man's shoes as he shuffles straight down the middle of the platform.

Someone grabs the underside of Cameron's arm and helps him up. It's the old woman with the magazine. She pats Cameron on the back and then immediately moves away. Cameron feels blood running down the side of his mouth. He touches it. It's brighter than he thought it would be. Orange-red, like in the movies.

A loud whoosh announces the train is coming. It thunders down the tracks, bright and steely. The doors slide open and a tourist family steps out. They are wearing denim shorts and I heart NY T-shirts, expectant grins on their faces, bright plastic bags swinging from their hands. They look around, not sure where to go, but excited all the same.

The people waiting on the platform climb aboard quickly, eager to move on to the next thing. Down the track, the blind man is stepping onto a train car. People part to let him pass.

Cameron stands near the open doorway, which will only be open for a few more seconds. If he gets on the train, he will have to explain the blood spots on his shirt collar. He could call it off, say he's sick.

But he's already here. He can't change direction. Cameron steps onto the train just before the doors close. The cold, recycled air wraps around him as the train lurches forward, accelerates, and barrels into the dusk.

THE BITTER CRIMSON
KATHRYN WELLS

The sun was setting, spreading gold onto the walls of the room. I stood up from my desk and walked to the window, looking out at the grounds below. I could see them outside enjoying a game of catch, my husband watching over them. They were so young, so full of life.

The clock struck six, rousing me from my thoughts and I began the routine of dressing for dinner. I chose the green velvet gown. The weight of it made me feel strong, and the movement kept me womanly.

As I descended the stairs to the dining room, a tremor ran through me, making my grip on the rail feeling weak. A nausea rose swiftly inside me so that I had to stop. I calmed myself as I had done many times before; I could not appear frail in front of them. I could not.

When I entered the dining room, I found them all seated and waiting, my girls in identical yellow frocks, and my husband in his usual dining jacket.

'Mother, you're late,' Liza said as I took my seat. It was true, the clock showed that it was thirty-five minutes past six. Dinner was strictly at six thirty; I had never been late before.

'I'm sorry my darlings, but I had the most awful time pinning my hair. It just wouldn't stay,' I said dramatically. They both giggled. 'I hope you're not terribly cross with me.'

'We could never be cross with you, Mother,' Freya said. I smiled warmly at them, but I noticed that my husband's brow was creased in a deep frown. He knew why I had been late.

'Well, now that we're all here, would you care to bring out the first course, Henry?' he asked our butler. Henry dashed off to fetch a delicious starter of shrimp in a delicate sauce. I savoured each mouthful.

When the meal was over, I saw the girls to bed, and then met my husband in the gardens. We walked together, arm in arm and I revelled in the warmth of him. The air was particularly fresh, and the stars sparkled brightly. It seemed the perfect evening.

We came upon a table set with red wine, and he lit a perfumed candle for me. He knew how much I loved them.

'Is it ready?' I asked.

'Yes,' he said, handing me a glass already full. 'Are you sure you want to?'

'More than you can know, my love.' I took the glass to my lips and swallowed, watching the single tear roll down his cheek.

HOW TO COOK EGGS
EDEL WILLIAMS

    She had to admit that sitting here in the hot sun was not the best of places to be. The wraparound veranda offered little in the way of real protection from the midday heat, and at this time of day, it was steamy and blisteringly hot. You could boil an egg on the wooden steps, and she knew that because as a child her Da had showed her just how quickly it would fry there. Two steps down to the left on the front of the porch was the very spot he had cracked one open, and on a stinking hot day in July, much the same time as it was now, the pair of them had watched it cook. She remembered watching its clear membrane quickly turn a milky white and the buttery sunshine of the yolk firm up just ever so slightly. That's the way she loved it, just barely cooked, so that it was still full of gooey deliciousness. Too cooked and the yellow became solid and powdery while the white became a rubber disc. It almost made her gag when she had to eat it that way, and her Ma had always cooked the eggs like that; too done.

  Her Da said the best way to eat an egg was raw, but she couldn't quite get used to the slime of it like that either. She used to feign sickness when she watched him crack the egg and just suck the inside straight into his mouth, swallow and then smack his lips together, as he winked at her. Then they would both laugh as if it was some sort of shared secret. She remembered the taste of the eggs her Da used to cook. Oh, how she savoured the remembered taste of those eggs.

    She recalled the smell of her Da too, the slight tobacco aroma she'd get when she put her head on his shoulder and the smell of sweat if it was late in the evening after he'd come in from his days work in the fields. Her Da used to call that the sweet smell of honest to goodness hard work when she'd wrinkle her nose at him, and he'd tell her there was no shame in that odour – it was a 'righteous perfume'. That had been such a long time ago when he had been a younger man. Her Da was dead now, coming up on five years. Sissy said that once Ma died Da's world stopped turning, that Ma had been the Sun to Da's Earth and without her, he was just too bereft and broken. He just seemed to get smaller and smaller every day until he just gave up and died of a broken heart, nine months after Ma had passed. He was two years short of his seventieth birthday. All they had left of Ma and Da was this house and its small now dried up and neglected garden, and Sissy said that they could take the house over her 'goddamn dead body'.

Sissy was her older sister by two hours. Ma used to say that when Sissy was born, Savannah was so delighted to have her belly all to herself that she didn't want to come out. Savannah leaned back hard into the rocking chair and wiped the sweat from her head with the back of her hand. It was a scorcher today, the sun was literally sizzling in the cobalt, cloudless sky which meant there was not a wisp of relief. She could hear the buzzing of flies and the rhythmic ticking of crickets off somewhere to her left. Looking off into the distance, the green of the faraway hills shimmered in the heat, gently rippling like the surface of a calm lake.

She didn't know how they'd ended up here. She didn't know how she'd ended up sitting here on their old porch in the mid-day July Sun holding a shotgun. Da used to say that while shotguns have enormous energy, they don't have great power.

"Anything over 120 pounds wouldn't be too damaged by the pellet spread fired from your average shotgun" he'd say.

"Unless of course you were standing at close range, then it would tear a hole in you the size of a fist". And Da's fists had been huge. Da had taught Savannah and Sissy to shoot when they were old enough to hold the shotgun, and Ma had hated that. Sissy had always been that bit bigger, but when Savannah held the gun upright, it barely stood two inches past her shoulders. Now, the shotgun lay with its solid weight across her lap. She didn't like the feel of the metal in her hands, she never had, so in that regard Savannah was more like her mother. On a day like today the metal heated up quickly, so she had placed it instead across her skirted legs as she rocked gently on the chair as far out of the sun as the porch would allow.

Oh, she had loved her Da very very much. She had been Da's girl, while Sissy had been Ma's favorite, one for each of them, her Da used to say. Above all else, they both had felt very loved. She cast her gaze over the remnants of her Ma's garden. Where once tomatoes, squash, cabbage, potatoes and roses used to grow, now the dirt was dry, cracked and lifeless. Without watering, nothing much would grow here, nothing other than scutch. The sun was just too hot. Her Ma used to call the scutch 'Devil's grass' and she'd curse as she'd spend hours pulling it up from her vegetable patch, only for it to come back again the following week. If she closed her eyes tight enough, she could just about see her Ma out there in her wide brimmed straw hat, tied under her chin with a neat little bow, bending down, cussing softly as she pulled at the grass. Ma would then gently caress the almost ripe vegetables, willing them to redden, or darken so that she could pick them, wash them and put them on their plates for tea. Perfect balls of wholesome sunshine her Ma used to call her tomatoes, and they had tasted like no shop bought tomato Savannah would ever buy. Sweet and juicy and bursting with flavor, she'd had to slurp up the insides as soon as she bit through the skin, or else it would drip down her chin and be lost.
She licked her lips, as much from the memory as the thirst she could feel coming on.

Savannah sat lost in her memories for a long time. Her parents were gone, this house was falling to ruin, the garden was long dead. What was she here for? What was she protecting?
They hadn't realized that the small mortgage left on the property had not been fully paid. Da died so quickly after Ma, that they had been left reeling in shock and the anguish of loss. Sissy said the banks were going to take the house 'over her goddamn dead body', but neither she nor Sissy had lived in it for many years.
They had their own houses now, with their own children, their own men who worked hard in the fields and came home to noise and laughter and fresh cooking on the stove. It had been many years since she visited their parents' grave when all she could do was double over with the torment of their loss as tears streamed

down her face, leaving her exhausted. Like today, she could think of them, and their memories brought sadness instead of agony and some time in the future, she knew their memories would bring a quiet contentment. But this house, this was forsaken, derelict. Her Ma and Da weren't here any more. She looked around at the dead garden, the shabby paint flaking off the outside of the house. Even the porch had felt a bit soft under her foot. She unshelled the shotgun and picked up the discarded red buck-shots. She got up, leaned the empty shotgun against the rocking chair and stepped down the four steps off the porch, glancing one last time at the place where she and her Da had cooked the egg, walked out into the midday sun, and didn't look back.

BYSTANDER
IONA WINTER

I woke from a dream, my body swaying as a building might in an earthquake—in all directions at once. Vivid images surged through my mind's eye.

A door to the past flung open, and I am sucked through as though underwater with muffled hearing and disembodied voices that demand my attention.

I am a bystander, caught between the present and history. My arms weighted, like the sinkers Uncle used when he took us fishing. I recall how solid they felt in my hands.

***

The party was in full swing. People spilled through the door and soon it became standing room only. Empty beer bottles lined themselves up on the kitchen bench.

Mum swayed to the music, topped up drinks, and occasionally left the lounge to make sure we were still asleep. She had one eye on the bedroom door, to ensure nobody disturbed us kids.

Everyone was having fun, and the music grew steadily louder.

Mum went to check on us again but Dad bailed her up in the kitchen. 'Where the fuck are you going?'

'To check on the kids,' she said.

'No, you're not, you're hooking up with Henry.'

'What?' Mum replied, her voice lowered.

'I've seen you coming back together twice.'

'Oh, come on, you know how I get when it comes to parties,' she said.

Dad grabbed her arm, twisted it, and through his teeth snarled, 'Don't lie to me, bitch.'

'I'm not.'

'Yes, you fucking well are,' he spat.

'C'mon man, leave your missus alone and have another beer,' said Sid, a workmate of Dad's.

He stepped between them holding out a bottle like a peace offering. Sid caught Mum's eye and signalled with a flick of his head, get the hell out of here.

Mum turned cautiously towards the bedroom.

'That's right slut, run away,' Dad sneered, and launched the bottle at her head.

Mum watched its trajectory in slow motion, before it smashed on the wall beside her. She stood still, observing amber liquid run down the white paint.

Dad went back to the party, laughing.

Mum moved down the hallway and felt for the bedroom door handle.

'Arsehole,' she whispered.

Switching on the bedside lamp, Mum woke us with an embrace.

'Mum?' I said.

'We're going, and I need you to stay quiet please,' she said.

'Aw…but it's really late,' I whined.

'I know, but it's not safe for us here,' she said.

'Is it Dad?' I asked.

'Later, just put a jumper on okay?' Mum replied.

Moving fast she reached for our schoolbags, stuffing them with underwear and changes of clothing.

Mum reached for the shoebox hidden at the back of the cupboard, after the last time Dad had lost the plot. Lifting the lid, she felt for the notes—nothing.

'Shit.'

She hushed us as we crept out of the house via the back door. With my sister Livy on her shoulder, bags on the other and me holding her hand, we headed to the car.

Dad put his head out the window and jeered, 'Where the hell are you going to go?'

With urgency Mum unlocked the car, and deposited us inside. But then Livy sat upright and shouted, 'Mum!'

Bracing herself, she turned to face Dad as he sauntered out of the house calling, 'Wanna come back inside babe?'

By now people were looking out the windows and someone had turned the music down.

'No, we're going. Just let us leave okay?'

'Get moving then bitch, and take this with you!' Pulling the ring from his finger, Dad threw it.

Mum watched it sail through the air and land on the driveway in front of her, where it clinked and rolled to a halt. In disbelief, she reached for it.

Dad launched himself, hands tight around Mum's throat, squeezing hard. People ran out of the house. They grabbed at him but he held fast. Boozey breath, spittle flying, Dad eyeballed her.

Mum lashed out, punching his face. Blood splattered from his nose, and his hands fell slack. Instinctively she ran.

Panicking, Mum pushed down the car locks and fumbled with the key in the ignition.

Dad lurched towards us, blood covering his face and shirt.

The engine started.

We were all crying; our faces glistened in the shifting light. I cradled Livy's head in the crook of my arm.

As if she were disconnected, Mum watched Dad slam his fists down on the bonnet, over and over again. She paused.

'Fuck off you fucking whore!' he screamed.

Mum threw the gear stick into reverse and accelerated down the driveway.

Something inside her snapped, as if it was comical, 'He looks like a madman,' she laughed.

***

And so, I woke with my heart thumping, to the smell of booze from Dad's breath, and Mum's fear taut beneath my skin.

I fumbled for the light and woke the dog, who sat upright on the bed and barked. The dreaming's started up again. Each time, my right ear becomes muffled as if holding a shell and listening for the sea.

Hearing Dad's voice reminds me of the past, deep-set in my bones. In the early morning light, I imagine a movement in the corner of the room and freeze.

'It'll be okay with the light on', I whisper, just like when I was a kid.

I don't want these pictures etched inside me of the bathroom in that house. The seventies baby-pooh coloured tiles, and filthy bath that Mum scrubbed for hours each time we went back.

I remember lying down once with a split lip, fingering the grout between those tiles and wondering why Mum put up with it. At the time, I guess she didn't feel she was worth much more. She hung around waiting for Dad to love her, and us.

Some snapshots cannot be erased.

Printed in Great Britain
by Amazon